To Mum and Dad

Preface

Professor Sealy is undoubtedly correct and far-sighted to point out

> 'One area where I suspect that we all succumb to the temptation to keep yesterday's law alive is that of minority shareholders and their remedies. We teach the "alteration of articles" cases, from *Allen v Gold Reefs* to *Greenhalgh*, as the living law when surely today the *Greenhalgh*-type victims would have an unanswerable case of unfairly prejudicial conduct under s.459. So would the petitioners in many of the early "just and equitable" winding up cases. And this could well be true of the "variation of rights" cases like *White v Bristol Aeroplane Co*. Why take up valuable lecturing time dwelling on arguments based on these now superseded issues? Should we not mercifully draw the curtain over *Greenhalgh* and assume that he would now get a better deal from a judge empowered to have regard to enforceable considerations? The amendment of s.459 by the 1989 Act should also, of course, open the door to a wholesale rewriting of *Foss v Harbottle*, (although I doubt whether our judges have much stomach for this challenge): the question is, do we still deal with *Foss* in all its complex detail just because that mass of teasing and testing case-law is there?'
>
> ('Company Law Through the Cases' in *Examining the Law Syllabus, Beyond The Core* (ed. Birks), Oxford University Press, 1993, p.37).

This book attempts to put aside the yesterday's law on minority shareholders' protection in company law, for the law in this area is today developing very rapidly and galloping in a different direction. Practitioners, teachers and students of company law alike need to change their emphasis and take a new approach in their treatment of minority shareholders' protection. Thus, much of this book is devoted to a detailed examination of the unfair prejudice remedy under s.459.

I am grateful to the Law School, University of East Anglia for its research scholarship, without which it would have been impossible for me to research into much of what is the basis of this book. I also wish to express my gratitude and indebtedness to Simon Goulding of UEA for his advice and encouragement and patient reading and comments of early drafts. I am extremely grateful to my colleague, Andrew Hicks, who very patiently read the drafts and made valuable detailed comments at a time when it would have been extremely pleasant to go outdoors and do something else. John Lowry of Sussex University has also very kindly made constructive comments on the final drafts. I also wish to thank Anne Waters for typing the table of cases, Mervyn Bennun and Kate Tyler for solving problems I faced in word-processing earlier drafts of this book and Laura Chapman and Beth Sargeant for reading the proofs. For tolerating my long absence and neglect during the period of my research and writing up this book, Deav-Tieng Teo deserves very special thanks.

I am also grateful to Jo Reddy, Sonny Leong, Edmund Latham and the production team at Cavendish Publishing Ltd for their enthusiasm and friendly assistance in the preparation of this book.

I have attempted to state the law as at 15 December 1993 based on materials available to me.

S H Goo
Exeter

Acknowledgement

The author wishes to thank Her Majesty's Stationery Office for allowing the reproduction of the prescribed form set out in Appendix 1 to this book. The author also wishes to thank Blackstone Press Ltd. and the authors of the *Inns of Court School of Law Manual on Chancery Practice* (1991/92 edition) for allowing the production of a fictitious petition set out in Appendix 2 to this book which is based on that in the *Manual* (at pp 315-317).

Contents

Preface i

Acknowledgement iii

Table of Cases ix

Table of Statutes xvii

1 Minority Shareholders' Actions in General 1
- 1.1 Introduction 1
- 1.2 Common law: majority rule and its exceptions 2
- 1.3 The scope of fraud on minority exception 3
  - (a) Fraud 4
  - (b) Wrongdoer control 5
- 1.4 Problems of common law protection 6
- 1.5 Personal right action 10
- 1.6 Just and equitable winding up and its limitations 13
- 1.7 History of s.459 of the Companies Act 1985 15

2 The Unfair Prejudice Remedy: Preliminary Matters 17
- 2.1 Who can petition under s.459? 17
  - (a) Member 19
  - (b) Persons to whom shares have been transferred or transmitted by operation of law 20
  - (c) Member alleged to have been erroneously registered as such 22
- 2.2 What needs to be shown? 22
  - (a) Company's affairs 23
  - (b) Act or omission of company 26

3 Interests of Member Qua Member 31
- 3.1 Qua member 31
- 3.2 Petitioner's legitimate interests 34
  - (a) Exclusion from management 35
  - (b) Excessive remuneration 37
  - (c) Inadequate dividends 37
  - (d) 'Take-over' situations 38
  - (e) Retaining the proportionate shareholding 39
  - (f) Alteration of articles of association 39
  - (g) Breach of directors' duties 40
  - (h) Decisions to continue trading at a loss 46
- 3.3 Circumstances in which no legitimate expectation can be inferred 46
- 3.4 Interests arising from personal rights of shareholders 49
- 3.5 Legitimate expectation not transmissible by law 49

4 The Concept of Unfair Prejudice 51
4.1 General 51
4.2 Impropriety or illegality not a requirement 52
4.3 Both unfairness and prejudice needed 53
4.4 Prejudice 53
4.5 Exercise of legal right may still be unfairly prejudicial 54
4.6 Conduct prejudicial to all members 57
4.7 Test of unfairness 58
4.8 Factors courts take into account 59
(a) The petitioner's conduct 59
(b) Offer made to buy out the petitioner 61
(c) Alternative remedy 69
(d) Motive of oppressor 70
(e) Delay in petitioning 76
(f) Other relevant factors 76
4.9 Conclusion 77

5 The Application of Section 459 79
5.1 Exclusion from management 79
5.2 Breach of directors' duties 80
5.3 Excessive remuneration 86
5.4 Inadequate dividends 87
5.5 Take-over situations 88
(i) Misleading information or advice 88
(ii) Compulsory acquisition under s.429, Companies Act 1985. 90
(iii) Breach of City Code 93
5.6 Alteration of articles 94
5.7 Miscellaneous 97
(a) Variation of class rights 97
(b) Autocratic behaviour and disregard of proper procedure 97
(c) Decisions to continue trading at a loss 98
(d) Failure to provide information requested 98
(e) Lack of probity 98

6 Procedural Aspects 101
6.1 The Courts 101
6.2 Procedural provisions 101
6.3 Parties to the s.459 petition 104
6.4 Service out of jurisdiction 106
6.5 Petition to strike out or stay proceedings 106
6.6 Advertisement of petition 108

6.7 Interlocutory orders 108
(a) Injunction 108
(b) Appointment of a receiver 111
(c) Interim payment order 111
6.8 Discovery of documents 113
6.9 Section 459 of the Companies Act 1985 and s.122(1)(g) of the Insolvency Act 1986 115
(a) Striking out a s.122(1)(g) petition 115
(b) Using s.459 as an alternative in s.122(1)(g) petition 116
(c) Section 122(1)(g) as an alternative to a s.459 order 117
(d) Conclusion 119
6.10 Indemnity as to costs 119
6.11 Security for costs 122
6.12 Interest prior to judgment 123
6.13 Escape clauses 123

7 Remedies 125
7.1 Final orders 125
7.2 Valuation of shares 128
(a) Basis of valuation 130
(b) Factors affecting the basis of valuation 133
(c) Date of valuation 135

8 Conclusions 139

Appendix 1 143

Appendix 2 145

Index 149

Table of Cases

A & BC Chewing Gum Ltd., Re [1975] 1 WLR 579 114
A Company (No 002612 of 1984), Re 57
Abbey Leisure Ltd., Re [1990] BCC 60 (CA) 66-68, 107, 115, 117, 141
Alexander v Automatic Telephone Co. [1900] 2 Ch 56 (CA) 4, 6
Allen v Gold Reefs of West Africa Ltd.
[1900] 1 Ch 656. ....3, 12, 40, 70, 74-75, 94-96
Allen v Hyatt (1914) 30 TLR 444 ....40, 88
American Cyanamid v Ethicon Ltd [1975] AC 396 109-111
Ampol Petroleum v R W Miller (Holdings) Ltd.
[1972] 2 NSWLR 850 94
Antigen Laboratories Ltd., Re [1951] 1 All ER 110n 10, 15
Ashburton Oil NL v Alpha Minerals NL
(1971) 123 CLR 614 (H Ct of Aus) 40
Automatic Self-Cleansing Filter Syndicate Co. Ltd.
v Cunninghame [1906] 2 Ch 34 27
Baltic Real Estate Ltd., Re [1992] BCC 629 105-106
Bamford v Bamford [1970] Ch 212 ....4, 42, 72
Barron v Potter [1914] 1 Ch 895 14
Bayswater Trading Co. Ltd., Re [1970] 1 WLR 343 18
Beattie v Beattie [1938] Ch 708 11
Bellador Silk Ltd., Re [1965] 1 All ER 667 ....16, 31
Bird Precision Bellows Ltd., Re [1984] 3 All ER 444,
[1984] Ch 419, [1984] 2 WLR 869,
affd [1985] 3 All ER 523, [1986] 2 WLR 158,
[1986] Ch 658 ....36, 67, 93, 130-135, 138
Blue Arrow plc [1987] BCLC 585, Re 34, 36, 57
Bond v Barrow Haematite Steel Co. [1902] 1 Ch 353 87
Boswell (Steels) & Co. Ltd., Re (1989) 5 BCC 145 65
Bovey Hotel Ventures Ltd., Re
(unreported, 31 July 1981) 43, 51, 53, 57-58, 73, 81
Breckland Group Holdings Ltd. v
London & Suffolk Properties Ltd. [1989] BCLC 100 27
British Holdings plc v Quadrex [1989] 3 All ER 492 112-113
Britoil [1990], Re BCC 70, CA 91
Brown v British Abrasive Wheel Co. Ltd. [1919] 1 Ch 290 ....12, 70
BSB Holdings Ltd., Re [1992] BCC 915 ....24, 105
Buenos Ayres Great Southern Railways Co. Ltd. v Preston
[1947] Ch 384, [1947] 1 All ER 729 87
Bugle Press Ltd., Re [1961] Ch 270, CA 90-91, 93
Burland v Earle [1902] AC 83 ....2, 4, 40, 71
Cade (J E) & Son Ltd., Re [1991] BCC 360; [1991] BCLC 213 ....10, 33, 47, 107
Canniford v Smith, Financial Times, December 21, 1990 120
Carrington Viyella plc, Re (1983) 1 BCC 98 ....45, 57
Castleburn Ltd., Re (1989) 5 BCC 652 ....64, 132
Charnley Davies Ltd, Re [1990] BCC 605 26
Charter Oil Co. Ltd. v Beaumont (1967) 65 DLR (2d) 112 (BCCA) 12
Charterbridge Corporation Ltd. v Lloyds Bank Ltd.
[1969] 3 WLR 122; [1969] 2 All ER 1185; [1970] Ch 62 26

Chez Nico (Restaurants), Re [1991] BCC 736 92-93
Clemens v Clemens Bros. Ltd. [1976] 2 All ER 268 ....3, 6, 39, 70-71, 83, 140
Coleman v Myers [1977] 2 NZLR 225 ....40, 88, 90
Company (No. 00330 of 1991) ex p. Holden, Re a
[1991] BCLC 597 ....65, 67, 141
Company (No. 00370 of 1987) ex p. Glossop, Re a
(1988) 4 BCC 507; [1988] BCLC 570 ....38, 57
Company (No 005685 of 1988)
ex p. Schwarcz (No. 2), Re a [1989] BCLC 427 40
Company (No. 00314 of 1989) ex p. Estate Acquisition
and Development Ltd. and Others, Re a [1991] BCLC 154 ....107, 115-116
Company (No. 00477 of 1986), Re a (1986) 2 BCC 99;
[1986] BCLC 376 ....22, 32, 34, 36, 43, 70, 82
Company (No. 00596 of 1986), Re a [1987] BCLC 133 ....109, 111
Company (No. 00687 of 1991), Re a [1992] BCLC 133 ....108, 118
Company (No. 00789 of 1987) ex p. Shooter, Re a,
sub nom Nuneaton Borough AFC Ltd (1989) 5 BCC 792 ....20, 53, 127
Company (No. 00823 of 1987), Re a The Times 26 July 1989 87
Company (No. 001126 of 1992), Re a [1993] BCC 325 105
Company (No. 001363 of 1988) ex p. S-P, Re a
(1989) 5 BCC 18; [1989] BCLC 579 ....107, 115-117, 119
Company (No. 001761 of 1986), Re a [1987] BCLC 141 ....23-24, 52-54
Company (No. 002470 of 1988) ex p. Nicholas, Re a
[1991] BCLC 480.24-25, 60, 76, 107, 115
Company (No. 002567 of 1982), Re a [1983] BCLC 151 ....32, 69
Company (No 002612 of 1984), Re a (1984) 1 BCC 99;
[1985] BCLC 80, see also Cumana Ltd, Re a
(Appeal Judgment) 39, 57, 72, 110, 135
Company (No. 003096 of 1987), Re a (1987) 4 BCC 80 ....33, 67-69, 107, 115
Company (No. 003160 of 1986), Re a [1986] BCLC 391 ....19, 21, 35
Company (No. 003843 of 1986), Re a (1987) 3 BCC 624;
[1987] BCLC 562 ....33, 67-69
Company (No. 004175 of 1986), Re a [1987] BCLC 574 ....108, 111
Company (No. 004377 of 1986), Re a
[1987] 1 WLR 102 ....36, 61-62, 64, 67, 79, 132
Company (No. 004475 of 1982), Re a [1983] Ch 178 ....27, 32
Company (No. 004502 of 1988), ex p. Johnson, Re a
[1992] BCLC 701. 120
Company (No. 005134 of 1986) ex p. Harries, Re a
[1989] BCLC 383 76
Company (No. 005136 of 1986), Re a,
sub nom Re a Sherborne Park Residents Co. Ltd
(1986) 2 BCC 99, 528 [1987] BCLC 82 ....11, 41, 44-45, 71, 80, 120
Company (No. 005287 of 1985), Re a [1986] 1 WLR 281 ....43, 70
Company (No. 006834 of 1988) ex p. Kremer, Re a
(1989) 5 BCC 218; [1989] BCLC 365 ....62, 64, 66-69, 127, 132
Company (No. 007281 of 1986), Re a [1987] BCLC 593 104
Company (No. 007623 of 1986), Re a [1986] BCLC 362 ....61, 65, 69, 73, 132

Company (No. 007828 of 1985), Re a (1986) 2 BCC 98 21
Company (No. 008126 of 1989), Re a (1992) BCC 542 125
Company (No. 008699 of 1985), Re a (1986) 2 BCC 99;
[1986] BCLC 382 ....32, 38, 43-44, 58, 72, 82, 89, 93
Company ex p. Burr, Re a [1992] BCLC 724 ....46, 70, 87, 107
Company, Re a [1983] 1 WLR 927; [1983] 2 All ER 854 ....62, 72
Company, Re a [1986] BCLC 68 ....70, 105, 126
Company, Re a [1985] BCLC 80,
see Company, Re a (No. 002612 of 1984)
Cook v Deeks [1916] 1 AC 554 (PC) 4, 80
Cooper v The Premier Trust [1945] OR 35 12
Crossmore Electrical and Civil Engineering Ltd., Re
(1989) 5 BCC 37, ...114, 118, 120
Cumana Ltd., Re (1986) 2 BCC 99, 453,
[1986] BCLC 430 (CA) 36-37, 39, 43, 57, 72, 81, 123, 128, 135-136
Cumbrian Newspapers Group Ltd. v Cumberland &
Westmorland Herald Newspaper & Printing Co. Ltd.
[1987] Ch 1; [1986] 2 All ER 816 97
Currie v Cowdenbeath Football Club Ltd.
[1992] BCLC 1029 35
D R Chemicals Ltd., Re (1989) 5 BCC 39 ....43, 68, 72, 76, 131, 134, 137
Dafen Tinplate Co. Ltd. v Llanelly Steel Co.
[1920] 2 Ch 124 ....70, 75
Daniels v Daniels [1978] Ch 406 .4, 8
Dennis (W) and Sons Ltd. v West Norfolk Farmers'
Manure and Chemicals Co-operative Co. Ltd. [1943] Ch 220 113
Devlin v Slough Estates Ltd. [1983] BCLC 497 13
Disderi & Co., Re (1870) LR 11 Eq 242 20
Dunford & Elliott Ltd. v Johnson & Firth Brown Ltd.
[1977] 1 Lloyd's Rep 505 93
Ebrahimi v Westbourne Galleries, see Westbourne Galleries, Re
Edwards v Halliwell [1950] 2 All ER 1064 ....2, 7, 10, 12
Elder v Elder & Watson Ltd. (1952) SC 49 ....15-16, 31, 51, 80
El Sombrero Ltd., Re [1958] 3 All ER 1 56
Eley v Positive Government Security Life Assurance Co. Ltd.
(1876) 1 Ex D 88 ....11, 79
Elgindata Ltd., Re [1991] BCLC 959, The Times, June 18 1992 ....34, 38, 45-46, 81, 85, 88, 120-121, 126, 131, 137
Esso Standard (Inter-America) Inc. v
J W Enterprises [1963] SCR 144, 37 DLR (2nd) 598 92
Estman Co. (Kilner House) Ltd. v GLC [1982] 1 WLR 2;
[1982] 1 All ER 437 4
Evertite Locknuts Ltd., Re [1945] Ch 220 92
Evling v Israel & Oppenheimer Ltd. [1918] 1 Ch 101 13
Ferguson v Maclennan Salmon Co. Ltd. [1990] BCC 702 113

Five Minute Car Wash Service Ltd., Re [1966] 1 WLR 745 ....15, 46, 83-85
Foss v Harbottle (1843) 2 Hare 461 ....1, 3, 6-7, 9-11, 15, 41, 45, 52, 72, 77, 81, 83, 121, 139-140
Fraser v Whalley (1864) 2 Hem & M 10 ....13, 40
Galloway v Halle Concerts Society [1915] 2 Ch 233 13
Garage Door Associates, Re [1983] BCLC 164 22
German Date Coffee Co., Re (1882) 20 Ch D 169 14
Gething v Kilner [1972] 1 WLR 33740, 88
Ghyll Beck Driving Range Ltd., Re [1993] BCLC 1126 ....80, 99, 129-130
Glamorganshire Banking Company, Re (1884) 28 Ch D 620 8
Gold Coast Selection Trust v Humphrey [1948] AC 459 129
Gordon v Elliman (1954) 119 NE 2d 331 49
Grant v UK Switchback Railways Co. (1888) 40 Ch D 135 ....8, 12, 43
Greenhalgh v Arderne Cinemas Ltd. [1946] 1 All ER 512; [1950] 2 All ER 1120; [1951] Ch 286 ....12, 39-40, 70, 74-75, 96
Greenough v Gaskell (1833) 1 My & K 98 113-114
Grierson, Oldham & Adams Ltd., Re [1968] Ch 17; [1967] 1 WLR 385; [1967] 1 All ER 192 (Ch) 91, 93
Hailey Group Ltd., Re [1993] BCLC 458....................25, 55, 82, 128
Halt Garage, Re [1982] 3 All ER 1016....................86
Harmer (H R) Ltd., Re [1958] 3 All ER 689 ....11, 16, 22, 31, 97, 128
Harrods (Buenos Aires) Ltd., Re [1991] BCLC 666 106
Hayes v Bristol Plant Hire Co. Ltd. [1957] 1 WLR 499....................7
Heron International v Grade [1983] BCLC 244 (CA) 40, 88
Hickman v Kent or Romney Marsh Sheep-Breeders' Assn [1915] 1 Ch 881 ....11, 32
Hoare & Co. Ltd., Re (1933) 150 LT 374 91-92
Hogg v Cramphorn Ltd. [1967] Ch 254....................6, 8, 40, 44, 72, 83
Hope v International Financial Society (1876) 4 Ch D 327 12
Howard Smith Ltd. v Ampol Petroleum Ltd. [1974] AC 821 (PC)....................40, 51, 94
Howie & Ors v Cramford [1990] BCC 330 132
Hydrosan Ltd., Re [1991] BCC 19 113-114
Irvine v Union Bank of Australia (1877) 2 AC 366....................8, 12
Island Export Finance Ltd. v Umunna [1986] BCLC 460....................83
James Pilkin & Co. Ltd., Re (1916) 85 LJ Ch 318 20
Jermyn Street Turkish Baths Ltd., Re [1970] 1 WLR 1194; [1971] 1 WLR 1042 ....15-17, 19, 22-23, 86
Jesner & Anor v Jarrad Properties Ltd. & Ors (1992) BCC 807....................76, 117
JN2 Ltd., Re [1978] 1 WLR 183....................17, 22
John Smith's Todcaster Brewery, Re [1953] Ch 308 (CA) 12
Johnson v Hall (1957) 10 DLR (2d) 243 (BCSC)....................12
Kaye v Croyden Tramways Co. [1898] 1 Ch 358 (CA) 12
Kenyon Swansea Ltd., Re (1987) 3 BCC 259; [1987] BCLC 514 ....23, 83, 120

Lee v Chou Wen Hsien [1985] BCLC 45 7
Ling Beng Sung v Kong Thai Sawmill (Miri) Sdn Bhd
[1976] 1 MLJ 59 10
Loch v John Blackwood Ltd. [1924] AC 783 14
London School of Electronics Ltd., Re
[1986] Ch 211, [1985] BCLC 273 ....36, 43, 57,
59-60, 81, 135, 137
Lonrho v Shell Petroleum Co. Ltd. [1980] 1 WLR 627 114
Lundie Bros. Ltd., Re [1965] 1 WLR 1050 31
MacDougall v Gardiner (1875) 1 Ch D 13 ....2, 10, 13, 43
Malaga Investment Ltd., Re (1987) SLT 603 110
Marx v Estates & General Investments Ltd.
[1975] 3 All ER 1064; [1976] 1 WLR 380 121
McCusker v McRae (1966) SC 253 98
McGuinness & Anor, Petitioners, sub nom
McGuinness v Bremner Plc (1988) 4 BCC 161,
(1988) SLT 891, [1988] BCLC 673 ....54, 56-57, 128
Menier v Hoopers Telegraph Co. (1874) 9 Ch App 350 4
Meyer Douglas, Re [1965] VR 638 18
Meyer's Case (1954) SLT 273 57
Milgate Developments Ltd., Re [1991] BCC 24 120
Mills v Mills (1938) 60 CLR 150.76
Morgan v 45 Flers Avenue Pty. Ltd. (1986) 10 ACLR 692 ....23, 25
Mosely v Koffyfontein Mines Ltd. [1904] 2 Ch 108 (CA) 12
Mozley v Alston (1847) 1 Ph 790 3, 13, 42
Murray's Judicial Factor v Murray & Sons [1993] BCLC 1437 ....8, 34, 98
Newhart Developments Ltd. v Co-operative
Commercial Bank Ltd. [1978] QB 814 26
Ngurli Ltd. v McCann (1953) 90 CLR 425 (H Ct of Aus) 40
Noble (R A) & Sons (Clothing) Ltd., Re
(1983) BCLC 273 ....51, 53, 59-60, 80, 117
North West Transportation Co. Ltd. v Beatty
2[1887] 12 AC 589 71
Northern Counties Securities Ltd. v
Jackson and Steeple Ltd. [1974] 1 WLR 1133 ....27-28, 71
Norvabron Pty., Re (No. 2) Ltd. (1987) 11 ACLR 279 52
Nuneaton Borough Association Football Club Ltd., Re
see Company (No. 00789 of 1987) ex p. Shooter, Re a
OC (Transport) Services Ltd., Re.136
Opera Photographic Ltd., Re [1989] BCLC 763 56
Pappaioannoy v The Greek Orthodox Community
of Melbourne (1978) 3 ACLR 801 13
Pavlides v Jensen [1956] Ch 565 ....4-5, 7-8
Pender v Lushington (1877) 6 Ch D 70 (CA) 12-13, 43
Pennell Securities Ltd. v Venida Investments Ltd.
(unreported 25 July 1974, noted 44 MLR 40 (1981)) 6, 39
Percival v Wright [1902] 2 Ch 421 ....40, 71, 80, 88
Peso Silver Mines v Cropper (1966) 58 DLR (2d) 1 83

Phillips v Manufacturers' Securities Ltd. (1917) 116 LJ 290 71
Pickering v Stephenson (1872) LR 14 Eq 322 120
Piercy v S. Mills & Co. Ltd. [1920] 1 Ch 77 40
PMPA Insurance Co. Ltd. v New Ireland Assurance Co., Irish Times, 23 October 1975 (Irish H.C.) 35
Postgate & Denby (Agencies) Ltd., Re [1987] BCLC 8 ....47, 64, 109
Prudential Assurance Co. Ltd. v Newman Industries Ltd. (No. 2) [1982] Ch 204 ....5-7, 10, 13, 41-42, 44, 80, 141
Pulbrook v Richmond Consolidated Mining Co. (1878) 9 Ch D 610 7
Punt v Symons & Co. Ltd. [1903] 2 Ch 506 40
Quickdome Ltd., Re (1988) 4 BCC 296, at 300
Quin & Axtens Ltd v Salmon sub nom Salmon v Quin & Axtens Ltd[1909] 1 Ch 311 [1909] AC 442 ....7, 11-12, 27
R v Board of Trade ex p. St Martins Preserving Co. Ltd. [1965] 1 QB 603 ....24, 26
Railway Time Tables Publishing Co., Re (1889) 42 Ch D 98 20
Rayfield v Hands [1960] Ch 1 11
Regal (Hastings) Ltd. v Gulliver [1942] 1 All ER 378 ....7, 71-72, 80, 82-83
Rica Gold Washing Co., Re (1879) 11 Ch D 36 15
Ricci Burns Ltd. v Toole [1989] 3 All ER 478 113
Richmond Hill Hotel Co., Re (1867) LR 2 Ch App 527 20
Ringtower Holding plc, Re (1989) 5 BCC 82; [1989] BCLC 427 ....33-34, 40, 47, 96, 127
Russell v Northern Bank Development Corp Ltd. [1992] BCLC 1016, HL 34
Ryan v South Sydney Junior Rugby League Club Ltd. (1974) 3 ACLR 486 (NSW) 13
St Piran Ltd., Re [1981] 3 All ER 270 93
Salmon v Quin & Axtens Ltd see Quin & Axtens Ltd v Salmon
Sam Weller & Sons Ltd., Re (1989) 5 BCC 810; [1990] BCLC 80 ....38, 57, 71, 85, 87-88
Scottish Co-operative Wholesale Society Ltd. v Meyer [1958] 3 All ER 66; [1959] AC 324 ....16, 23, 25, 31, 53, 81, 98, 130, 136, 141
Shanning International v George Wimpey International [1988] 3 All ER 475 113
Shinlar v Northan [1960] 2 All ER 239 60
Short v Treasury Comrs [1948] AC 534 129
Shuttleworth v Cox [1927] 2 KB 9.75, 95
Sidebottom v Kershaw, Leese [1920] 1 Ch 154 75
Simpson v Westminster Palace Hotel Co. (1860) 8 HL Cas 712 12
Smith & Fawcett, Re [1942] Ch 304 80
Smith v Croft (No. 2) [1987] BCLC 355; [1988] Ch 114 ....5, 27
Smith v Croft [1986] 1 WLR 580; [1986] 2 All ER 551 ....37, 86, 120
Soundcraft Magnetics Ltd. ex p. Nicholas, Re The Times, 10 July 1992 25

Southern Foundries v Shirlaw [1940] AC 701 60
Stewarts (Brixton) Ltd., Re [1985] BCLC 4 ....25, 70, 81
Sticky Fingers Restaurant Ltd., Re [1992] BCLC 84 56
Sussex Brick Co. Ltd., Re [1961] Ch 289n 92
Sweny v Smith (1869) LR 7 Eq 324.13
Tecnion Investments Ltd., Re [1985] BCLC 434, CA 114
Unisoft Group Ltd. (No. 1), Re [1993] BCLC 1292, CA 122
Vujnovich & Anor v Vujnovich (1989) 5 BCC 740, PC;
[1990] BCLC 227, PC 107, 115, 119
Wallersteiner v Moir (No. 2) [1975] 2 QB 373 ....9, 120-121
Watts v Midland Bank plc [1986] BCLC 15 26
Westbourne Galleries Ltd., Re [1970] 1 WLR 1378;
[1970] 3 All ER 374; [1971] 1 All ER 561;
[1971] 2 WLR 618 CA; revised sub nom
Ebrahimi v Westbourne Galleries Ltd.
[1972] 2 All ER 492; [1973] AC 360 ....14-15, 22-23, 34, 72, 119
White v Bristol Aeroplane Co. [1953] Ch 65 (CA) 12
Whitechurch Insurance Consultant Ltd., Re [1993] BCLC 1359 ....56, 119
Whitechurch Insurance Consultants Ltd., Re [1993] BCLC 1359
Whitehouse v Carlton Hotel Pty. Ltd.
[1987] 162 CLR 285 (H Ct of Aus) 40
Whitla Holdings Pty. Ltd., Re (1982) 7 ACLR 348 8
Whyte, Petitioner, Re (1984) SLT 330 ....23, 55
Williams & Humbert Ltd. v W & H Trade Marks (Jersey) Ltd.
[1986] AC 368, HL 107
Wondoflex Textiles Pty. Ltd., Re [1951] VLR 458 60
Wood v Odessa Waterworks Co. (1889) 42 Ch D 636 11-12
Woodhouse & Co. Ltd. v Woodhouse (1914) 30 TLR 559 113
XYZ Ltd., Re [1987] 1 WLR 102 81
Yenidje Tobacco Co. Ltd., Re [1916] 2 Ch 426 14
Young v Bristol Aeroplane Co. [1944] KB 718 113

Table of Statutes

Companies Act 1948
s 26(2) 18
s 132 55
s 210 .... 1, 2, 10, 15, 16, 17, 18, 22, 23, 25, 31, 32, 46, 51, 52, 53, 58, 77, 80, 83, 84, 86, 97, 115, 125, 128, 139

Companies Act 1980
s 9 97
s 17 97
s 75 .... 2, 16, 32, 55, 110, 139
s 125 97
s 127 97

Companies Act 1985 .... 18, 109
s 9 39
s 14 .... 11, 140
s 22 19
s 22(1) 19
s 22(2) 18, 19, 20
s 35(2) 12
s 35(3) 12
s 151(1) 82
s 151(2) 82
s 303 54
s 359 .... 19, 20
s 368 56
s 371 56
s 429 .... 90, 92, 93
s 459 .... 2, 3, 14, 15, 16, 17, 19, 20, 21, 23, 26, 28, 29, 33, 37, 40, 41, 42, 43, 45, 47, 49, 51, 52, 53, 54, 56, 57, 58, 60, 61, 62, 64, 65, 66, 67, 68, 69, 70, 71, 72, 76, 77, 79-99, 101, 104, 105, 107, 108, 109, 110, 113, 114, 115, 116, 117, 119, 120, 121, 123, 125, 126, 128, 132, 134, 137, 139, 140, 141, 142
s 459(1) 17, 18, 27, 108, 111, 112
s 459(2) 18, 20, 21, 50
s 459(3) 141
s 460 .... 2, 16, 112
s 461 .... 2, 16, 59, 66, 104, 109, 111, 117, 123, 129, 130, 132
s 461(1) 108, 111, 112, 125, 135
s 461(2) 112, 125
s 461(2)(c) 44, 45, 126
s 461(2)(d) 112, 123, 126, 130, 135
s 461(3) 126

Companies Act 1985 (cont)
s 518 ... 24
s 726(1) ... 122
s 744 ... 101
Part XVII ... 21, 101, 102, 103, 106, 108, 125

Companies Act 1989
s 145 ... 17
Sched 19, para 11 ... 57

Insolvency Act 1986 ... 26
s 6 ... 26
s 27 ... 26
s 117(1)(2)(5) ... 101
s 122(1)(g) ... 2, 13, 14, 33, 66, 67, 107, 115, 116, 117, 119, 141
s 124 ... 14
s 125(2) ... 67, 115, 117
s 127 ... 118, 119

Supreme Court Act 1981
s 37 ... 109, 111, 112
s 37(1) ... 108

Chapter 1

Minority Shareholders' Actions in General

1.1 Introduction

There are many ways in which non-controlling shareholders in a company can be 'squeezed out'[1] or their interests in the company prejudiced. In some respects shareholders of public companies are in a better position in that they are able to realise their investment if need be. Furthermore, listed companies are subject to stock market control, and bad publicity of majority's unfair conduct towards the minority may affect the company's profitability and share value. For minority shareholders in an unlisted company, there is no such readily available market. Publicity is unlikely to affect substantially the majority's interest in the company but may make it even more difficult for the minority to realise their shares in the company. Even if the minority could find a buyer, the price they would get for their shares is not likely to reflect their true worth. There may also be restrictions in the company's articles on a member's right to transfer his shares.

For shareholders who want to resort to litigation, there are a number of possibilities. First, a shareholder may bring a derivative action, where there is fraud on the minority and the wrongdoers are in control to prevent the company from suing, as an exception to the rule in *Foss v Harbottle*.[2] It will be seen[3] that the technicality and doctrinal obscurity of the rule in *Foss v Harbottle* has often meant that shareholders are refused a remedy as a matter of procedure, even though the merits of the case justify a remedy being granted. The shareholder may choose to bring a personal action under s.14 of the Companies Act 1985, if he can show that some personal rights conferred upon the shareholders by the memorandum and articles of association or the Companies Acts have been infringed. Where a number of shareholders have suffered an infringement to the same personal rights, a representative action may be brought on behalf of the group. It is, however, not without difficulties alleging breach of personal rights.[4] Prior to the enactment of s.210 of the

---

1 Being driven out of a position of management or ownership or both. For the methods of 'squeeze out' see Chesterman, *Small Businesses*, 2nd ed. pp. 151-152, and Hadden, *Company Law and Capitalism*, 2nd ed. p. 240.

2 (1843) 2 Hare 461.

3 See paras. 1.2-1.4 below.

4 See para. 1.5 below.

Companies Act 1948, minority shareholders were often forced to use the 'sledge-hammer' device of petitioning for the winding up of the company under what is now s.122(1)(g) of the Insolvency Act 1986. This was clearly unsatisfactory, particularly where the company was a going concern.[5] Following the recommendations of the Cohen Committee,[6] s.210 was passed in an attempt to provide a remedy for the minority against oppressive conduct by the majority and as an alternative to s.122(1)(g). Section 210 however soon became a dead duck as it was too restrictively applied. As a result, it was replaced by s.75 of the Companies Act 1980 which adopted the changes proposed by the Jenkins Committee.[7] The provisions in s.75 are today contained in s.459 to s.461 of the Companies Act 1985 as amended by the Companies Act 1989. Section 459 now allows a member of a company to petition on the ground of unfair prejudice. There has recently been an explosion of litigation under the section and the section presumably also enables many more disputes to be settled out of court. 'It is possible that, in the not too distant future, derivative actions can be relegated to an historical footnote only'.[8] This book is thus principally about minority action under s.459. But an attempt is made here to identify the problems and limitations of other types of minority actions.

1.2 Common law: majority rule and its exceptions

All powers of a company are in theory exercised by one or other of its own organs: the shareholders in the general meeting and the board of directors. Each of these bodies generally makes its decision by majority vote. Minority shareholders who are unhappy with the decision of the majority can only bring a personal action if the decision of the majority is illegal or *ultra vires* the memorandum of association, or infringes the member's personal rights conferred by the Companies Act or the articles of association.[9] Problems arise where the alleged wrong is done to the company or is an act which the majority is entitled to do lawfully or at least, entitled to ratify. In those cases the minority can get very little help, as the courts are extremely reluctant to review complaints about such acts. In order to redress the wrong the action should *prima facie* be brought by the company itself.[10] This rule is laid down

5 See para. 1.6 below.
6 Cmnd. 6659, para. 60.
7 Cmnd. 1749.
8 Gower's *Principles of Modern Company Law*, 5th ed. 1992, at 670.
9 *Edwards v Halliwell* [1950] 2 All ER 1064 at 1067, per Jenkin LJ (CA). For personal right action see para. 1.5 below.
10 Per Lord Davey in *Burland v Earle* [1902] AC 83, at 93. See also Mellish LJ in *MacDougall v Gardiner* (1875) 1 Ch 13, at 25.

in the well-known case of *Foss v Harbottle*.[11] It springs from two related concepts:[12] (a) that a company is a legal entity distinct from its shareholders; and (b) that a corporate group cannot function effectively unless the will of the majority generally prevails.

This democratic principle of majority rule means that those who control more than half of the votes on the board or at a shareholders' meeting - and, indeed, those who command a good deal less than a majority of the votes but manage to exercise *de facto* control - thus have substantial power. It is obvious that the law must provide some remedies in cases where such majority power has been abused. The law has to strike a delicate balance between safeguarding the company's legitimate business from being obstructed by tiresome complaining minorities on the one hand, and restraining unfair and wrongful acts which the majority can exploit to its own advantage thereby prejudicing the legitimate interests of the minority, on the other hand.

The judiciary has made some attempts to combat the injustice that may arise in the application of the rule in *Foss v Harbottle*. Thus there is an exception to this rule where the decision of the majority is a fraud on the minority. There is seemingly also an exception in cases where the act done, although regular in form, is unfair and oppressive as against the minority.[13]

1.3 The scope of fraud on minority exception

With the comparatively liberal interpretation of s.459 by the judiciary today, cases on the rule of *Foss v Harbottle* and its exceptions are probably less significant. However, to appreciate the difficulties faced by a dissentient minority in bringing an action for a wrong allegedly done to the company, it is perhaps useful to mention briefly the scope of the fraud on minority exception to the rule in *Foss v Harbottle* which has occasioned considerable litigation and presented significant difficulties to the dissentient shareholder in his path to litigation.

The fraud on minority exception is essentially a procedural device created by the court to allow the complaining shareholders to bring an action in their own names. Such a procedure is called a derivative action. It is available where the directors against whom the relief is sought themselves hold and

11 See also *Mozley v Alston* (1847) 1 Ph 790.

12 See Wedderburn [1957] CLJ 193, at 196. See, too, R. Hollington, *Minority Shareholders' Rights* (London 1990) Chapter 1.

13 *Clemens v Clemens Bros. Ltd.* [1976] 2 All ER 268; *Allen v Gold Reefs of West Africa* [1900] 1 Ch D 656.

control the majority of the shares in the company, and will not permit an action to be brought in the name of the company. It is designed to give a remedy for a wrong which would otherwise escape redress. It is obvious that in such an action the plaintiff cannot have a larger right to relief than the company itself would have if it were the plaintiff. The plaintiff cannot complain of acts which are valid if done with the approval of the majority of the shareholders, or are capable of being confirmed or ratified by the majority.[14]

(a) Fraud

A common thread running through the cases is that the minority can only bring a derivative action where the acts complained of are of a fraudulent character; where there is a 'fraud on minority'. In the absence of such fraud, a transaction authorised or ratified by the wrongdoing directors at a general meeting cannot be set aside.[15] Where fraud can be established, neither the wrongdoing directors nor the shareholders in general meeting can validly ratify the alleged wrong.[16]

Fraud in this context is not confined to literal or common law fraud and it is not always necessary for the plaintiff to allege fraud as such.[17] Fraud on the minority is a non-ratifiable wrong which includes misappropriation of corporate property,[18] *mala fide* abuse of power[19] or discrimination,[20] and self-serving negligence.[21] A *bona fide* abuse of power can be ratified by the majority.[22] So can a mere negligent exercise of directors' powers which does not benefit the wrongdoers themselves at the expense of the company.[23] If the directors sell their own property to the company at an inflated value it is also ratifiable.[24]

---

14 *Burland v Earle* [1902] AC 83.

15 *North-West Transportation Co. Ltd. v Beatty* (1887) 12 App Cas 589 (PC).

16 *Cook v Deeks* [1916] 1 AC 554 (PC); *Menier v Hoopers Telegraph Co.* (1874) 9 Ch App 350.

17 *Daniels v Daniels* [1978] Ch 406; but see *Pavlides v Jensen* [1956] Ch 565, where Danckwerts J held that the minority action failed on two grounds, the first being that the sale of the company's mine at a gross undervalue was not alleged to be fraudulent or *ultra vires*, but merely negligent and therefore open to ratification. (The other was that no sufficient control was exercised by the alleged wrongdoers to enable them to stifle proceedings in the name of the company against them.)

18 *Cook v Deeks* [1916] 1 AC 554 (PC).

19 *Alexander v Automatic Telephone Co.* [1900] 2 Ch 56 (CA).

20 *Estman Co. (Kilner House) Ltd. v GLC* [1982] 1 WLR 2; [1982] 1 All ER 437.

21 *Daniels v Daniels* [1978] Ch 406, at 414. Templeman J effectively extended the meaning of fraud to cases where directors used their powers intentionally or unintentionally, fraudulently or negligently in a manner which benefited themselves at the expense of the company.

22 *Bamford v Bamford* [1970] Ch 212.

23 *Pavlides v Jensen* [1956] Ch 565.

24 *Burland v Earle* [1902] AC 83, but this will today be covered by ss.320-22 of the Companies Act 1985.

(b) Wrongdoer control

In addition to establishing a non-ratifiable wrong done to the company, the plaintiff must also show that there was sufficient control exercised by the alleged wrongdoers to enable them to stifle any attempt to institute proceedings in the name of the company. The question is: Was the plaintiff being improperly prevented from bringing these proceedings on behalf of the company? If it is an expression of the corporate will of the company by an appropriate independent organ that is preventing the plaintiff from prosecuting the action, he is not improperly prevented.[25] Control may include *de facto* control of the company by the wrongdoers as well as *de jure* control.[26] It would also include a situation where a majority of the board of directors are deceived by the wrongdoer with the result that the question of civil proceedings will never be put to, and be properly considered by, the shareholders.

The court can investigate the conduct of the voting and count heads to see what the other shareholders, independent of the plaintiffs and the wrongdoers, think should be done.[27] The appropriate independent organ capable of reviewing the matter will vary according to the constitution of the company concerned, but will usually be the general meeting. The defendants will, in most cases, be disqualified from participating in the vote expressing the corporate will. Where the majority of independent shareholders would vote against legal proceedings, no action in the company's name would lie.

A minority shareholder would, therefore, be advised, before commencing proceedings in the name of the company, to invite the board or a meeting of shareholders to consider initiating an action on the basis of the evidence he collects in support of that action. Where this has not been done, the judge trying the preliminary issue of *locus standi* may grant a sufficient adjournment to enable a meeting of shareholders to be convened by the board.[28] This is to enable the judge to reach a conclusion as to wrongdoer control in the light of the conduct of, and proceedings at, the meeting.

---

25 Per Knox J in *Smith v Croft (No. 2)* [1988] Ch 114, at 184C-F, 184H-185E. In *Pavlides v Jensen* [1956] Ch 565 the action failed because *inter alia* there was no *de jure* voting control of the company by the wrongdoers which could enable them to improperly prevent legal proceedings.

26 *Prudential Assurance Co. Ltd. v Newman Industries (No. 2)* [1982] Ch 204, at 219E and 221G.

27 *Smith v Croft (No. 2)* [1988] Ch 114, 184C-F. In Knox J's view, the independent shareholders are not the plaintiffs or the defendants, neither are they members who vote with a view to supporting the defendants rather than securing benefit to the company, or persons whose vote in the situation is such that there is a substantial risk of that happening (186D-F).

28 *Prudential Assurance v Newman (No. 2)* [1982] Ch 204, at 222A.

If a minority brings an action on behalf of the company, the defendants may apply for the action to be struck out.[29] Where this happens, the judge must attempt to avoid a full-dress trial. At the same time, on trials of a preliminary point of law, he must not decide the preliminary issue on the hypothesis that all the allegations in the statement of claim of fraud and control are facts.[30]

1.4 Problems of common law protection

Although the minority may be able to sue on behalf of the company if the fraud on minority exception can be established, it is often a formidable task to do just that. Professor Sealy has succinctly pointed out some of the following problems:[31]

(i) It is difficult to distinguish between wrong done to the company (where the rule in *Foss v Harbottle* applies) and a wrong done to members personally (where the rule does not apply). One source of confusion, long recognised, is the use of the representative form[32] for the derivative action coupled with the failure to recognise that the same act can be both a wrong to the company and a wrong to one or more of the individual shareholders.[33] Because such an action is normally brought in representative form, with the company named as a defendant, it is not easy to discern whether a company is a wrongdoer or the victim or possibly both.[34] It would be a futile exercise to attempt any such analysis if the only relief sought is declaratory or injunctive,

---

29 Where this happens, there is a dilemma in that if, on such application, the plaintiff can require the court to assume as a fact every allegation in the statement of claim, as in a true demurrer, the plaintiff will frequently be able to outmanoeuvre the primary purpose of the rule in *Foss v Harbottle* by alleging fraud and control by the fraudster. If on the other hand, the plaintiff has to prove fraud and control before he can establish his title to prosecute his action, then the action may indeed be fought to a conclusion before the court can decide whether or not the plaintiff should be permitted to prosecute it. In the latter case the purpose of the rule in *Foss v Harbottle* disappears: *Prudential Assurance v Newman (No. 2)* [1982] Ch 204 (CA), at 219F-H.

30 *Prudential Assurance v Newman (No. 2)* [1982] Ch 204, at 221G-H.

31 See Sealy 'Problem of Standing, Pleading and Proof in Corporate Litigation' in *Company Law in Change* (ed Pettet, 1987).

32 A derivative action *must* be brought in the representative form, whereas personal actions to enforce shareholders' rights *may* be brought in such form: RSC, Ord 15, r.12.

33 The Court of Appeal in *Prudential* case has shown its reluctance to accept that the members and the company could be victims of the same wrong, because the members had not suffered independent damage.

34 See cases on alterations of articles allegedly not made '*bona fide* for the benefit of the company as a whole'; similar variations of class rights; 'oppression' cases such as *Clemens v Clemens Bros. Ltd.* [1976] 2 All ER 268, and *Pennell Securities Ltd. v Venida Investments Ltd.* (25 July 1974, unreported); *Hogg v Cramphorn Ltd.* [1967] Ch 254, and other 'proper purposes' decisions; *Alexander v Automatic Telephone Co.* [1900] 2 Ch 56, where the directors made discriminatory calls on shares.

where there is little on the surface to distinguish the action from a derivative suit. As a result of many poorly reasoned, illogical or inconsistent judicial pronouncements, the rule in this area is in impenetrable disarray.[35]

(ii) One difficulty shown by *Prudential Assurance Co Ltd. v Newman Industries Ltd. (No. 2)*[36] is the *prima facie* case which must be shown by the plaintiff in a derivative suit. The court would not allow a full scale trial to take place and at present, the best that it can do is to adjourn the matter while a shareholders' meeting is held, at which the question whether to litigate or not is put. The general meeting may not have the constitutional power to vote on such an issue. Whether the board is for some reason incompetent to act may be a question which can be resolved only after evidence has been heard.[37] Without hearing evidence, the court is in no position to know whether there is a serious risk that the meeting will not come to an informed decision.[38]

(iii) There is the unresolved problem of ratifiable and non-ratifiable wrongs which is shown by *Cook v Deeks*[39] and *Regal (Hastings) Ltd. v Gulliver*.[40] These decisions are supposedly distinguishable on the grounds that the former involved misappropriation of corporate assets, but the latter involved misappropriation of business opportunity - somewhere between the two cases and somewhere between *Daniels v Daniels*[41] and *Pavlides v Jensen*,[42] there is a grey area in which it is difficult to draw a line

(iv) Similarly, there is a difficulty in distinguishing between a breach of the articles of association which is serious enough to amount to a wrong done to the company, and one which is only an internal irregularity. Where articles require a special majority, the majority cannot ratify a wrong by ordinary resolution.[43] However, on other occasions the court allowed ratification by ordinary resolution on the ground that they involved only minor internal

35 See Sealy, op. cit. In *Lee v Chou Wen Hsien* [1985] BCLC 45, director was precluded by rule in *Foss v Harbottle* from challenging decision of fellow directors to expel him from office because it was a wrong done to company and his injuries were coincidental by-products. Contrast *Pulbrook v Richmond Consolidated Mining Co.* (1878) 9 Ch D 610, wrongful exclusion of director was held to be an individual wrong: applied in *Hayes v Bristol Plant Hire Co. Ltd.* [1957] 1 WLR 499.

36 [1982] Ch 204.

37 Wedderburn (1976) 39 MLR 327, at 328.

38 See also Sealy (1987) CLJ 398.

39 [1916] 1 AC 554.

40 [1942] 1 All ER 378, HL.

41 [1978] Ch 406.

41 [1978] Ch 406.

42 [1956] Ch 565.

43 *Edwards v Halliwell* [1950] 2 All ER 1064; *Quin & Axtens v Salmon* [1909] AC 422.

irregularities and were not an attempt to alter the articles.[44] But drawing the line between the two categories is not easy.

(v) Although it has been held that it is not necessary to plead equitable fraud with some particularity in the case of self-serving negligence,[45] the constraints regarding the pleading and proof of fraud misconceived by counsel has been encouraged by the courts. This can be an unnecessary deterrent to a minority shareholder's action.[46] In *Re Whitla Holdings Pty. Ltd.*, an action based on breach of fiduciary duty was dismissed because the alleged 'fraud' was not particularised in the pleadings.[47] Similarly, in *Pavlides v Jensen*, it was held that the minority action failed partly because the grossly undervalue sale was not alleged to be fraudulent but merely negligent.[48]

(vi) As the court insists on the discovery of documents and correspondence reasonably necessary to the conduct of the proceedings, to mount a successful derivative action the minority invariably needs to gain access to detailed internal accounts and records of the company to enable him to formulate any precise allegation against the wrongdoers. But this is generally denied.[49] The company's annual accounts and reports, various statutory minute books and registers to which members have access will not usually be sufficient.[50] To get detailed and up to date financial accounts, they need the co-operation of the company's auditor which may not always be forthcoming. In respect of the day-to-day management of the company's affairs, insider information is much needed if a minority is to succeed in bringing an action.[51]

44 Eg *Grant v UK Switchback Rly* (1888) 40 Ch D 135; *Irvine v Union Bank of Australia* (1877) 2 App Cas 366. But in *Hogg v Cramphorn* [1967] Ch 254, an individual shareholder was allowed to sue and was heard all the way to judgment even though the wrong was one which was within the competence of the company to put right.

45 *Daniels v Daniels* [1978] Ch 406, per Templeman J at 413H-414B.

46 See Sealy, 'Problem of Standing, Pleading and Proof in Corporate Litigation' in *Company Law in Change* (ed Pettet, 1987).

47 (1982) 7 ACLR 348.

48 [1956] Ch 565.

49 Although in *Re Glamorganshire Banking Company* (1884) 28 Ch D 620, Bacon VC (at 625) said that if fraud or inaccuracy were suggested the court would exercise its discretion to see that justice was done, the conventional legal wisdom normally denies the shareholder any right of access.

50 The Cadbury Committee points out that the basic weakness in the current system of financial reporting is the possibility of different accounting treatments being applied to essentially the same facts, with the consequence that different results or financial positions could be reported, each apparently complying with the overriding requirement to show a true and fair view: Cadbury Committee, The Financial Aspects of Corporate Governance, 1 December 1992, para 4.47.

51 Hadden, *Company Law and Capitalism*, 2nd ed., at 280-282. In *Murray's Judicial Factor v Murray & Sons* [1993] BCLC 1437, while recognising that a member was entitled to examine the accounting records of the company and that an order might be made to enable a member to inspect the books of account, the Court of Session, Inner House (1st division) held that a member was not entitled to know the basis of a valuation of the company property or the identity of the valuer. It was sufficient that he was told what the valuation was (at 1451f).

The Cadbury Committee[52] points out that shareholders need a coherent narrative report and accounts, supported by the figures of the company's performance and prospects. It recommends that the board of directors should present a balanced and understandable assessment of the company's position.[53] It also recommends that balance sheet information should be included with interim reports.[54] Although it advocates for the highest level of disclosure consonant with presenting reports which are understandable, it recognises the need to avoid damage to their competitive position by detailed reporting.[55] These recommendations if adopted may help minority shareholders to get more information to support their claims. But they are unlikely to eliminate the problem altogether.

(vii) A minority shareholder who brings a derivative suit may have a right to an indemnity against the company in respect of his costs if he has acted in good faith and reasonably in bringing proceedings.[56] Provided the authority of the court is obtained in advance, the minority is reasonably safe from having to pay the costs of an unsuccessful action themselves. But they will have to take the risk of paying for counsel's opinion, which the court may require before sanctioning further proceedings at the company's expense.[57] In determining whether such an order is to be made the court has to decide whether an independent board of directors or shareholders would in the circumstances have properly authorised an action in the name of the company.[58] The minority may also have to persuade other shareholders to vote in favour of proceedings against the wrongdoer at any shareholders' meeting, which the court may require to be summoned. If further proceedings are not sanctioned by the meeting or the court any costs incurred will have to be paid by the minority. Given that it is difficult for the minority to gain detailed internal information, it is equally difficult to persuade other shareholders and the court to sanction proceedings in order to secure the costs.

(viii) There are far more fundamental problems which may not be resolved even if Parliament were to pass a law abolishing the rule in *Foss v Harbottle*.[59] The first problem is the inherent unsuitability of our traditional adversarial procedure for the purpose of an action brought by a minority

52 Cadbury Committee, The Financial Aspects of Corporate Governance, 1 December 1992, para. 4.50.
53 Ibid., para. 4.50.
54 Ibid., para. 4.56.
55 Ibid., para. 4.51.
56 *Wallersteiner v Moir (No. 2)* [1975] 2 QB 373.
57 Hadden, at 279-280.
58 Ibid., at 222-3.
59 Sealy, op. cit.

shareholder. As already mentioned, our rules of company law give a shareholder virtually no rights of access to 'inside' corporate information. Procedural rules require an orderly sequence of pleading without allowing discovery until the issues are well defined. Such an instinctive desire to have the security of the familiar adversarial framework persists even after the enactment of s.210 of the Companies Act 1948. A rule which required the petitioner to specify from the outset the relief that he was seeking was devised.[60]

Closely related to such procedural difficulties is the problem of the court's unwillingness and inability to hear a case. The Court of Appeal's concern in the *Prudential* case, about the expense and injustice which could be caused by a full scale trial of the preliminary issue of *locus standi* which the plaintiff might ultimately lose, is understandable. But the only alternative suggested, that a once-for-all ruling had to be given without any evidence being heard at all, is equally undesirable.[61]

1.5 Personal right action

A member can bring a personal action for breach of personal rights which arise from the Companies Acts,[62] the memorandum and articles of association, or a separate shareholders' agreement. He may also bring a representative action on behalf of a group of members whose same personal rights have been infringed. In these actions where breach of personal rights is alleged, the rule in *Foss v Harbottle* does not apply. However, the dilemma is that it has long been regarded as settled that a wrong which is done to the company cannot be a wrong done to the member personally.[63] The problem which arises in many cases is the difficulty of identifying with any degree of precision whether a wrong is done to the company or to the members personally.[64]

---

60 *Re Antigen Laboratories Ltd.* [1951] 1 All ER 110n. Warner J expressed a similar view in *Re J E Cade & Son Ltd.* [1991] BCC 360, at 368F, a recent case on s.459. But as the form set out in the schedule to the Companies (Unfair Prejudice Applications) Proceedings Rule 1986 envisages, it is possible for the petitioner to add 'such other order may be made as the court thinks fit' in the petition. Judges in other jurisdictions such as in *Ling Beng Sung v Kong Thai Sawmill (Miri) Sdn Bhd* [1976] 1 MLJ 59, in which the Malaysian Federal Court, not specifically aided by the pleadings, made a series of detailed orders dealing with matters ranging from the destiny of the company's yacht to the amount of notice to be given of directors' meetings, have seen no need to limit their own scope for creative action in this way.

61 Sealy, op. cit.

62 Eg ss.4 and 9 of the Companies Act 1985 protecting members' rights in the memorandum and articles from being altered without a special resolution in general meeting; ss.125 to 127 of the same Act regulating variation of class rights and ss.428 to 430F giving minority who are subject to compulsory acquisition in a take-over rights to challenge the acquisition.

63 See eg *MacDougall v Gardiner* (1875) 1 Ch 13, at 25; *Edwards v Halliwell* [1950] 2 All ER 1064, at 1066g-h, *Prudential Assurance v Newman Industries (No. 2)* [1982] Ch 204, at 224A-D.

64 See para. 1.4(i) above

Furthermore, where a member alleges breach of rights conferred on him by the articles of association in his capacity as an outsider, eg a solicitor or a director of the company, it is not entirely clear whether he will succeed in his action. The contractual effect of rights conferred by the memorandum and articles under s.14 has been the subject of great academic debate and various views have been put forward. Under s.14 of the Companies Act 1985, memorandum and articles of association constitute a contract between the company and its members[65] and are enforceable amongst the members *inter se*.[66] But the orthodox view is that s.14 only gives memorandum and articles of association contractual effect insofar as they confer rights or obligations on the member qua member.[67] Wedderburn suggested that every member has a right to see that the company is run according to the articles, except for those articles already identified as concerning internal procedures only.[68] And since articles constitute a contract between the company and its members, a member can sue in a personal action even if that has the effect of enforcing rights conferred on him or anyone else otherwise than as a member, so long as he sues as a member.[69] This view has not yet received support in judicial dicta. The academic debate is an ongoing one, but it is perhaps rendered less significant today as a result of the development of s.459.

It is also not well settled whether a member can bring a personal action against wrongdoing directors for breach of duties.[70] This is because it is said that directors owe their duties to the company, are the duties also owed to a member personally and only in very limited circumstances, the precise scope of which is not well defined, are the duties also owed to a member personally. More recently, Hoffmann J suggested in very general terms that the directors' duty to issue shares for a proper purpose was owed to the members, not the company.[71] It is however difficult to say whether Hoffmann J's view is supported by authorities.

---

65 *Hickman v Kent* or *Romney Marsh Sheep-Breeders' Assn* [1915] 1 Ch 881.

66 *Wood v Odessa Waterworks Co.* (1889) 42 Ch D 636, *Rayfield v Hands* [1960] Ch 1.

67 *Hickman*'s case, supra, *Eley v Positive Government Security Life Assurance Co. Ltd.* (1876) 1 Ex D 88, *Beattie v Beattie* [1938] Ch 708. Gower's *Principles of Modern Company Law*, 5th ed., 1992, pp.285-288.

68 Wedderburn (1957) CLJ 194, at 214-215, also (1958) CLJ 93.

69 Wedderburn, ibid., citing *Quin & Axtens v Salmon* [1909] 1 Ch 311; *Re H R Harmer* [1958] 3 All ER 689. In *Quin*'s case, Farwell LJ said (at 319) that Salmon has a right to prevent the attempt to alter, by a simple resolution instead of a special resolution, the terms of the contract between the parties. Such a general right to enforce the articles would therefore appear to offend the rules in *Foss v Harbottle* (1843) 2 Hare 461 itself, which prevent action by minority shareholders for internal irregularities. For other views see Drury [1986] CLJ 219, Prentice (1980) Co. Law 179, Gregory (1981) 44 MLR 526, Goldberg (1972) 35 MLR 363, (1985) 48 MLR 158.

70 See Chapter 3, para. 3.2 (g). Beck ((1974) 52 Can Bar Rev 159, at 171-172) suggested that any breach of director's duty should give rise to a personal action.

71 *Re a Company (No. 005136 of 1986)* (1986) 2 BCC 99, 528 [1987] BCLC 82. Sub nom *Re Sherborne Park Residents Co. Ltd.*

The other potential obstacle in a member's personal action is the rule that the court will not interfere with matters of pure internal management of the company.[72] Quite what are treated as minor internal irregularities which are ratifiable and not actionable and what are more serious breaches of articles is uncertain. It is therefore difficult to lay down any generally accepted test of what is and what is not an actionable personal right. It is perhaps easier to list personal rights that had been recognised (not intended to be exhaustive) as follows:[73]

(1) The right to receive timely[74] and informative[75] notice of company meetings.

(2) The right to vote at such meetings and have votes recorded.[76]

(3) The right to have a properly executed proxy accepted.[77]

(4) The right to inspect certain of the corporation's records.[78]

(5) The right not to have class rights varied or abrogated.[79]

(6) The right not to have some right conferred upon them by articles or by-laws infringed.[80]

(7) The right not to have the internal corporate structure altered in a manner that amounts to a fraud on the minority.[81]

(8) The right to enforce a declared dividend as a legal debt.[82]

(9) The right to sue in respect of a decision to enter into an *ultra vires*[83] or illegal[84] transaction.

(10) The right to challenge a special resolution to alter the company's articles which was not passed *bona fide* in the interest of the company.[85]

72 *Grant v UK Switchback Railways Co.* (1888) 40 Ch D 135 and *Irvine v Union Bank of Australia* (1877) 2 App Cas 366.

73 *Mayson, French & Ryan on Company Law*, 10th ed., at 555-556.

74 *Charter Oil Co. Ltd. v Beaumont* (1967) 65 DLR (2d) 112 (BCCA).

75 *Kaye v Croyden Tramways Co.* [1898] 1 Ch 358 (CA).

76 *Pender v Lushington* (1877) 6 Ch D 70 (CA).

77 *Johnson v Hall* (1957) 10 DLR (2d) 243 (BCSC).

78 *Cooper v The Premier Trust* [1945] OR 35.

79 *White v Bristol Aeroplane Co.* [1953] Ch 65 (CA); *Greenhalgh v Arderne Cinemas* [1950] 2 All ER 1120; *Re John Smith's Todcaster Brewery* [1953] Ch 308 (CA).

80 *Wood v Odessa Waterworks* (1889) 42 Ch D 636 (to have a dividend paid in cash where articles so specify); *Quin & Axtens Ltd. v Salmon* [1909] AC 442; *Edwards v Halliwell* [1950] 2 All ER 1064 (to have the articles observed if they specify a certain procedure to be followed in a particular instance).

81 *Brown v British Abrasive Wheel Co.* [1919] 1 Ch 290.

82 *Mosely v Koffyfontein Mines Ltd.* [1904] 2 Ch 108 (CA).

83 *Simpson v Westminster Palace Hotel Co.* (1860) 8 HL Cas 712. See also s.35(2) and (3) of Companies Act 1985 (as amended by s.108 of the Companies Act 1989).

84 *Hope v International Financial Society* (1876) 4 ChD 327.

85 *Allen v Gold Reefs of West Africa Ltd.* [1900] 1 Ch 656.

(11) The right to challenge a resolution that was not properly adopted because votes cast against it were improperly rejected.[86]

(12) The right to challenge a decision by directors to allot shares where the decision is not *bona fide* in the company's interests or is for an improper purpose.[87]

(13) The right to challenge a decision of the members to pay a dividend that was less than the memorandum required to be paid.[88]

(14) The right to challenge an irregular forfeiture of shares by directors.[89]

(15) The right to challenge the improper conduct of elections of directors or other officers.[90]

(16) The right against directors for breach of fiduciary duties in causing the company to levy calls on shares of some shareholders but not others.[91]

On the other hand, a member cannot enforce any right to have a poll taken where to do so would be futile.[92] He does not have a right to have company accounts prepared in accordance with the requirements of the Companies Act,[93] or to have directors retire in accordance with the articles.[94] Nor can he sue wrongdoing directors for loss in the value of his shares where that wrongdoing had caused damage to the company and the shareholders' loss is only consequential to it.[95]

1.6 Just and equitable winding up and its limitations

A member often petitions under s.122(1)(g) of the Insolvency Act 1986 for the company to be wound up on the ground that it is just and equitable to do so. This was a very popular remedy in the days when minority actions were litigated with great difficulties at common law. But it was an unsatisfactory remedy particularly where the company was a going concern. It was also

86 *Pender v Lushington* (1877) 6 Ch D 70.
87 *Fraser v Whalley* (1864) 2 Hem & M 10.
88 *Evling v Israel & Oppenheimer Ltd.* [1918] 1 Ch 101.
89 *Sweny v Smith* (1869) LR 7 Eq 324.
90 *Ryan v South Sydney Junior Rugby League Club Ltd.* (1974) 3 ACLR 486 (NSW); *Pappaioannoy v The Greek Orthodox Community of Melbourne* (1978) 3 ACLR 801.
91 *Galloway v Halle Concerts Society* [1915] 2 Ch 233.
92 *MacDougall v Gardiner* (1875) 1 ChD 13 (CA).
93 *Devlin v Slough Estates Ltd.* [1983] BCLC 497. (The Cadbury Committee does not appear to have made any recommendation to redress this problem.)
94 *Mozley v Alston* (1847) 1 Ph 790.
95 *Prudential v Newman (No. 2)* [1982] Ch 204 at 223 (CA).

frequently used in conjunction with, and as alternative to, s.459 until the recent Practice Direction which draws attention to the undesirability of including as a matter of course a prayer for winding up as an alternative to relief under s.459.[96]

The circumstances in which it would be just and equitable to wind up a company are extremely wide. Lord Wilberforce in the landmark case of *Re Westbourne Galleries* suggested that a company can be wound up on the just and equitable ground not only where there is a breach of rights and obligations defined by the Companies Act and the articles of association, but also where there is a breach of equitable rights, obligation and legitimate expectations, if the company is formed or continued on the basis of a personal relationship, involving mutual confidence, or if there is an agreement or understanding giving members equitable rights, obligations or expectations (in *Westbourne Galleries* case, that all or some of the members shall participate in the conduct of the business), or if there is a restriction on the transfer of the members' interest in the company.[97] Other circumstances where winding up is just and equitable are cases where a member can show a justifiable loss of confidence in the probity of the majority,[98] where there is a total deadlock[99] in the management of the affairs of the company,[100] or where the main objects for which the company was formed cannot now be achieved.[101]

Relief will however be refused if the court is also of the opinion that some other remedy, for example relief under s.459, is available to the petitioners and that they are acting unreasonably in seeking to have the company wound up instead of pursuing that other remedy.[102] The availability of relief under s.459 has perhaps placed some limitations on the application of s.122(1)(g).[103] Other limitations are procedural. Under s.124 of the 1986 Act, only a contributory who has had shares allotted to him or held by him and registered in his name for at least six months during the 18 months before the commencement of the winding up may apply for a winding up order under s.122(1)(g). A contributory who has not held shares for the requisite period of time may petition under s.122(1)(g) only if the number of members is reduced

96 Practice Direction (winding up: petition by contributory) (Ch 1/90) [1990] BCLC 452 dated 22 February 1990.

97 [1973] AC 360, at 379 E-G.

98 *Loch v John Blackwood Ltd.* [1924] AC 783.

99 This is rare as the chairman will often have a casting vote to break the deadlock at board level, and if this does not solve the problem, the matter will be decided by the general meeting: *Barron v Potter* [1914] 1 Ch 895.

100 *Re Yenidje Tobacco Co. Ltd.* [1916] 2 Ch 426.

101 *Re German Date Coffee Co.* (1882) 20 Ch D 169.

102 Section 125(2) of the Insolvency Act 1986.

103 See Chapter 6, para. 6.9 below.

below two or the shares have devolved on him through the death of a former holder. A contributory is any person who is liable to contribute to the assets of a company in the event of its being wound up.[104] A fully paid-up member who is not liable to contribute has to show that he has a tangible interest in the winding up.[105] A petitioner must also come with clean hands, and so his petition may be rejected if the matters complained of were largely due to his own misconduct.[106]

1.7 History of s.459 of the Companies Act 1985

Section 210 of the Companies Act 1948 was introduced as a result of the recommendation made by the Cohen Committee[107] to provide protection for a minority shareholder who was a victim of oppression and who did not wish to take the drastic step of winding up the company. The section allowed any member of a company to petition to the court if the affairs of the company were being conducted in a manner oppressive to some part of the members (including himself). If the court was satisfied that the facts would justify a winding-up order on the just and equitable ground, and that this would unduly prejudice that part of the members, it had power to make such order as it thought fit to end the matter complained of.

Section 210 was intended to provide an individual member remedies free from the restrictions of the *Foss v Harbottle* rule. It had the advantage over just and equitable winding up of being less draconian and more flexible; it enabled the court to impose whatever solution it considered appropriate. Although the section was intended to be an efficient and effective alternative remedy[108] to just and equitable winding up and other common law protections, this objective was not achieved. Proceedings were soon pushed into an adversarial straitjacket.[109] The petitioner had to prove oppression qua member.[110] Mere negligence and mismanagement were excluded from the scope of the section.[111] Excessive remuneration was held not to be oppression,[112] neither was a breakdown of relationships between

---

[104] Section 79 of the Insolvency Act 1986.
[105] *Re Rica Gold Washing Co.* (1879) 11 Ch D 36.
[106] *Re Westbourne Galleries Ltd.* [1972] 2 All ER 492, at 507, [1973] AC 360, at 387, per Lord Cross. A petitioner under s.459 does not have to come with clean hands although his conduct will be taken into account: see Chapter 4 para. 4.8(a) below.
[107] Cmnd. 6659.
[108] Cmnd. 6659, p. 95.
[109] *Re Antigen Laboratories Ltd.* [1951] 1 All ER 110n.
[110] *Elder v Elder & Watson Ltd.* (1952) SC 49; *Re Westbourne Galleries Ltd.* [1970] 1 WLR 1378.
[111] *Re Five Minute Car Wash Service Ltd.* [1966] 1 WLR 745.
[112] *Re Jermyn Street Turkish Baths* [1971] 1 WLR 1042.

participants.[113] Petitioners had to show that they had a tangible interest in the outcome,[114] but to wind up the company would be unfairly prejudicial to the petitioner.[115] The petitioner ought not to petition under s.210 for any collateral purpose.[116] The conduct complained of had to be of a continuing nature.[117] A remedy was sometimes denied because alternative forms of relief were thought more appropriate.[118]

Although the parliamentary draftsman maybe partially at fault, the problem was more a matter of judicial psychology than inadequate drafting.[119] There are only two reported cases in the UK where petitioners successfully relied on the section[120] - a disappointing record when compared with the just and equitable ground for winding up. The two decisions related to circumstances very different from those in which the Cohen Committee envisaged that the section was most likely to be employed.[121] The wider application of the section in the two cases was of course desirable as it would advance the remedy.[122] What is unfortunate is that other applications, in the circumstances which the Committee did envisage, were unsuccessful.[123]

The Jenkins Committee recommended certain changes which were adopted by Parliament in the form of s.75 of the Companies Act 1980 and contained today in s.459 to s.461 of the Companies Act 1985. There is now a new spirit in the air with s.459 of the 1985 Act (as amended) where, *inter alia*, 'unfairly prejudicial conduct' has replaced the requirement of 'oppression'.

---

113 *Elder v Elder & Watson Ltd.* (1952) SC 49.

114 *Re Bellador Silk Ltd.* [1965] 1 All ER 667, but see Lord Denning's dicta in *Scottish Co-operative Wholesale Society v Meyer* [1959] AC 324 (s.210 was not limited to cases where the company was still in active business. It could apply even though the business of the company had been brought to a standstill).

114 Section 210, CA 1948.

116 *Re Bellador Silk Ltd.* [1965] 1 All ER 667.

117 *Re Jermyn Street Turkish Baths Ltd.* [1971] 1 WLR 1042.

118 Ibid.

119 Sealy, op. cit.

120 *Re H R Harmer Ltd.* [1958] 3 All ER 689 and *Scottish Co-operative Wholesale Society v Meyer* [1959] AC 324.

121 Unreasonable refusal to pass transfer so as to force a sale to themselves at a low price and taking excessive remuneration so as to leave nothing for distributions by way of dividend. (Cmnd. 6659, paras. 58 and 59).

122 Lord Denning clearly agreed that this should be so ([1957] AC 324, HL., at 369).

123 A personal representative who was refused registration could not claim to be a member and therefore could not petition under s.210 and excessive remuneration was held not covered by the section: *Re Jermyn Street Turkish Baths Ltd.* [1971] 1 WLR 1042 (CA) (for a different view see Pennycuick J at first instance [1970] 1 WLR 1194 (Ch Division)).

Chapter 2

The Unfair Prejudice Remedy: Preliminary Matters

Section 459(1) of Companies Act 1985 as amended by s.145 of Companies Act 1989 (Schedule 19, para. 11)[1] provides that:

> 'A member of a company may apply to the court by petition for an order under this Part on the ground that the company's affairs are being or have been conducted in a manner which is *unfairly prejudicial to the interests of its members generally or of some part of its members* (including at least himself) or that any actual or proposed act or omission of the company (including an act or omission on its behalf) is or would be so prejudicial.'

2.1 Who can petition under s.459?

In accordance with the judicial policy of non-intervention, a petitioner under s.459 must establish *locus standi* from the outset. Failure to do so will prevent the petitioner from petitioning, regardless of the merits of the case. This is not to drive a litigant from the judgment seat, or to do any injustice to him, but merely to require him to establish his right to present a petition before he is permitted to take a step which has such an immediate and potentially damaging effect on the company.[2]

Section 459(1) provides that a member of the company may petition. One of the problems of the old s.210 was the question of the *locus standi* of a trustee in bankruptcy, personal representative of a bankrupt or deceased member. In *Re Jermyn Street Turkish Baths Ltd.*,[3] Pennycuick J held that on the facts the petitioners had in fact become registered as members and therefore their status was beyond question.[4] He went on to hold that even without registration, the petitioners, as personal representatives of a deceased

---

1 Came into force on 4 February 1991: Companies Act 1989 (Commencement No. 8 and Transitional and Saving Provisions) Order 1990 (SI 1990 No. 2569), Article 4(e).

2 Per Brightman J in *Re JN2 Ltd.* [1978] 1 WLR 183, at 188c (a case of just and equitable winding up).

3 [1970] 1 WLR 1194.

4 Sealy argued ([1970] CLJ 215, at 216) that Pennycuick J had failed to consider the latter part of Article 21 of Table A (1929) when he quoted the first part of it, and notices of general meetings were not at any time sent to the representatives nor apparently asked for by them, which would have been done if they were thought to have become members. It is submitted that Sealy had overlooked the finding of the judge. The company secretary wrote to the company's auditor, on 21 November 1961, that they 'have duly registered the Administrators in the company's books'. The register of

member, had to be regarded as members of a company for the purposes of s.210.[5] However, although it was a welcome and valuable ruling, it was necessarily *obiter*, as on the facts the personal representatives had been registered as members. It was also contrary to the Australian decision in *Re Meyer Douglas.*[6] Furthermore s.26(2) of the CA 1948 (now s.22(2) of CA 1985) limited the definition of membership to 'every other person who agrees to become a member of a company *and* whose name is entered in its register of members ...'. A personal representative, who agrees to become a member of a company but whose name is not yet entered in its register of members, cannot be regarded as a member for the purposes of the provisions in the Companies Act 1985.[7] So despite Pennycuick J's interpretation, it would seem that personal representatives of a deceased member could not be regarded as a member before registration.[8] This is certainly unfortunate and undesirable as one of the species of oppression which the Cohen Committee had in mind was that of the personal representative who was refused by the company directors to register as the holder of a deceased member's shares and who was therefore forced to sell at whatever price the shareholders, often the majority, saw fit to pay.[9]

In view of the uncertainty and the extremely disadvantageous position of a successor in title, s.459(2), implementing the recommendations of the Jenkins Committee,[10] further extends the application of s.459(1) 'to a person who is not a member of a company but to whom shares in the company have been transferred or transmitted by operation of law, as those provisions apply to a

members kept by the company also revealed that on the same page of the register where Littman's name appeared, as the holder of 50 shares, 'the administrator of' was added before 'Littman', and then the names and addresses of the administrators and 'Registered 21 November 1961' followed ([1970] 1 WLR 1194, at 1204H-1205A). Article 21 was irrelevant because the directors had not exercised their powers under it. As no particular form was required by statute or under the articles for registration of personal representatives in the register of members of the company, the nature of the entry in the company's register depended on the intention of the parties. On the facts, the administrator had requested to be registered which the company duly did.

5 [1970] 1 WLR 1194, at 1205G. He applied, by analogy, Buckley J's decision in *Re Bayswater Trading Co. Ltd.* [1970] 1 WLR 343 which held that for the purpose of s.353 of the Companies Act 1948, the word 'member' had to include representatives of a deceased member. However, as s.26(2) was not considered by Buckley J, the case may be *per incuriam*. See also current Table A Articles 29-31 which entitle a personal representative to the shares of the deceased and to be registered as a member.

6 [1965] VR 638, (Supreme Court of Victoria) (s.16(5) of the Companies Act 1961 provides that members includes 'every other person who agrees to become a member of a company and whose name is entered in its register of members'. Gowans J held that the personal representative of a deceased member was not, before being registered, a member, and therefore was not competent to lodge a petition as a member under s.186 of the 1961 Act, which was similar to s.210 of the English Companies Act 1948); Sealy [1970] CLJ 215, at 216.

7 Rajak [1972] 35 MLR 156.

8 See Cmnd. 1749, para. 209.

9 Cmnd. 6659, para. 58.

10 Cmnd. 1749, para. 212(f).

member of the company; and reference to a member or members are to be construed accordingly'.

Therefore, to have the right to present a petition, the petitioner has to be either a member as defined in s.22 of the CA 1985, or a person to whom shares in the company have been transferred or transmitted by operation of law.[11] This will now be considered in more detail.

(a) Member

Section 22(1) of the 1985 Act provides that 'the subscribers of a company's memorandum are deemed to have agreed to become members of the company, and on its registration shall be entered as such in its register of members'. Section 22(2) further provides that 'every other person who agrees to become a member of a company and whose name is entered in its register of members is a member of the company'. The provision in s.22 has the advantage of certainty, as it can be more readily determined who are the persons registered as members at a given time. Problems, however, occur where errors have been made in the making of entries in the register of members. Though a person can, and should, bring an action for rectification of the register of members pursuant to s.359 of the 1985 Act, before presenting a petition under s.459, the real issue is whether that person, having obtained rectification, can complain about conduct unfairly prejudicial to himself at a time when he was not registered as a member but was entitled to rectification of the register. There has been no case law as yet on this point, though clearly such an action should lie.[12]

An ancillary issue where a person is not a subscriber but has been registered as a member is whether the word 'agrees' in s.22(2) is satisfied by a mere assent of the prospective member or whether a contract (an agreement in

---

11 Pennycuick J's *obiter dictum* in *Re Jermyn Street Turkish Baths* [1970] 1 WLR 1194 seems redundant now.

12 Prentice argues ((1988) 8 OJLS 55, at 62) that a transferee of shares should be able to seek relief for unfairly prejudicial conduct which occurred before he became a member. Robin Hollington (*Minority Shareholders' Rights* (1990), at para. 4-003) said that it was implicit in *Re Quickdome* (1988) 4 BCC 296 that a person entitled to rectification of the register could complain about that conduct, although obviously much would depend on the circumstances. With respect, the author finds it difficult to understand how such an inference could be drawn from Mervyn Davies J's judgment. Mervyn Davies J's judgment concerned petition by a person to whom shares were allegedly transferred and not a person who was entitled to be registered as a member; and Mervyn Davies J made no mention on the latter (see Mervyn Davies J's judgment at 300-301, (1988) 4 BCC 296). The Court's reluctance to allow shareholders to whom shares are not properly transmitted by operation of law (*Re Quickdome*, supra, *Re a Company (No. 003160 of 1986)* [1986] BCLC 391 at 393) shows that the petitioner must be a member at the time the act took place. So it is likely that the court may refuse a petition by a person who was not registered at the material time but was entitled to rectification.

the technical sense) between the prospective member and the company is necessary.[13] This issue was raised in *Re Nuneaton Borough Association Football Club Ltd.*[14] where the Chancery Division thought that the section contemplated 'an agreement in the technical sense between the prospective member and the company'. Fox LJ in the Court of Appeal said that he was not sure precisely what the deputy judge meant by 'an agreement in the technical sense' - whether he meant a contract or some bilateral agreement falling short of a contract. However he concluded that as a matter of English the word 'agrees' was satisfied by mere assent - to accept favourably ... to accede, to consent to, a conclusion with which Nicholls and Ralph Gibson LLJ agreed. He did not think that a contract was necessary and thought that the section made no reference to any bilateral element.[15] Nicholls LJ said that the 'contract' interpretation of the word 'agrees' was also rejected by a contextual approach to interpretation. First, the 'contract' interpretation does not produce a workable result in the case of a person who acquired his shares from a transferor as, in the normal way, a transferee of shares does not enter into a binding contract with the company prior to being entered on its register. Secondly, the company is protected by s.22(2) by stipulating that a further requisite of membership is entry in the register of members maintained by the company. As the register may be rectified by the court under s.359 in cases where there is no true consent on the part of the would-be member or an entry is made in error or without due authority, the requirement that there must be a prior binding contract between the company and the would-be member serves no useful purpose.[16] It was, therefore, held that what was needed was the unilateral consent of the prospective member.[17]

(b) Persons to whom shares have been transferred or transmitted by operation of law

Personal representatives, administrators of estates of deceased persons or trustees in bankruptcy are now given *locus standi* to bring a s.459 petition. However, a strict interpretation of the provision in s.459(2) has been applied by the court.

---

13 The issue of agreement does not arise in the case of a subscriber, as a subcriber is deemed to have agreed to become the member of the company (s.22(1)), and what is necessary is the registration of his membership by the company.

14 (1989) 5 BCC 377. See also Lowry (1992) JBL 186.

15 Ibid., at 380c. *Re Railway Time Tables Publishing Co.* (1889) 42 Ch D. 98, *Re Disderi & Co.* (1870) LR 11 Eq 242, and *Re James Pilkin & Co. Ltd.* (1916) 85 LJ Ch 318 were cited.

16 (1989) 5 BCC 377, at 382H-383C.

17 *Re Richmond Hill Hotel Co.* (1867) LR 2 Ch App 527 was held inapplicable by Nicholls LJ as being a case merely of an example of a set of circumstances in which an apparent consent was, in law, no consent at all.

First, the word 'transferred' in s.459(2) contemplates at least that a proper instrument of transfer should have been executed and delivered to the transferee or the company in respect of the shares in question. It was held in *Re a Company (No. 003160 of 1986)* that it was not sufficient that there should be an agreement for transfer.[18]

In *Re Quickdome Ltd.*[19] a company had been bought off the shelf and the subscribers (the company formation agents) had executed stock transfer forms in blank without naming the transferees. Unfortunately, the purchasers never registered any share transfers. When one of them petitioned under s.459, Mervyn Davies J held that she had no *locus standi* to present a petition under Part XVII of the 1985 Act since she was not registered as a shareholder and was not named as a transferee in the stock transfer forms. He found that no proper instrument of transfer had been executed as the transfer relied on was a blank as to the name of the transferee. The fact that she had an equity to have the transfer completed in her favour provided no assistance as the equity sprang from the share transfer agreements and the words of Hoffmann J in *Re a Company (No. 003160 of 1986)* showed that it was not sufficient that there be an agreement for transfer.

Secondly, the phrase 'transmitted by operation of law'[20] refers to a legal process by which the legal title passes, even though there be some further act (such as registration) to be done, and does not cover the creation of an equitable interest, for example, under a trust. The mere assertion that constructive trust arises (which is frequently a remedy imposed on the conscience of the person affected, rather than an existing legal act) cannot possibly amount to a transmission by operation of law.[21]

In *Re a Company (No. 007828 of 1985)*[22] the argument was rejected that the petitioners had agreed to acquire shares in the company, that they were the equitable owners of the shares, and consequently were persons to whom the shares had been transmitted by operation of law.

18 Per Hoffmann J (1986) 2 BCC 99, 276 at 99, 279 affirmed by Mervyn Davies J in *Re Quickdome Ltd.* (1988) 4 BCC 296, at 300.
19 See Fox and Bastin (1989) 133 SJ 474.
20 The typical case of shares transmitted by operation of law would be a person entitled to shares upon the death or bankruptcy of a shareholder.
21 *Re a Company (No. 007828 of 1985)* (1986) 2 BCC 98, 951, at 98, 954.
22 Ibid.

(c) Member alleged to have been erroneously registered as such

Where the respondent alleges that the petitioner has been erroneously registered as such and seeks to strike out the petition, whether the petition will be stayed or struck out pending resolution of this dispute or not is a matter of convenience, not a matter of law. The general rule in the case of a contributory's winding up petition is to require determination of the dispute before presentation of the petition.[23] This rule seems to have less force in the case of unfair prejudice petition. In *Re Garage Door Associates*[24] Mervyn Davies J refused to strike out a petition where the petitioner was alleged to have no beneficial interest in the capital of the company. It was held that the issue as to share ownership could be determined in the course of the petition.

2.2 What needs to be shown?

Having established *locus standi*, the petitioner must show that the company's affairs are being, or have been, conducted in a manner which is unfairly prejudicial to his interest qua member,[25] or that the company's act (actual or proposed) or omission is, or would be, so prejudicial.

Section 210 of the 1948 Act was limited to conduct of a continuing nature and did not apply to isolated acts of oppression which did not exist at the time the petition was presented.[26] Thus directors' improper overriding of a resolution of the shareholders properly passed in the general meeting to sell a lease which the company possessed was thought, as an isolated incident, not to be a sufficient ground for an order under s.210 which required a course of oppressive conduct continuing up to the date of the petition.[27]

In *Re Jermyn Street Turkish Baths Ltd.*,[28] Buckley LJ said that an allegation that the directors had improperly allotted shares to themselves would not be sufficient under s.210 as the terms of s.210 made it clear that the oppression complained of had to be operative at the time when the petition was filed.[29]

---

23 Per Brightman J in *Re JN2 Ltd.* [1978] 1 WLR 183, at 188.
24 [1983] BCLC 164.
25 See Chapter 3 para. 3.1 below. The qua member requirement is somewhat redundant in quasi-partnership company cases: see *Re a Company (No. 00477 of 1986)* [1986] BCLC 376.
26 See Roxburgh J's judgment at first instance in *Re Harmer* quoted by Jenkin LJ in the Court of Appeal [1959] 1 WLR 62, at 84.
27 *Re Westbourne Galleries Ltd.* [1970] 1 WLR 1378, at 1390G; [1970] 3 All ER 374, at 385a.
28 [1971] 3 All ER 184; [1971] 1 WLR 1042.
29 [1971] 3 All ER 184, at 198; [1971] 1 WLR 1042, at 1058H; see also Pennycuick J's dictum at first instance [1970] 3 All ER 57, at 66g; [1970] 1 WLR 1194, at 1207C.

Although it may be argued that such situations as happened in *Re Westbourne Galleries Ltd.*[30] and *Re Jermyn Street* may be regarded as giving rise to 'continuing' wrongs on the ground that the company and its shareholders continued to be deprived by such oppressive conduct, and that this element of continuity was present so long as the company neglected to remedy the oppressive conduct, the courts were not impressed by this argument. This unsatisfactorily restrictive approach of the courts to limit the application of s.210 to conduct which was of a continuous nature conflicted with the principle laid down in the House of Lords in *Scottish Cooperative Wholesale Society v Meyer* that the court in construing s.210 had to have regard to business realities and not legal technicalities.[31] Implementing the Jenkins Committee's recommendation,[32] s.459 now applies to isolated acts as well as a course of conduct. An isolated past act or omission[33] is sufficient. The courts also have jurisdiction to remedy a proposed future act or omission.[34] However, as was required under s.210, the actions complained of under s.459 must consist of the conduct of 'the company's affairs' or an 'act or omission of the company (including an act or omission on its behalf)'.[35]

The first limb of s.459(1) deals with the way in which the company's affairs 'are being or have been conducted'. It does not seem to provide a remedy for the way in which the company's affairs would be conducted in the future. The second limb deals with actual or proposed acts or omissions of the company (including one on its behalf) which are or would be unfairly prejudicial. However it is not entirely clear[36] if Parliament intended to introduce any real distinction between 'company's affairs' and 'act or omission of the company'. The meaning of 'company's affairs' and 'acts or omissions of the company' will now be considered.

(a) Company's affairs

There is no definition of what constitutes the 'affairs' of the company in the context of s.459. It has been held to be a phrase with a 'wide meaning'[37] and

30 [1970] 1 WLR 1378; [1970] 3 All ER 374.
31 [1959] AC 342, at 343.
32 Cmnd. 1749, at paras. 202, 212(b).
33 Section 459(1). *Scottish Co-operative Wholesale Society v Meyer* [1959] AC 342, at 362.
34 *Re Whyte* 1984 SLT 330; *Re Kenyon Swansea Ltd.* (1987) 3 BCC 259.
35 See *Re a Company (No. 001761 of 1986)* [1987] BCLC 141, at 144f-g.
36 Prentice (1988) 8 OJLS 55, at 68-72 seems to suggest that they are different as he dealt with the two limbs under quite different headings.
37 *Morgan v 45 Flers Avenue Pty. Ltd.* (1986) 10 ACLR 692, at 704: a case of s.260 of the Australian Corporation Law/Act 1989.

to be capable of covering a company's 'good will, its profits or losses, its contracts and assets including its shareholding in and ability to control the affairs of a subsidiary, and perhaps in the latter regard a subsidiary ...'.[38] In *Re BSB Holdings Ltd.*,[39] the transfer of broadcasting business which was originally carried out by the parent company to its wholly owned subsidiary and the subsequent merger of the subsidiary with a third company was held to be conduct in the affair of the parent company. In *Re a Company (No. 002470 of 1988) ex p. Nicholas*,[40] it was held by the Court of Appeal that the withholding of money owed to a subsidiary company by a parent company that exercised financial control over it could constitute acts done in the conduct of the subsidiary's affairs.

In *Re a Company (No. 001761 of 1986)*,[41] Harman J made a distinction between conduct 'in the company' and conduct '*dehors* the company'.[42] Conduct such as being 'rude, domineering, disruptive and aggressive towards [customers] and members of staff of the company at the [company] premises'; trying 'to get more money for the company in a somewhat abrasive fashion'; asking 'the secretary to park the director's car'; 'aggressive and unhelpful [behaviour], causing [one] to avoid her'; 'service on the company of a notice under s.518 [of the CA 1985] requiring repayment of a loan'; in her personal interest asking the others in a board meeting, in their personal and individual capacity, to transfer their shares to her and to resign as directors, have been held not to be 'conduct of or in the company's affairs'.[43] They are acts by the respondent in her personal capacity and *dehors* the company.

In *Re a Company (No. 001761 of 1986)*,[44] the principal allegation of unfair prejudice was that the respondent, a shareholder in the company, had, without informing the other shareholders, paid off the company's bank loan and had taken a transfer of the bank's security. Harman J held that the respondent's approach to the bank, with a view to paying off the bank, must have been an act in the personal capacity of the respondent, and the failure to give notice to the company was an act of no effect whatever. Harman J further explained conduct '*dehors* the company' by the example of a director who stole cash from the

---

38 *R v Board of Trade ex p. St Martins Preserving Co. Ltd.* [1965] 1 QB 603. This definition was given in the context of s.432(2) CA 1985. There is no reason why such generous definition should not be adopted in interpreting the same phrase in s.459 so as to maximise the protection afforded to minority shareholders.

39 [1992] BCC 915.

40 [1992] BCC 895.

41 [1987] BCLC 141.

42 Ibid., at 148a.

43 Ibid., at 145-6.

44 Ibid.

company's safe. The act would constitute conduct by a director in his personal capacity. It would make no difference if he had abused his position as a director to effect the theft. It would, however, be otherwise if the director in question used his dominant position in the company to stifle any proceedings by the company against himself, which will then constitute an 'affair of the company'.

In *Scottish Co-operative Wholesale Society Ltd. v Meyer*[45] an old s.210 case, the conduct of the SCWS as shareholders of STM was said expressly by Lord Morton[46] to be conduct not in the affairs of STM, but was conduct in the affairs of the SCWS. Viscount Simonds and Lord Denning[47] thought that that conduct by itself would not be enough. Lord Keith, however, concluded his minority judgment on the broader ground that conduct by the shareholder of its own affairs might amount to oppressive conduct in the company's affairs.[48] However, Viscount Simonds, Lord Denning and Lord Morton all agreed that the inaction of directors who knew of the damaging course of conduct by the shareholder (a course of conduct which if called to the company's attention, the company would probably have been able to ratify), was *conduct in the affairs of the company* and oppressive.

In *Re Stewarts (Brixton) Ltd.*[49] a director's conduct in setting up a rival business and/or channelling work which rightfully belonged to the company to the new company in breach of his fiduciary duties to the company, (or in breach of his duties as a partner in a quasi-partnership company), was held to be positive misconduct in relation to the affairs of the company. Similarly, the making of calls on partly paid-up shares was conduct of the affairs of the company.[50]

In an Australian case[51] which deals with the issue in the important context of groups, the court held that a person appointed to the board of directors of

45 [1958] 3 All ER 66. See also *Re a Company (No. 002470 of 1988) ex p. Nicholas* [1991] BCLC 480 in which Harman J held that conduct of parent company in remunerating its directors highly out of its profit was not conduct in the affairs of the subsidiary. Parent company's failure to pay its debts to its subsidiary was not *per se* an act in the business of the subsidiary. As the parent company's failure to pay such debts was due to genuine financial difficulties, the *Meyer*'s case was distinguished. On appeal, the Court of Appeal held that the parent company's failure to pay its debts to its subsidiary was an act in the subsidiary's affairs. But the Court of Appeal agreed that the failure was not *unfairly* prejudicial ([1992] BCLC 895, sub nom *Re Soundcraft Magnetics Ltd. ex p. Nicholas*, The Times, 10 July 1992).

46 [1958] 3 All ER 66, at 74.

47 [1958] 3 All ER 66, at 71, 87.

48 [1958] 3 All ER 66, at 85.

49 [1985] BCLC 4.

50 *Re Hailey Group Ltd.* [1993] BCLC 459 at 469b.

51 *Morgan v 45 Flers Avenue Pty. Ltd.* (1986) 10 ACLR 692.

one company by another company was not acting in the affairs of the appointing company when voting at a meeting of the board of the company to which he had been appointed. This decision was probably based on the difficult requirement that a director must consider the interests of the company of which he was a director and not to be influenced by the interests of the company appointing him,[52] and that therefore in dealing with the affairs of the former company he was not acting with respect to the affairs of the appointing company. This requirement is somewhat unrealistic and is regularly infringed in practice. Where activities are carried on in group form, the economic reality of group activity should be recognised and the manner in which the affairs of one member of the group are conducted should, in most circumstances, be treated as part of the affairs of other group members.

Can the meaning of 'company's affairs' extend to the conduct of a company's subsidiary affairs by a receiver? It was so extended in a case involving the powers of inspectors.[53] Although the court would be vigilant to prevent s.459 from being used so as to impede a receiver in carrying out his normal functions[54] there is no reason why the phrase should not bear a similar meaning in s.459. So if the receiver's conduct has caused unfair prejudice to a shareholder, the latter should be given standing to bring an action under the section as receivership should not be allowed to deprive a shareholder of the protection of s.459 (this is of course assuming that the shareholders remain entitled to a surplus of assets after the receivership is complete).

Section 459 would probably not, however, extend to the activities of an administrator or to a voluntary arrangement, as similar provisions are now provided by the Insolvency Act 1986 to protect the interests of creditors and members in both of these situations.[55]

(b) Act or omission of company

First, before a proposed act justifies relief under s.459, it should have reached such a degree of maturity that there is a strong likelihood that it will be implemented by the company. For example, mere discussion over certain

52 See *Charterbridge Corporation Ltd. v Lloyds Bank Ltd.* [1969] 3 WLR 122; [1969] 2 All ER 1185; [1970] Ch 62.

53 *Ex p. St. Martins Preserving Co. Ltd.* [1965] 1 QB 603.

54 See *Newhart Developments Ltd. v Co-operative Commercial Bank Ltd.* [1978] QB 814; *Watts v Midland Bank plc* [1986] BCLC 15.

55 Sections 6 and 27 of the 1986 Act respectively. See eg *Re Charnley Davies Ltd.* [1990] BCC 605. See also Gower's *Principles of Modern Company Law*, 5th ed., 1992, at 758-760.

activities that the company might enter into, such as, a new line of business outside the expertise of the directors, has been held not to be an act of the company.[56]

Secondly, for any actual or proposed act or omission to come within s.459(1) it must be that 'of the company'. Where the act is that of the board, this requirement would be clearly satisfied.[57] The acts of an individual to whom the powers of the board have been delegated or authorised by the board would be treated as those of the company. To afford a wider protection against unfairly prejudicial conduct by the board, acts done by the board of directors *ultra vires* the articles of association should now also be considered as acts of the company since such acts would now be binding on the company in a contract with an outsider.[58] This would seem to be so even though no personal action at common law lies in respect of an *ultra vires* act done in fulfilment of a legal obligation arising from a previous act of the company,[59] and even though shareholders may by special resolution relieve the directors from personal liability arising from an *ultra vires* transaction.[60]

There are, however, some matters in relation to which the directors are not competent to act on behalf of the company, the relevant authority being the company in general meeting. The acts of shareholders with respect to matters over which they had exclusive competence would of course be acts of the company.[61] Acts of shareholders in general meeting in matters other than those within their exclusive competence are, however, not treated as those of the company. In *Northern Counties v Jackson & Steeple*[62] Walton J agreed with Mr Instone's submission that:

---

56 *Re a Company (No. 004475 of 1982)* [1983] Ch 178.

57 A company as such is only a juristic figment of the imagination. There must be someone who acts on behalf of the company. The Board of Directors has the general power of management under Article 70, Table A, Companies (Table A to F) Regulations 1985 (SI No. 805). Their acts must, therefore, be the acts of the company itself. Shareholders do not have a general supervisory power (*Automatic Self-Cleansing Filter Syndicate Co. Ltd. v Cunninghame* [1906] 2 Ch 34; *Salmon v Quin & Axtens Ltd.* [1909] 1 Ch 311, CA; *Breckland Group Holdings Ltd. v London & Suffolk Properties Ltd.* [1989] BCLC 100). They may, however, have power on other matters.

58 Section 35A, s.35B (as amended by s.142, CA 1989) and s.711A (as amended by s.142, CA 1989).

59 Section 35(2) of CA 1985 (as amended by s.108, CA 1989).

60 Section 35(3) of CA 1985 (as amended by s.108, CA 1989).

61 See Walton J in *Northern Counties v Jackson & Steeple* [1974] 1 WLR 1133, at 1143h. Such instances are special resolutions passed by shareholders to alter the article of association under s.9, CA 1985; ratifications by shareholders of a breach of duty by the directors: Wedderburn, *'Trust, Corporation and Worker'* (1985) 23 Osgoode Hall L J 203, at 221; independent shareholders' decisions when the board or majority delinquent shareholders resolve not to bring an action against errant directors: *Smith v Croft (No. 2)* [1987] BCLC 355.

62 [1974] 1 WLR 1133.

> 'Although it is perfectly true that the act of the members, in passing certain special types of resolutions, binds the company, their acts are not the acts of the company. There would ... be no real doubt about this, were it not for the use of the curious expression 'the company in general meeting' - which, in a sense, drags in the name of the company unnecessarily. What that phrase really means ... is 'the members (or corporators) of the company assembled in a general meeting', and that if the phrase is written out in full in this manner it becomes quite clear that the decisions taken at such a meeting, and the resolution passed thereat, are decisions taken by, and resolutions passed by, the members of the company, and not by the company itself.'[63]

Walton J went on to explain that this was because a shareholder was voting as a person owing no fiduciary duty to the company and was not an agent of the company. His reasoning initially seems consistent with the concept of separate legal personality where shareholders are normally treated as entities separate from the company. However, it produces illogical results in certain cases. In many situations the members' resolutions, by binding the company, will in fact cause the company to act, or omit to act, in a certain manner which might be unfairly prejudicial to the minority shareholder's interests, but would not be treated as acts of the company following Walton J's dictum. They may not be acts or omissions performed or omitted to be performed 'on its behalf' either. It is submitted that Walton J's dictum should not apply to s.459 because when the court is confronted with unfairly prejudicial conduct and called upon to look into the justice and equity of a case, the court should treat the resolution of shareholders in general meeting as an act of the company. Therefore, not only the formal acts of the shareholders should be treated as those of the company, but also the informal acts of shareholders, which have constitutional status.

From the discussion above, it appears that the meaning of the 'affairs of the company' is wider than and includes the meaning of 'act or omission of the company'. Section 459, as currently reads, does not seem to allow a petition to be made if the company's affair *will* be conducted in an unfairly prejudicial manner. Whereas an act of the company which *would* be unfairly prejudicial is covered by the section. Given that Walton J's dictum contemplates circumstances in which shareholders' acts in general meeting will not be treated as the act of the company, if such acts were to have unfairly prejudicial effect in future no petition would lie. This artificial distinction is clearly undesirable. It is therefore submitted that the section should be amended to make it plain that where a company's affairs are being or have been conducted in a manner which is or would be unfairly prejudicial to the

63 *Northern Counties v Jackson* [1974] 1 WLR 1133, at 1144c-e.

interests of its members generally or of some part of its members (including at least himself) relief under the section should be available. The amendment should also make it clear that for the purposes of s.459, act or omission of a company should include any acts of shareholder which have constitutional status. Alternatively, a broader definition of 'conduct in the company's affairs' may be adopted to counteract Walton J's narrow approach.

Having established that the conduct complained of is the way in which the company's affairs are being or had been run, or is an act or omission of the company, as mentioned, the petitioner must also show that his interest is unfairly prejudiced by such conduct. The concept of unfair prejudice is the crux of the relief under s.459 and will be discussed in Chapter 4. But first, a detailed account of the interests of shareholders entitled to be protected will be made in Chapter 3.

Chapter 3

Interests of Member Qua Member

3.1 Qua member

It was repeatedly held, under s.210 of the 1948 Act, that the oppression to members had to be suffered by the petitioner in his capacity as a member as such and not, for example, as a director or creditor.[1] Such an interpretation resulted in the remedy sometimes being denied in the very circumstances in which it was most needed, such as where a shareholder was denied a role in the board. This was particularly so in the case of a small private company where the primary interest of the members was to secure for themselves remunerative employment as directors, the payment of dividends being relatively less important. And it was primarily to remedy this type of oppression in the private company that the Cohen Committee recommended s.210.[2] Despite the thorough analysis of s.210 made by the Jenkins Committee, no recommendation was made with respect to this aspect of its operation.

---

1 See *Elder v Elder & Watson Ltd.* [1952] SC 49, at 57; *Re Lundie Brothers Ltd.* [1965] 1 WLR 1050, at 1058; *Re H.R. Harmer Ltd.* [1959] 1 WLR 62, at 83, 87; *Re Bellador Silk Ltd.* [1965] 1 All ER 667. These cases are arguably inconsistent with the view taken in *Scottish Co-op Wholesale Society v Meyer* ([1959] AC 324 at 343) that in construing s.210 the court had to have regard to business realities and not legal technicalities. But in *Re H R Harmer* ([1958] 3 All ER 689, at 703I; [1959] 1 WLR 62, at 83), although Jenkins LJ agreed in principle with the qua member requirement, he said that the sons as members, and not merely as directors, were oppressed by the father's autocratic conduct and that the fact that the oppressed members were also directors was not a disqualifying circumstance in seeking relief under s.210. It has been suggested (Wedderburn, (1966) MLR 321, at 323) that this was because the alleged oppression also resulted in a breach of articles of association, when directors could, as members, stand on their rights 'to have its affairs conducted in accordance with its articles' (to quote Jenkin LJ, at 704). Wedderburn argued that this was why the sons who were both shareholders and directors were nevertheless given relief against the father, and because there had been no breach of articles in *Elder*, *Lundie*, and *Bellador*, the petitioners could not complain in a capacity as a shareholder. Rajak ((1972) 35 MLR 156, at 160) seemed to support this view when he said that had the father been astute enough to provide a constitutional framework for his actions, the petition under s.210 would have failed in limine since they would have failed to show oppression of themselves qua members. It is probably true that certain breach of articles could be oppressive to a member in his capacity as a member in certain circumstances. However, whether all breaches automatically result in a director being oppressed in his capacity as a member is a very controversial issue. For conflicting views see Wedderburn [1957] CLJ 193, [1958] CLJ 93; Gower's *Priciples of Modern Company Law* (5th ed. 1992) at 282-288; Drury [1986] CLJ 219; Prentice (1980) Co. Law 179; Gregory (1981) 44 MLR 526; Goldberg (1972) 35 MLR 363, (1985) 48 MLR 158.

2 Cmnd. 6659, para. 61.

In the early days of the unfair prejudice remedy (or what was then s.75 of the Companies Act 1980), the notorious 'qua member' limitation[3] was regarded as a limitation on the scope of the remedy. Lord Grantchester was of the opinion, *obiter*,[4] that the section, like the old s.210, was confined to conduct affecting a member qua member.

This narrow view quickly found disfavour. In *Re a Company (No. 002567 of 1982)*,[5] Vinelott J saw 'considerable force' in an argument that where there was unfair exclusion from the management of the affairs of the company, though the petitioner's strict rights as a shareholder may not be affected, his interest under the agreement, express or implied, that he would be allowed to participate and to be paid remuneration was affected. In conclusion, he thought it unlikely that the legislator could have intended to exclude from the scope of s.459 a petition by a shareholder/director in these circumstances. This view is certainly to be welcomed.

The same approach was taken[6] in *Re a Company (No. 008699 of 1985)*[7] where Hoffmann J said that he found this distinction between member and outsider rights difficult to follow.[8] However, in *Re a Company (No. 00477 of 1986)*[9] he accepted in principle that the section must be limited to conduct which was unfairly prejudicial to the interests of the members as members and that it could not extend to conduct which was prejudicial to other interests of persons who happened to be members.

Hoffmann J went on (quoting Lord Wilberforce in *Re Westbourne Galleries*[10]):

3 Derived by analogy from what is now s.14 of the Companies Act 1985 (See *Hickman v Kent or Romney Marsh Sheep-Breeders' Assn.* [1915] Ch. 881.) and later applied in s.210 of the 1948 Act.

4 *Re a Company (No. 004475 of 1982)* [1983] Ch 178, at 190, [1983] 2 All ER 36, at 44. The failure of the directors to formulate a scheme of reconstruction under what is now s.110 of the Insolvency Act 1986, or a scheme of purchase under what is now s.162 of the Companies Act 1985, was held not to amount to unfairly prejudicial conduct to the petitioners qua members because the statutory provisions did not create any interest until such schemes were adopted. For criticisms, see Davies [1983] JBL 486 and McMullen (1983) CLJ 205 (the latter pointed out that, if the strict qua member requirement is needed, a dismissed director could not complain of his removal *per se* in a petition under s.459 but would have to use the more drastic remedy of a winding up petition under s.122(1)(g) of the Insolvency Act 1986).

5 [1983] 1 WLR 927, at 933.

6 However, Hoffmann J's approach was based on the ground that the section uses the word 'unfairly' whereas Vinelott J took a different line that the word 'interests' should be given a wide interpretation. The result is nevertheless the same.

7 [1986] BCLC 382.

8 Ibid., at 387e.

9 [1986] BCLC 376, at 378h-i.

10 [1973] AC 360, at 379.

'[Section 459's] application must take into account that the interests of a member are not necessarily limited to his strict legal rights under the constitution of the company. The use of the word "unfairly" in s.459, like the use of the words "just and equitable" in [s. 122(1)(g)], enables the court to have regard to wider equitable considerations ... They are a recognition of the fact that "a limited company is more than a mere entity, with a personality in law of its own: that there is room in company law for recognition of the fact that behind it, or amongst it, there are individuals with rights, expectations and obligations *inter se* which are not necessarily submerged in the company structure."

Thus, in the case of the managing director of a large public company who is also the owner of a small holding in the company's shares, it is easy to see the distinction between his interests as a managing director employed under service contract and his interests as a member. In the case of a small private company in which two or three members have invested their capital by subscribing for shares on the footing that dividends are unlikely but that each will earn his living by working for the company as a director, the distinction may be more elusive. The member's interests as a member who has ventured his capital in the company's business may include a legitimate expectation that he will continue to be employed as a director, and his dismissal from that office and exclusion from the management of the company may therefore be unfairly prejudicial to his interests as a member.'[11]

This desirable relaxation of the qua member limitation on s.459 has been supported by dicta in subsequent first instance English cases. Thus, in *Re Ringtower Holding plc*,[12] Peter Gibson J said that as the interests of the members that the section protected were not confined to their strict legal rights under the company's constitution, they might have a legitimate expectation as members that the company's affairs would be conducted in a particular way. However, the courts have continued to emphasize that their interests as members depend on, *inter alia*, proof of a legitimate expectation and do not arise simply from the nature of the company.[13]

11 Ibid., at 378i-379h.

12 (1989) 5 BCC 82, [1989] BCLC 427.

13 *Re a Company (No. 003843 of 1986)* [1987] BCLC 562; *Re a Company (No. 003096 of 1987)* (1988) 4 BCC 80; *Re Ringtower Holding plc* (1989) 5 BCC 82; [1989] BCLC 427. In *Re J E Cade & Son Ltd.* [1991] BCC 360, it was held that the petitioner's interest in the quasi-partnership company did not include his interest as the owner of the farm used by the company. When his interest as the owner of the farm was allegedly affected, he was not affected qua member.

3.2 Petitioner's legitimate interests

Closely related to the qua member requirement is the concept of unfair prejudice to the 'interests' of members. So what are the interests of a member? No guidance is provided by the legislation. Hoffmann J said:

> 'I bear in mind that Lord Wilberforce added [in the *Westbourne Galleries* case] that in most companies and in most contexts, whether the company was large or small, the member's rights under the articles of association and the Companies Act could be treated as an exhaustive statement of his interests as a member. He mentioned various features typically present in cases in which further equitable considerations might arise: a personal relationship between shareholders involving mutual confidence, an agreement that some or all should participate in the management and restrictions on the transfer of shares which would prevent a member from realising his investment.'[14]

As it is unlikely that the parties' relationships will be definitively set out in the memorandum or articles of association, the courts will thus have to identify any additional interests by looking beyond the legal entity of the company to the individuals within it, and by having regard to their rights, expectations, and obligation *inter se*.

Where there is an express mutual understanding or agreement,[15] which is not incorporated into the articles of association, that the affairs of the company will be run in a particular manner, the court may be prepared to regard that as part of the members' interests under the section. This applies to quasi-partnership companies,[16] but does not seem to apply to public limited companies.[17]

In the absence of such an express agreement, whether the court is willing to find that an implied agreement gives rise to a legitimate expectation or interest will depend on the issues involved and the nature of the companies in question and the pre-incorporation history (eg how the business had been run before incorporation) or any other relevant circumstances.[18] The structure of a

---

14 *Re a Company (No. 00477 of 1986)* [1986] BCLC 376 at 379e.

15 An agreement outside the articles of association between shareholders as to how they would exercise their voting rights on a resolution to alter the articles was not necessarily invalid: *Russell v Northern Bank Development Corp Ltd.* [1992] BCLC 1016, HL.

16 See *Re a Company (No. 00477 of 1986)*, ibid; Peter Gibson J's dictum in *Re Ringtower Holding plc* (1989) 5 BCC 82, at 93D-H, [1989] BCLC 427, at 440b-g.

17 See *Re Blue Arrow* [1987] BCLC 585, at 590e-h.

18 See *Murray's Judicial Factor v Murray & Sons* [1993] BCLC 1437 at 1449a-b. In *Re Elgindata Ltd.* [1991] BCLC 959, the petitioner's appointment as a non-executive director gave him a legitimate expectation to be consulted on policy matters relating to the company's affairs.

company has a direct bearing on the nature of the entitlements of a shareholder. Although it is difficult to define precisely the differing types of companies, at the extremes there is a clear distinction between a publicly quoted company and a quasi-partnership company. In the case of a public company, there is usually no underlying personal relationship and employment is rarely an incident of membership. The shareholders are more interested in dividend yield, capital appreciation and possible take-over bids, but less concerned with the day-to-day running of the company.[19] The interests of a member in a quasi-partnership company are in employment and participation, in the status quo, in the proper conduct of the company's affairs and in their financial position.[20]

The legitimate interests of shareholders in both quasi-partnership companies and public limited companies in various situations are considered below in detail. The circumstances in which such interests may be unfairly prejudiced will be considered in Chapter 5.

(a) Exclusion from management

This is one of the most common forms of oppression alleged. The petitioners must establish a clear link between their capacity as members and their interest in management.[21] In a quasi-partnership company, the court is more likely to imply a mutual agreement or understanding that all the members will take part in the management of the company's affairs even in the situation of a joint venture between, say, A, B and C where A and B are the active participants and directors, while B's shares are held by his nominee C.[22] In such a case, can C, as a shareholder, complain about the unfair exclusion by A of B? The issue is whether C has a legitimate expectation that B could not be excluded from business participation. This was the issue the court had to consider in *Re a Company (No. 003160 of 1986)*[23] where the husband, a joint venturer in the company, whose shares were temporarily registered in his wife's name, was discharged as an employee. Hoffmann J having held that the husband had no *locus standi* nevertheless contemplated a very wide concept of legitimate expectation:

---

19 See Afterman, *Company Directors and Controllers* (1970), at 9-12. See also *PMPA Insurance Co. Ltd. v New Ireland Assurance Co.*, Irish Times, 23 October 1975 (Irish H.C.), where Kenny J said: 'The interest of a member of a public company is, first, that the company should be carried on successfully, that the maximum of dividends should be paid consistent with commercial prudence and that the assets should if possible be increased.'

20 See Hanningan, (1988) LMCLQ 60, at 63; Prentice, (1988) 8 OJLS 55, at 61.

21 *Currie v Cowdenbeath Football Club Ltd.* [1992] BCLC 1029.

22 *Re a Company (No. 003160 of 1986)* [1986] BCLC 391.

23 [1986] BCLC 391.

'The jurisdiction to remedy conduct 'unfairly prejudicial' to the interests of members enables the court to protect not only the rights of members under the constitution of the company but also the rights, expectations and obligations of the individual shareholders *inter se* ... In the typical case of the corporate quasi-partnership these will include the expectations that the member will be able to participate in the management of the company and share in its profits through salaried employment. As at present advised, I do not see why, if such was the understanding between the parties, it should not also include an expectation that a nominee member's husband and beneficiary should enjoy such rights and benefit.'[24]

Indeed, *Re Whyte*[25] indicates that the section can even be used by members, in appropriate circumstances, to prevent the removal of directors other than themselves.

Where the articles have provided a machinery for the purchase of the departing member's shares at a fair value, then it is arguable that no implied mutual agreement that the petitioner will not be excluded from management can be made, as the articles have contemplated such an exclusion.[26]

As mentioned, shareholders of a public company are not interested in the day-to-day management, therefore the relaxation of the qua member requirement by Hoffmann J does not seem to affect their position where the issue is exclusion from management. If they become dissatisfied then they can always sell their shares on the open market. In *Re Blue Arrow plc*,[27] the petitioner complained about being removed from her position as non-executive president of the company. The company was a public company which had been floated on the Unlisted Securities Market. The petitioner could not establish any expectation that she would not be removed from office by alteration of the company's articles of association. Vinelott J held that it was impossible in public companies to infer any legitimate expectation to remain president from arrangements outside those embodied in the formal constitution of the company as outside investors were entitled to assume that the whole of the constitution was contained in the articles, read, of course, with the Companies Acts.[28]

24 (1986) 2 BCC 99, 276 at 99, 281.

25 1984 SLT 330. Other cases where exclusion has been accepted by the court as capable of amounting to unfair prejudice are *Re Cumana Ltd.* [1986] BCLC 430 (CA), *Re London School of Electronics Ltd.* [1986] Ch 211, *Re Bird Precision Bellows Ltd.* [1984] 2 WLR 869 and *Re a Company (No. 00477 of 1986)* [1986] BCLC 376.

26 See eg *Re a Company (No. 004377 of 1986)* [1987] 1 WLR 102; [1987] BCLC 94. See Chapter 4, para 4.8 (b)(i).

27 [1987] BCLC 585.

28 Ibid., at 590g-h.

(b) Excessive remuneration

As a member in a quasi-partnership has an interest in the proper running of the company and also a financial interest, excessive remuneration is clearly detrimental to those interests. Although it has traditionally been difficult to challenge the appropriateness of remuneration, for the courts regard the question of quantum as being a matter for internal management,[29] the courts have now indicated that s.459 can be used to challenge these payments. In *Re Cumana Ltd.*,[30] Vinelott J found, *inter alia*, and the Court of Appeal agreed, that remuneration of some £365,000 over a 14-month period, given the circumstances of the company, was clearly excessive and unfairly prejudicial to the petitioner's interests.

In the case of a public limited company, excessive remuneration can be detrimental to dividend yield and capital appreciation. In principle, it may thus be prejudicial to the shareholders' interests. Therefore, s.459 could in principle be useful in public limited companies where the issue is not exclusion from management but excessive remuneration.

It is interesting to note that the Cadbury Committee[31] recognises that shareholders are entitled to a full and clear statement of directors' present and future benefits, and of how they have been determined.[32] Remuneration of directors should be both fair and competitive[33] and a remuneration committee should be set up to recommend to the board the remuneration of directors.[34] The members of the committee should be persons who have no personal interest in the outcome.[35]

(c) Inadequate dividends

Does a shareholder have an interest in the recommendation and declaration of dividends where funds are available for that purpose? In a quasi-partnership, it would seem to depend on the basis on which the petitioner had joined the company and profits were to be distributed. If the petitioner has contributed relatively substantial amounts of capital to the company and is not receiving

---

29 See Parkinson (1984) 134 NLJ 130; *Smith v Croft* [1986] 1 WLR 580.
30 (1986) 2 BCC 99, 453.
31 Cadbury Committee, The Financial Aspects of Corporate Governance, 1 December 1992.
32 Ibid., para. 4.40
33 Ibid., para. 4.44.
34 Ibid., paras. 4.42, 4.44.
35 Ibid., para. 4.44.

any dividend while the others are receiving directors' remuneration, then the court could possibly imply that there is a mutual understanding that dividends will be paid whenever funds are available for such purpose.[36]

As shareholders in a public limited company are interested in dividend yield, a failure to recommend and declare dividend when funds are available for that purpose is clearly prejudicial to their interests.[37] There are of course circumstances in which such prejudice may not be unfairly so.[38]

(d) 'Take-over' situations

As a shareholder in a quasi-partnership is normally financially and personally committed to the company, a share acquisition offer to buy out the majority may be prejudicial to the minority's interest to the extent that a change of control may threaten his participation in the management. In time, however, the situation may change and the company may cease to be a commercially viable entity. In such cases, a share acquisition offer, though prejudicial in this respect, may not be unfairly so if it would be in the interest of the company as a commercial entity that the majority be acquired by outsiders.

Where the minority is also persuaded by the majority to sell his shares, he has an interest in being able to sell his shares at the best price.[39]

In a public listed company, although shareholders are interested in take-over bids, as they are less personally committed to the ownership and control of the company and may freely sell their shares on the open market, it seems less possible for the court to infer a mutual understanding that the company will not subject itself to possible take-over bids.

36 The Jenkins Committee was of the opinion that such conduct should be within the new section: see Cmnd. 1749 (1962), para. 212. Vinelott J has also expressed the view that a shareholder may well have an interest in the declaration of dividends: see (1985) 6 Co. Law 21, at 31. See *Re Sam Weller & Sons Ltd.* [1990] BCLC 80, cf *Re a Company (No. 00370 of 1987) ex p. Glossop* [1988] BCLC 570.

37 Warner J in *Re Elgindata Ltd.* [1991] BCLC 959, at 991b said that a failure to declare and a failure to pay a dividend after it had been declared can both be unfairly prejudicial.

38 See Chapter 5, para. 5.4 below.

39 Per Hoffmann J in *Re a Company (No. 008699 of 1985)* [1986] BCLC 382, at 387b, where it was held that the directors of a company had acted in a manner unfairly prejudicial to the interests of the petitioners by favouring a lower bid for the company's shares from a company promoted by the directors in preference to a higher bid from a trade competitor.

(e) Retaining the proportionate shareholding

Where the position is not governed by the articles of association or the Companies Act, whether a member has a legitimate expectation not to have his shareholding diluted will depend on the precise arrangement and agreement which led to the incorporation of the company.[40] Where they have bargained for the percentage of shares each is initially to hold, that might arguably give rise to such a legitimate expectation. Where a party acquires certain shares, after the company is incorporated, from his fellow shareholders, without new agreement as to the maintenance of status quo on shareholding, then there is probably no legitimate expectation that their shareholding will not subsequently be diluted. In a quasi-partnership company, the proportionate shareholding held by each shareholder is often of great importance.[41] The courts may be ready to infer that there is a mutual understanding that the status quo of shareholders will not be altered. Any attempt to dilute a shareholder's holding in the company will be prejudicial to his interests.[42]

In public limited companies, every shareholder is entitled to buy and sell his shares on the open market as he pleases as long as the regulations of the City Code on Takeovers and Mergers are observed. However, as allotment of shares can only be made by directors with express authority given either in the articles or by a resolution in general meeting, and an allotment by the directors to dilute the minority shareholders' holding is an improper purpose hence a breach of directors' duty, such an allotment will be prejudicial to shareholders' interests, by reason of the breach, though it may not be unfairly so.[43]

(f) Alteration of articles of association

A company has a power to alter its articles of association by special resolution under s.9 of the Companies Act 1985. Such power is to be exercised *bona fide*

---

40 Though not in Table A, articles of association commonly provide that the directors shall offer any new issue of shares to all members in proportion to their existing holdings unless a general meeting by special resolution directs otherwise. In many cases, the position is now governed by ss.89-96 of CA 1985.

41 See cases of attempted dilution such as *Clemens v Clemens Bros. Ltd.* [1976] 2 All ER 268; *Pennell v Venida Investments Ltd.* (unreported 25 July 1974, noted 44 MLR 40 (1981)); *Greenhalgh v Arderne Cinemas Ltd.* [1946] 1 All ER 512.

42 See eg *Re a Company (No. 002612 of 1984)* [1985] BCLC 80 (decision of the Court of Appeal is reported as *Re Cumana Ltd.* [1986] BCLC 430); *Re a Company (No. 007623 of 1986)* [1986] BCLC 362.

43 See Chapter 5.

for the benefit of the company as a whole.[44] Thus, a shareholder cannot challenge an alteration which was carried out in accordance with the *Allen v Gold Reefs of West Africa*[45] principle.[46] However, as s.459 does not require any impropriety or illegality on the part of the oppressors, such an alteration may potentially be unfairly prejudicial to a shareholder's other interests. This applies to both public companies and quasi-partnership companies, depending on the types of interests affected by the alteration. Thus, in *Greenhalgh v Arderne Cinemas Ltd.*,[47] if Mr Greenhalgh could have established that there was an understanding that the existing members were to have first option on any shares which were for sale, the alteration would have been prejudicial to his interests for the purposes of s.459. In *Re Ringtower Holding plc*,[48] Peter Gibson J accepted the contention that a special resolution validly passed according to the tests in *Greenhalgh* could nevertheless amount to unfair prejudice.[49]

(g) Breach of directors' duties

It is trite law that directors owe fiduciary duties and duty of care to the company.[50] In only very limited circumstances are directors held to owe such duties to shareholders personally.[51] Therefore, at common law, shareholders can only challenge a breach of such duties if they can either establish that there is a breach of personal right[52] or there is a fraud on minority. Thus it is

44 *Allen v Gold Reefs of West Africa Ltd.* [1900] 1 Ch 656.

45 [1900] 1 Ch 656.

46 Eg *Greenhalgh v Arderne Cinemas Ltd.* [1950] 2 All ER 1120, where the Court of Appeal upheld a proposed alteration which was intended to permit the direct sale of shares to an outsider, without having first to offer them to the existing shareholders, provided that the sale was approved by an ordinary resolution of the company in general meeting. The alteration was found to be merely a relaxation of a very stringent provision and as such was *bona fide* for the benefit of the company as a whole notwithstanding the fact that in practice it only relaxed the position vis-à-vis the majority, who could then sell directly to an outsider.

47 [1950] 2 All ER 1120.

48 (1989) 5 BCC 82, sub nom *Re a Company (No 005685 of 1988) ex p. Schwarcz (No. 2)* [1989] BCLC 427.

49 (1989) 5 BCC 82, at 102G.

50 *Burland v Earle* [1902] AC 83, at 93.

51 *Allen v Hyatt* (1914) 30 TLR 444; *Coleman v Myers* [1977] 2 NZLR 225; *Gething v Kilner* [1972] 1 WLR 337, [1972] 1 All ER 1164; *Heron International v Grade* [1983] BCLC 244 (CA); cf *Percival v Wright* [1902] 2 Ch 421.

52 There are authorities which suggest that a shareholder has a personal right to sue where directors have made a decision to allot shares which is not *bona fide* in the company's interests or is for an improper purpose: *Fraser v Whalley* (1864) 2 Hem & M 10; *Punt v Symons & Co. Ltd.* [1903] 2 Ch 506; *Piercy v S. Mills & Co. Ltd.* [1920] 1 Ch 77; *Hogg v Cramphorn Ltd.* [1967] Ch 254; *Ashburton Oil NL v Alpha Minerals NL* (1971) 123 CLR 614 (H Ct of Aus); *Howard Smith Ltd. v Ampol Petroleum Ltd.* [1974] AC 821 (PC); *Whitehouse v Carlton Hotel Pty. Ltd.* [1987] 162 CLR 285 (H Ct of Aus); *Ngurli Ltd. v McCann* (1953) 90 CLR 425 (H Ct of Aus); see also Beck (1974) 52 Can Bar Rev 159, at 171-174.

not surprising that there have been suggestions for a liberalisation of the personal rights category which will have the effect of circumventing the rule in *Foss v Harbottle*.[53] It has also been suggested that any breach of a director's fiduciary duty should give a shareholder a personal cause of action.[54] It used to be thought that where the wrong complained of damaged the rights of individual members in the sense of lowering the value of their shares, as well as being a breach of duty to the company, the individual members could sue for the damage to themselves as proper plaintiffs and so avoid the rule in *Foss v Harbottle*.[55] This extension of personal rights has apparently been precluded by the case of *Prudential Assurance v Newman (No. 2)*.[56] The Court of Appeal indicated that it would be alert to any attempt to use the personal action as a means of circumventing the rule in *Foss v Harbottle*.[57] In the *Prudential* case the claim was based on the loss suffered by the minority shareholders as a result of the directors' alleged fraud on the company. Because the company had lost money, the shareholders' expectations of profit had been diminished. The Court of Appeal rejected such an argument because the alleged loss to the shareholders was neither separate nor distinct from that suffered by the company. Only one loss had occurred and only one action by the company could be allowed.

Can breach of directors' duties be a subject matter of a petition under s.459? Can s.459 be used to circumvent the rule in *Foss v Harbottle*? Primarily, this depends on whether a shareholder has an interest or legitimate expectation in the proper running of corporate affairs. It seems clear from the section that where the directors owe a duty to the shareholders, in theory, a s.459 petition will be possible to remedy any breach of such duty provided the breach is unfairly prejudicial. However, the shareholder may simply bring a personal action at common law without relying on s.459. But it is clear from case law that directors do not normally owe duties to individual shareholders, and the articles rarely, if ever, expressly provide a right to sue for breach of directors' duties (so that no personal action can be brought); a shareholder can only bring a s.459 petition if he can show that he has an interest or legitimate expectation that directors will act in accordance with their duties owed to the company and that such interest or legitimate expectation has been unfairly infringed.

---

53 Beck (1974) 52 Can Bar Rev 159, at 171-172; Gower's *Principles of Modern Company Law* (4th ed.) at 318-320.

54 Beck, op. cit., at 171-172. A recent example of this approach is Hoffmann J's decision in *Re a Company (No. 005136 of 1986)* (1986) 2 BCC 99, 528.

55 See Charlesworth & Morse *Company Law*, (14th ed. 1991), at 447; see also Beck's suggestion (op. cit., at 171-172) that in many cases in which there was a breach of directors' duties, the real aggrieved party who had suffered direct detriment was an individual shareholder.

56 [1982] 2 WLR 31 (CA).

57 See also Farrar's *Company Law* (3rd ed. 1991) at 447-449.

Given the fact that s.459 is intended to provide protection to shareholders' *interests* rather than *rights*, Beck's submission[58] and analysis that any breach of directors' duties gave a shareholder a personal cause of action, though made in relation to shareholders' derivative action and personal action and rejected by the Court of Appeal in the *Prudential* case, is nevertheless useful and relevant to analysing a member's interests in the context of a s.459 petition.

As Beck suggested,[59] one should approach this issue by asking who, in reality, is the aggrieved party and not by the mechanistic application of the formula that the director is an agent, the company is the principal and therefore action for breach of directors' duties such as fraud, negligence, or irregularity is only at the suit of the company, and that shareholders have no personal interest in it. Most cases of fraud will clearly involve a misappropriation by the director to the detriment of the company. The company is the only proper complainant. But a variety of other cases in which the directors act improperly, for instance wrongful allotment of shares, involve not merely a breach of duty by the agent, but a causing of the company to perform a corporate act in an improper or irregular manner to the direct detriment of particular shareholders, for which they ought personally to be able to sue. Only in the most theoretical sense may the company be said to have been injured by its directors' misuse of the power granted to them. A more realistic analysis is that by the misuse of their powers the directors have caused the company to act to the detriment of one group of shareholders and to the advantage of another - including, most likely, themselves. It should therefore follow, it is submitted, that the injured shareholders have a personal interest in this aspect of the proper running of corporate affairs by the directors in accordance with their duties. Such a view will not sit uncomfortably with that in *Bamford v Bamford*,[60] where Russell LJ said that the harm done by the directors (an improperly motivated allotment) was a harm done to the company, of which only the company could complain. Clearly the jurisprudence of s.459 encompasses a wider concept of 'interest' than was contemplated by the common law in that case.

What of certain breaches of articles of association which are regarded as mere internal irregularities? These irregularities are wrong done to the company and can be ratified by the majority.[61] It was, therefore, not actionable

58 Beck, op. cit., at 171-172.
59 Beck, ibid., at 172.
60 [1970] Ch 212.
61 See *Mozley v Alston* (1847) 1 Ph 790 where the articles contained a provision which required one-third of the directors to retire each year. It was alleged in a personal action that this had not been done. It was held that it was an injury to the company of which it alone could complain.

by a shareholder. Beck argued[62] that the decision in *Mozley v Alston*[63] had carried theory to an absurd point in holding that when directors unlawfully remained in office, it was the company that was primarily injured. He said that it was the shareholders' right to elect directors - a most important and meaningful act as shareholders. If this right was interfered with, it was they who were primarily injured and who should have standing to complain. He pointed out that the rule that internal irregularities can be ratified was difficult to reconcile with the view that the articles were in the nature of a contract between the members and the company. To allow a breach to be ratified was, in effect, to allow corporate business to be conducted as if the contract had been altered prior to the meeting when in fact it had not. Moreover, such a contractual alteration in the case of articles of association required a special resolution - a simple majority would not suffice. Even in cases like *Grant v United Kingdom Switchback Railways*,[64] and *Irvine v Union Bank of Australia*[65] where ratifications were permitted on the ground that they involved minor internal irregularities but not attempts to alter articles of association, as Beck pointed out, the courts were uncertain as to which procedural matters were to be treated as irregularities capable of ratification and which were to be treated as matters of substance that had to be adhered to.[66] It is submitted, again, that a shareholder has an interest or legitimate expectation in having the corporate affairs run in accordance with the articles of association.

The view submitted is not without judicial support.[67] In a number of cases the courts have found breaches of fiduciary duties to be unfairly prejudicial conduct.[68] In three recent cases[69] where the allegations in the petition referred to various breaches of duty by directors, Hoffmann J, who heard all three, clearly regarded allegations of breach of fiduciary duty as capable of establishing unfair prejudice to minority shareholders in a private company or a small public company. Even though the facts would have readily warranted the bringing of a derivative action, this would not bar a petition under s.459.[70]

62 Beck, op. cit., at 192.
63 (1847) 1 Ph 790.
64 (1889) 40 Ch D 135.
65 (1877) 2 App Cas 366.
66 For examples, compare *Pender v Lushington* (1877) 6 Ch D 70 with *MacDougall v Gardiner* (1875) 1 Ch D 13.
67 See Boyle, 'Judicial Interpretation of Part XVII of Companies Act 1985' in *Company Law in Change*, Current Legal Problems, 1987, at 26.
68 For examples see *Re Bovey Hotel Ventures* (unreported, 31 July 1981); *Re Cumana Ltd.* (1986) 2 BCC 99, 453, [1986] BCLC 430 (CA); *Re London School of Electronics Ltd.* [1986] Ch 211, [1985] BCLC 273, *Re D R Chemicals* (1989) 5 BCC 39.
69 *Re a Company* (No. 005287 of 1985) [1986] 1 WLR 281; *Re a Company (No. 008699 of 1985)* (1986) 2 BCC 99, 024; *Re a Company (No. 00477 of 1986)* (1986) 2 BCC 99, 171.
70 *Re a Company (No. 005287 of 1985)* [1986] 1 WLR 281, at 284.

Moreover, a breach of directors' duties not to mislead shareholders in take-over bids is capable of establishing unfair prejudice.[71] More recently, Hoffmann J in *Re a Company (No. 005136 of 1986)*[72] found that an exercise by directors of their fiduciary powers for an improper purpose, while technically a wrong done to the company, was substantially a complaint by a shareholder that his personal rights as a shareholder had been infringed. The basis of the complaint was that the allotment was alleged to be an improper and unlawful exercise of the powers granted to the board by the articles of association which constituted a contract between the company and its members. An abuse of power was found to be an infringement of a shareholder's contractual rights under those articles.

As has been pointed out,[73] any extension of the personal rights category suggested by Beck sits uneasily with the decisions in *Hogg v Cramphorn Ltd.*[74] and *Bamford v Bamford*[75] where improper allotments were referred to the general meeting for ratification, something which is irrelevant if an infringement of personal rights is involved.[76] While Hoffmann J's dictum in *Re a Company (No. 005136 of 1986)*[77] appears inconsistent with the *Prudential* case, it is in support of the view that a breach of directors' duties is at least prejudicial to the shareholders' interests as opposed to personal rights.

Another indication that the view submitted is plausible is the provision in s.461(2)(c) of Companies Act 1985. Following the recommendations of the Jenkins Committee,[78] s.461(2)(c) provides that the court may, *inter alia*, on a petition under the section, authorise 'civil proceedings to be brought in the name and on behalf of the company by such person or persons and on such terms as the court may direct'. This will enable the court to order a civil action against any outside wrongdoer where the board had refused to do so. It will also enable a minority who is unable to comply with all the conditions for bringing a derivative action, instead, to petition initially under the section and to ask for an order authorising it to institute proceedings in the name and on behalf of the company. The section can only be invoked when the court is satisfied that unfair prejudice has been established and, in such a case, once the full hearing has taken place the court will usually already be in a position to

71 *Re a Company (No. 008699 of 1985)* [1986] BCLC 382.
72 (1986) 2 BCC 99, 528 [1987] BCLC 82. Sub nom *Re Sherborne Park Residence*.
73 Farrar's *Company Law*, 3rd ed., at 448.
74 [1967] Ch 254.
75 [1970] Ch 212.
76 Farrar's *Company Law*, 3rd ed. at 448.
77 [1987] BCLC 82.
78 Cmnd. 1749, paras. 206, 207.

give a final remedy.[79] Would the court still make an order under s.461(2)(c)? It seems not. Because nothing more could be achieved by further proceedings. What then is the purpose of s.461(2)(c)? Surely it is not simply to facilitate a civil proceeding in favour of a minority because it creates double litigations. It is submitted that its main purpose is to declare that s.459 can be used to remedy a wrong done to the company, including breach of directors' duties.

It appears that the view submitted is particularly true in the case of a private company for the reasons suggested in the discussion above. In a public limited company with widely dispersed shareholdings, the issue is more complicated. In theory, there is no reason why Beck's analysis should not be accepted as supporting the view that shareholders in public limited companies also have an interest to see that directors will not be in breach of their duties owed to the companies. It is in this type of company that the restrictive aspects of 'fraud on minority' (especially wrongdoer control) prevent shareholders' derivative suits having much impact on the still serious problem of corporate abuse in public companies.[80] The court has shown its willingness to recognise such a legitimate expectation that the directors will act in accordance with their duties.[81]

Prior to the amendment made to s.459 by the 1989 Act, there was a suspicion that it may not be possible for a minority to use the section to surmount the *Foss v Harbottle* rule where the wrong has been done to the company as a whole, and therefore to all the members.[82] This doubt has now been resolved by the amendment under the 1989 Act.[83]

The view submitted, if correct, may eventually make the rule in *Foss v Harbottle* largely redundant.[84] It would also mean that shareholders have a legitimate expectation that directors would exercise a degree of care and skill in

---

79 Per Warner J in *Re Elgindata Ltd.* [1991] BCLC 959, at 961b-d. The petitioner sought in the alternative (to a share purchase order) an order authorising him to bring civil proceedings in the name and on behalf of the company against the respondents. But the counsel did not in the end ask the judge to make such order.

80 A problem recognised in Boyle, 'The Judicial Interpretation of Part XVII of the Companies Act 1985', *Company Law in Change*, Current Legal Problem, 1987, at 26.

81 Hoffmann J clearly regarded allegations of breach of fiduciary duty as capable of establishing unfair prejudice to minority shareholders in a private company or a small public company: *Re a Company (No. 005136 of 1986)* [1987] BCLC 82.

82 See eg *Re Carrington Viyella plc* ((1983) 1 BCC 98, 951, at 98, 959) where Vinelott J held that even if the petitioner could show that the board had acted in breach of duty in entering into the service agreement not in the interests of the company but for a collateral purpose, a case under s.459 had not been established because such a breach would affect all shareholders equally.

83 See Chapter 4, para. 4.6 below.

84 See Gower's *Principles of Modern Company Law*, 5th ed. 1992, at 603-606.

managing the company's affairs. There is little authority on the extent to which negligent or incompetent management of a company's business may be unfairly prejudicial.[85] The Jenkins Committee[86] intended that the reformed alternative statutory remedy might be used in this regard, although the courts decided otherwise[87] in the case of the old s.210. The problem is perhaps more of establishing unfairness, which will be discussed at Chapter 5 para. 5.2 below.

(h) Decisions to continue trading at a loss

Shareholders in both private and public companies have an interest in the profit-making of the companies. Where the company is trading at a loss, they have an interest in seeing that the companies take proper actions to prevent further losses. One such action may be for the company to cease trading immediately. If the majority shareholders or directors who are in control of the day-to-day management of the company decide to continue to trade when the company is failing to make a profit, the court may infer that the majority or directors' decision was influenced by a desire to remain in office. This could constitute unfair prejudice to the shareholders' interest.[88] However, if the company was also diversifying into more profitable areas, no such inference of unfairly prejudicial conduct could be made. The majority shareholders or directors are also entitled to take into account the employees' interests in continuation of their employment in deciding whether to continue to trade at a loss.

3.3 Circumstances in which no legitimate expectation can be inferred

Having discussed the situations in which interests or legitimate expectations can be inferred, it remains necessary to point out that there are also circumstances in which no such exercise can be made. A petitioner who alleges infringement of the equitable expectations supplementing his legal rights must be able to point to a special circumstance which creates such legitimate expectations.[89] Even in the case of small private companies, there are circumstances where the rights of members are limited to their strict legal

85 See Chapter 5, para. 5.2 and *Re Elgindata Ltd.* [1991] BCLC 959. See also Goo (1993) JBL 283; Griffin (1992) 108 LQR 389; Stapledon (1993) 14 Co. Law 94.

86 Cmnd. 1749 (1962), paras. 207-208.

87 *Re Five Minute Car Wash Service Ltd.* [1966] 1 WLR 745.

88 *Re a Company ex p. Burr* [1992] BCLC 724.

89 Eg in *Re Elgindata Ltd.* [1991] BCLC 959, the appointment as non-executive director gave the petitioner legitimate expectation to be consulted on corporate policy.

rights stated in the articles of association of the company or elsewhere. The joint venturers may have concluded detailed agreements which contemplate, *inter alia*, one party excluding the other from management. In such cases, the court is likely to hold that these agreements are exhaustive of the rights of the parties and there is no room for the superimposition of any such rights to management participation. Hoffmann J, in *Re Postgate & Denby (Agencies) Ltd.*,[90] said that s.459 enabled the court to give effect to the terms and understandings upon which the members of the company became associated but not to rewrite them. In this case, the non-voting equity shareholders alleged that their interests were being prejudiced by the proposal of the directors and holders of the voting shares to sell parts of the business to themselves without the approval of the equity shareholders. Hoffmann J held that there were no equitable considerations which extended the interests of the equity shareholders beyond their rights contained in the articles. There was no breach of the articles of association and the provisions of the Companies Acts in relation to conflicts of interest (neither was there any allegation of breach of fiduciary duty). As the articles expressly contemplated conflicts of interest on the part of directors and the exclusion of equity shareholders from voting notwithstanding their interests in the company, Hoffmann J thought that it was 'impossible to superimpose an obligation of fairness' requiring the approval of the equity shareholders to the proposed sales.[91]

It seems therefore that a member cannot complain about conduct in accordance with articles, especially if they have been deliberately inserted, unless he can show bad faith or impropriety or that the articles themselves are unfair (this aspect will be discussed below). And unless there are special circumstances present, for example, where the company was formed and run on the basis of mutual trust and confidence, the court will be very reluctant to extend the rights of members beyond those stated expressly in the constitution of the company. The court could give effect to equitable considerations arising from agreements or mutual understandings outside the constitution of the company, but could not superimpose further rights arising from its concept of fairness.[92] This is apparently due to the court's reluctance to interfere in contractual and commercial arrangements even though fairness might suggest the need for such intervention.

The court's reluctance to interfere is more apparent and firm in cases involving public limited companies. A recent example is the case of *Re Ringtower Holding plc*,[93] where the petitioners complained, *inter alia*, that

90 [1987] BCLC 8.
91 Ibid., at 14-15.
92 Warner J in *Re J E Cade & Son Ltd.* [1991] BCC 360, at 372B.
93 (1989) 5 BCC 82, at 94.

they had been wrongfully excluded from participation in management and that this constituted unfairly prejudicial conduct. Peter Gibson J held that where the parties had not only left the basis of their relationship to the articles of association but had also spelt out in detailed agreements all the matters which were to govern their relationship, then there was no room for claiming any legitimate expectation apart from those specified in the articles of association. Accordingly he ruled that while the constructive dismissal of the petitioners as directors and the subsequent failure to appoint them as directors of the company were wrongs done to them, they were not unfairly prejudicial to *their interests qua members* justifying an order under the section.

Similarly, in the case of *Re Carrington Viyella plc*[94] the petition was dismissed as vexatious and unfounded. There the petitioner claimed that ICI's failure to comply with its undertakings given to the government prior to the formation of Carrington Viyella plc was unfairly prejudicial to his interest and sought an order declaring that ICI was bound by its undertakings. Dismissing the petition, Vinelott J thought that other shareholders must have known that the undertakings 'were never intended to be immutable' and were always 'subject to change in the light of changed circumstances'. He said that:

> 'I can see no justification for claiming that because the existence of undertakings obtained by the Government in the public interest may have been a factor influencing the merits of potential investors acquiring shares of CV the shareholders of CV are entitled as a matter of private right to prevent ICI from voting its full strength without first approaching Government to obtain a release, modification or waiver of the undertakings. It seems to me that in so far as a potential investor paid regard to the undertakings he would have regard to the fact that the undertakings had been given and might be enforced by the Government if the public interests (which might not coincide with CV's commercial interests) so required. In doing so he would not be treating the undertakings as part of the constitution of CV or as in any way affecting the rights of shareholders *inter se*.'[95]

So it is more difficult to establish that his interest as a member is affected if he is directly affected by the majority's conduct as an official of the public company. So far as the shareholders of a public company are concerned, this qua member requirement remains a formidable hurdle for relief.

94 (1983) 1 BCC 98, 951.
95 Ibid., at 98, 957.

3.4 Interests arising from personal rights of shareholders

Apart from the interests given by the articles of association and the Companies Act or any legitimate expectations inferred by the courts, a minority may also petition under the section if his personal right has been unfairly infringed. The line between personal rights and corporate rights is not easily drawn. As already mentioned, there are perhaps two reasons for the difficulty. Firstly, there is the idea that all duties are owed by directors and officers exclusively to the corporation.[96] The fictional legal entity is viewed by the courts as an unbreachable barrier behind which the directors are generally safe from shareholders' personal action. Acts by the directors are readily seen as corporate acts. This is the natural result of the fact that a company acts only through its board of directors and occasionally its shareholders. Secondly, the form of the action is usually representative (as it may be when personal rights are being asserted, and as it must be in a derivative action).[97] The company and the wrongdoing directors are joined as defendants, so an argument for either cause of action is plausible.

Although it is difficult to lay down an accepted test of what is a personal right, existing cases which recognise certain personal rights are important in a petition under s.459 as they help determine the interests of a shareholder qua member.[98] These personal rights already recognised by the courts should also be recognised as shareholders' interests in all companies with regard a petition under s.459.

It is however necessary to add a word of caution. Although cases where personal rights have been recognised by the court may be relevant to determining shareholders' interests under s.459, the petition will only be successful if the petitioner can show unfairness. To this extent, an aggrieved shareholder whose personal right has been infringed may be advised to bring a personal action at common law, unless he prefers a more flexible remedy under the section.

3.5 Legitimate expectation not transmissible by law

When a member dies, his shares will be transmitted by law to his personal representatives. However, it has been recently held by the Court of Session, Inner House in *Murray's Judicial Factor v Murray & Sons*[99] that any

96 Fuld J in *Gordon v Elliman* (1954) 119 NE 2d 331, at 340-341.
97 RSC Ord 15, r 12.
98 For personal rights already recognised by the court, see Chapter 1, para. 1.5.
99 [1993] BCLC 1437.

legitimate expectation the deceased member has cannot be transmitted by law to his personal representatives under s.459(2). Thus, in a quasi-partnership although the deceased would have a legitimate expectation during his lifetime that he would continue to participate in the management and profits of the company, he had no legitimate expectation that his personal representatives should have such rights.[100] Neither could the personal representatives have enjoyed the deceased's legitimate expectation because it is not transmissible by law.[101]

100 Ibid., at 1449f.
101 Ibid., at 1455b

Chapter 4

The Concept of Unfair Prejudice

4.1 General

The departure from the wording of s.210 of the Companies Act 1948, which talked in terms of oppression, has considerably expanded the scope of the remedy.[1] While it follows that cases decided in favour of petitioners under s.210 would be similarly decided under s.459, it does not necessarily follow that cases which were unsuccessful under s.210 would be decided differently today under s.459. The matter depends upon the precise definition of unfair prejudice. The courts have rightly shown a reluctance to formulate a generally accepted or comprehensive definition, as this would have the undesirable effect of stultifying the very wide discretion conferred on them by the section.[2] Whether conduct is necessarily unfairly prejudicial will have to be evaluated against the nature of the firm and the interests of its members. However several principles by which the courts are guided can be detected from decided cases.

The courts are generally very reluctant to interfere in the affairs of companies and to impeach management with the benefit of hindsight on the business merits of a particular decision. As Lord Wilberforce stated in *Howard Smith v Ampol Petroleum Ltd.*:[3]

> 'There is no appeal on merits from management decisions to courts of law, nor will courts of law assume to act as a kind of supervisory board over decisions within the powers of management honestly arrived at.'

---

1 See Slade J in *Re Bovey Hotel Ventures Ltd.* (unreported, 31 July 1981) whose dictum was set out in the judgment of Nourse J in *Re R A Noble & Sons (Clothing) Ltd.* [1983] BCLC 273, at 290: 'For my own part, while I can think of many hypothetical cases that might fall within [s. 459] but not fall within s.210, I can think of no hypothetical cases which, though giving rise to the court's jurisdiction under s.210, would not give rise to such jurisdiction under [s. 459].'

2 In *Elder v Elder & Watson Ltd.* (1952) SC 49, Lord Cooper (at 55) said, with reference to the meaning of oppression in s.210, that 'the essence of the matter seems to be that the conduct complained of should at the lowest involve a visible departure from the standards of fair dealing, and a violation of the conditions of fair play on which every shareholder who entrusts his money to a company is entitled to rely.' The Jenkins Committee thought that Lord Cooper's view accorded with their view of the meaning of 'unfair prejudice' which was originally intended to be covered by s.210: see Cmnd. 1749, para. 204.

3 [1974] AC 821, at 832.

Many decisions taken by the majority which are not contrary to the articles of association or an Act of Parliament are a question of business judgment to be made by them. Whether their judgment is in the interest of the company (as would inevitably be asserted by the majority) is not always a suitable question for the judges to decide. However, it is questionable whether such a reluctance by the court should operate in the context of s.459 because the focal point of the court's enquiry here is the unfair impact of the company's conduct on the interests of the petitioners and this does not have as its central purpose the assessment of the business merits of the decision. An allegedly unfair prejudice may be caused by acts which are commercially unimpeachable. As the court will certainly have to weigh the business interests of the company against the impact on the interests of the petitioner, this traditional reluctance of the judiciary will inevitably affect the judgment of the court. It is, therefore, hoped that it will only operate, if at all, within a very narrow ambit when applying s.459.

4.2 Impropriety or illegality not a requirement

In determining whether conduct was unfairly prejudicial, the court looks at the impact and not the nature of the conduct. So it is not necessary for a petitioner to show any actual irregularity or an invasion of his legal rights or a lack of probity or want of good faith towards him on the part of those in control of the company.[4] No doubt such an infringement would normally be unfairly prejudicial to the petitioner, but were the courts to confine the granting of relief to situations where there has been an illegal act in the sense of involving some independent legal impropriety, s.459 would then merely become a procedural substitute for an exception to the rule in *Foss v Harbottle*. The requirement of impropriety as a condition for granting relief was undoubtedly the primary reason which caused the failure of s.210 in providing shareholders with adequate protection against oppression. Also, to require a petitioner to demonstrate an independent illegality would be implicitly to assume that a company's articles and memorandum completely encapsulated the parties' arrangements. This cannot realistically be done. Thus, while a particular act or omission may, ostensibly, be legally proper, it may nevertheless constitute unfair prejudice.[5]

4 *Re Norvabron Pty. (No. 2) Ltd.* (1987) 11 ACLR 279, at 290.

5 For example, a rights offer on a *pro rata* basis could be unfairly prejudicial to a shareholder where it was known that the shareholder did not have the resources to take up his allotment and the allotment was intentionally made to exploit this and to dilute his holdings in the company. Harman J was also prepared to hold that the making of a rights offer to soak up the funds of the petitioner so that he would lack the resources to bring an action against the company would constitute unfair prejudice: *Re a Company (No. 001761 of 1986)* [1987] BCLC 141, at 143e.

4.3 Both unfairness and prejudice needed

To succeed under s.459, it is necessary for the petitioner to show both unfairness and prejudice. The words 'in a manner which is unfairly prejudicial' plainly implies that there may be harm which is not unfair, and harm, to be within the section, must be unfair harm.[6] If a company retains its earnings for expansion purposes, this would be prejudicial to shareholders who did not have any employment relationship with the company. Their interest is to receive a tangible return for their investment. But it is not necessarily unfair unless perhaps the company pursues such a policy over a sustained and unreasonable period of time.

4.4 Prejudice

The circumstances in which prejudice may be suffered by members are almost unlimited. 'Without prejudice to the generality of the wording of the section, which may cover many other situations', Slade J in *Re Bovey Hotel Ventures Ltd.*[7] said:

> 'Prejudice includes cases where the value of his shareholding in the company has been seriously diminished or at least seriously jeopardised by reason of a course of conduct on the part of those persons who have had *de facto* control of the company.'

One classic example of such diminution in value is the old s.210 case of *Scottish Co-operative Wholesale Society v Meyer*[8] where the majority shareholders pursued a policy of running down the business of the company, to the benefit of their own competing business, thereby drastically reducing the value of the shares in the company. In *Re a Company (No. 00789 of 1987)*[9] Harman J held that the failure to conduct the affairs of a company properly from a procedural point of view could amount to unfair prejudice where the improprieties resulted in the invalidity of an allotment of shares to the petitioner.

However, s.459 cannot be limited to cases in which the value of members' shareholdings has been seriously diminished or jeopardised.[10] Where the

---

6 See Harman J in *Re a Company (No. 001761 of 1986)* [1987] BCLC 141, at 143e.
7 31 July 1981, unreported, but referred to in *Re R A Noble & Sons (Clothing) Ltd.* (1983) BCLC 273.
8 [1959] AC 324.
9 (1989) 5 BCC 792, at 800, 801.
10 Per Nourse J in *Re R A Noble & Sons (Clothing) Ltd.*, [1983] BCLC 273, at 291.

value of the petitioners' shareholdings has not been seriously diminished or jeopardised, the petitioner has to rely on the generality of the section's wording. This means that any harm done to the petitioners' legitimate right enjoyed by virtue of their shareholdings or any interests recognised by the court would constitute prejudice. So in a small private company formed as a quasi-partnership in which the joint venturers expect to share in the business by reason of their continued employment therein, the termination of employment is then clearly prejudicial to the interests of that joint venturer given that a wide meaning of 'interests' of members has been given by the court. In such a case, prejudice is obviously suffered even though there is no effect on the value of shares. In *McGuinness & Anor, Petitioners*[11] unreasonable delay in convening a meeting upon receipt of a member's requisition was held to constitute prejudice since 'justice delayed is justice denied' and 'delay is prejudicial to the interests of the petitioner who seeks to work out a legal remedy'.

However, prejudice of a speculative or vague nature will not be accepted. In *Re a Company (No. 001761 of 1986)*,[12] the principle ground of complaint was that the respondent had approached the company's bank, without notice to the company or the petitioners, and had paid off the loan which the company owed to the bank, and had taken a transfer of the bank's security. Harman J held that the failure by the respondent to give notice to the company or the petitioner had no effect whatsoever as they knew that the bank wanted repayment and it was open to them to organise repayment. The respondent's repayment to the bank and taking a transfer of the bank's mortgage was not prejudicial either, as the respondent had deprived the company of nothing and its position had not changed in any way.[13] The allegation that it was very bad luck on the petitioners that the respondent was able to find the money which they were unable to find was not sustainable either.

4.5 Exercise of legal right may still be unfairly prejudicial

As mentioned, conduct in accordance with the articles of association or the Companies Act cannot normally be challenged under s.459. However, the wider equitable considerations to which the court considering a s.459 petition may have regard include the question of whether it is inequitable to permit reliance on strict legal rights, such as the right under the Companies Act 1985, s.303, to dismiss a director by ordinary resolution of the members. In the case of a private or quasi-partnership company, it was held in *Re a Company (No.*

11 (1988) 4 BCC 161, at 167.
12 [1987] BCLC 141.
13 Ibid., at 147.

00477 of 1986)[14] that a member who had ventured his capital in a company's business on the basis that he would take part in its management had a legitimate expectation that he would continue to be a director of the company, so that his removal from the board, though legal, could be unfairly prejudicial to him.

In *Re Hailey Group Ltd.*[15] although the company was entitled to make calls on partly paid-up shares, where the making of calls was for the purpose of putting pressure on the petitioner perpetrated by the respondents, it was held to be prejudicial to the petitioner.[16]

Re Whyte, Petitioner[17] shows that the section can even be used by members, in appropriate circumstances, to prevent the removal of directors other than themselves. The managing director of a company (LGE) owned 49% of the shares of the company. Two other companies, G Ltd. and A Ltd., which were wholly-owned subsidiaries of a further company, R Ltd., held 51% of the shares between them. The board had six members, three non-executive directors who were nominees of G Ltd. and three executive directors including the petitioner. In May 1981, the company sued R Ltd. for £3, 890, 000. The board of the company remitted the conduct of the action to a committee of the three executive directors with full powers. In February 1983, G Ltd. and A Ltd. sought by requisition to convene an extraordinary general meeting under s.132 of the Companies Act 1948 to remove two of the existing directors (one executive director being nominee of LGE and the other, non-executive director being nominee of G Ltd., none of them being the petitioner) and to replace the executive director by the managing director of G Ltd. The requisitionists would have succeeded in having the necessary resolution passed. Having done so, they would be in a position to revoke the resolution delegating the conduct of the action against R Ltd. to the committee and thereafter the company's interests would be at the mercy of a board acting as nominees of the defenders. The managing director of LGE applied under s.75 of the Companies Act 1980 for orders restraining LGE from convening or holding the proposed extraordinary general meeting and from passing a resolution removing one of the directors and replacing him by the managing director of G Ltd., and against G Ltd. and A Ltd. restraining them from moving or voting in favour of such resolutions. As LGE's failure in the action would be wholly beneficial to G Ltd., whereas LGE's success in the action would be only 51% beneficial to G Ltd. and A Ltd. as shareholders of LGE, the deliberate proposal to alter the status quo was held to be unfairly

---

14 [1986] BCLC 376.
15 [1993] BCLC 459.
16 Ibid., at 469b.
17 1984 SLT 330.

prejudicial to the interests of the petitioner not just as a director but as a shareholder. It seems implicit from the case that although it was true that the respondents were doing no more than exercising their statutory right as majority shareholders to remove a director and thereby obtain control of the board by proper means, there was a legitimate expectation that where control was originally placed on a particular body, the composition of such a body could not be altered without 'any very good reason' so as to ensure a change of policy adopted by the new composition to the prejudice of other interest of the shareholders.

In a public limited company case, in *McGuinness & Anor, Petitioners*,[18] the directors were acting within the terms of the Companies Act and the articles in calling a requisitioned meeting for a date seven months after the date of the requisition. But the petitioners, as shareholders of not less than one-tenth of paid-up capital of the company, have a right to requisition an extraordinary general meeting in terms of s.368 of Companies Act 1985.[19] As one of the most valuable remedies which minority shareholders enjoyed by virtue of their holding shares of the required number, they were entitled to expect that that right could be exercised within a reasonable period. Regulation 37 of Table A, though not adopted by the company as part of its articles of association, reinforced the *prima facie* view that a delay of seven months between the lodging of a requisition and the holding of an extraordinary general meeting was unreasonably long. Such a delay without sound reason was held to be unfairly prejudicial to their interests as shareholders. This decision is a good example of the flexible nature of the protection provided by s.459 and indicates that strict compliance with formal legal rights, whether based upon the memorandum and articles of association or upon the Companies Act, may not *per se* be an answer to a claim of unfairly prejudicial conduct.

Where an application for an extraordinary general meeting of the company has been made by the respondent pursuant to s.371 of the Companies Act 1985, the mere fact that the petitioner has, at the date of the hearing of the s.371 application, petitioned under s.459 would not preclude the court from exercising its discretion under s.371.[20] On the other hand, if a s.459 petition is pending, it would be improper for the respondent to use s.371 indirectly to secure the removal of the petitioner.[21]

18 (1988) 4 BCC 161.

19 Now under s.368 as amended by Companies Act 1989 (Sched 19 para. 9) the directors, if requested to hold a meeting under this section, must fix the actual date of the meeting within 28 days of its being summoned.

20 *Re Whitechurch Insurance Consultants Ltd.* [1993] BCLC 1359; *Re El Sombrero Ltd.* [1958] 3 All ER 1; *Re Opera Photographic Ltd.* [1989] BCLC 763.

21 *Re Sticky Fingers Restaurant Ltd.* [1992] BCLC 84, at 88.

4.6 Conduct prejudicial to all members

Prior to the amendment made to s.459 by Schedule 19, para. 11 of the Companies Act 1989, it was not clear whether conduct by a company which *prima facie* affected all the members equally, such as the non-payment of a dividend, could never be conduct unfairly prejudicial to the interests of some part of the members.[22] The uncertainty has now been removed by the amendment.[23] The cases with regard to this point now appear to be of academic interest only.

---

22 Vinelott J in *Re Carrington Viyella plc* (1983) 1 BCC 98, 951 held that the court did not have jurisdiction under s.459 to deal with conduct that was indiscriminately prejudicial to the interests of all the members of a company. In *Re Blue Arrow plc* [1987] BCLC 585, he said that it was wholly inappropriate to pursue a claim under s.459 against directors' misleading information to members in a circular which prejudiced all members. On the other hand, Harman J recognised that some conduct, although affecting all members equally in one sense, could nevertheless be unfairly prejudicial to some members' interests. Refusing to strike out a petition under s.459, he held that a rights issue to all shareholders *pari passu* was capable of being unfairly prejudicial if it was known that some of the shareholders were unable to take up their rights (*Re a Company (No. 002612 of 1984)* [1985] BCLC 80). At the hearing, Vinelott J found as a fact that the rights issue was part of a scheme to reduce the petitioner's shareholding which was unfairly prejudicial to the interests of the petitioner ((1986) 2 BCC 99, 453) (approved by the Court of Appeal (1986) 2 BCC 99, 945 at 99, 500). However, later, in *Re a Company (No. 00370 of 1987)* ((1988) 4 BCC 507, at 511), Harman J distinguished his own previous ruling and those of Vinelott J and the Court of Appeal in *Re a Company* (*No 002012 of 1984*) on the ground that in the later case the board intended to discriminate and knew it was able to discriminate by making an offer purportedly to all which it knew well was one which not all could accept. He said that the conduct complained of must be conduct unfairly prejudicial to some part of the members because Parliament had provided something which affected a slice of the members and therefore no s.459 petition could possibly be based on conduct which had an equal effect on all shareholders and was not intended to be discriminatory between shareholders. Harman J's reasoning was erroneous because it effectively neutered the section by restricting its scope to cases of discrimination which were already actionable under the general law (see Instone (1988) JBL 410, at 411). His reasoning was rejected by Peter Gibson J in *Re Sam Weller & Sons Ltd.* ((1989) 5 BCC 810). Peter Gibson J said that the word 'interest' has an extended meaning and was wider than rights, and the element of unfairness made it possible that the interests of only some members might be unfairly prejudiced even though all the members were prejudiced by the conduct complained of. Lord Cooper also said, in *Meyer*'s case (1954 SLT 273, at 277), that the argument that the old s.210 was not available where all the members were in the same boat, was too narrow and placed an unintended emphasis on the words 'some part'. He added that when the section inquired whether the affairs of the company were being conducted in a manner oppressive to some part of the members, including the complainer, that question could still be answered in the affirmative even if, qua member, the oppressor had suffered the same or even a greater prejudice. It is submitted that Peter Gibson J and Lord Cooper's view is to be preferred. See also *Re Bovey Hotel Ventures Ltd.* (unreported, 31 July 1981); *Re Cumana Ltd.* [1986] BCLC 430, CA; *Re London School of Electronics Ltd.* [1986] Ch 211; *McGuinness & Anor, Petitioners* (1988) 4 BCC 161 which allowed petitioners to challenge conduct affecting all members.

23 For a different view see Griffin (1993) Co. Law 83, at 86.

4.7 Test of unfairness

As mentioned, the petitioner under s.459 must show that his interest has been prejudiced by the way in which the company's affairs have been conducted and the prejudice is an unfair one. Many petitions under the section were unsuccessful because the alleged prejudice was not unfair. The central theme of the section is the concept of unfairness. However, the significant issue which remains somewhat unclear is the extent to which prejudicial conduct is unfairly so. What then is the test of unfairness? Slade J said that the test of unfairness must be an objective, not a subjective, one:

> 'It is not necessary for the petitioner to show that the persons who have had *de facto* control of the company have acted as they did in the conscious knowledge that this was unfair to the petitioner or that they were acting in bad faith; the test, I think, is whether a reasonable bystander observing the consequences of their conduct, would regard it as having unfairly prejudiced the petitioner's interests.'[24]

> Hoffmann J in *Re a Company (No. 008699 of 1985)*[25] said that:

> 'Unfairness is a familiar concept employed in ordinary speech, often by way of contrast to infringement of legal right. It was intended to confer a very wide jurisdiction upon the court and I think it would be wrong to restrict that jurisdiction by adding any gloss to the ordinary meaning of the words.'

Armed with a wider power given by the section which replaced the old section 210 of the Companies Act 1948, the two statements represent a change of judicial attitude towards minority shareholders' protection in company law. The court is now prepared to look at alleged prejudicial conduct by the majority from an objective point of view and to give the section its natural meaning without any technical gloss. However, the test of unfairness is as vague as ever. What is fair or unfair must therefore depend on the circumstances of each case. A thorough examination of the cases reported so far reveals that the court is prepared to have regard to any circumstances that it considers to be relevant. Factors that have hitherto been taken into account include:

---

24 *Re Bovey Hotel Ventures Ltd.* (unreported 31 July 1981) cited by Nourse J in *Re RA Noble & Sons (Clothing) Ltd.* [1983] BCLC 273.

25 [1986] BCLC 382, at 388a.

(a) any misconduct on the part of the petitioner;

(b) any offer made to the petitioner;

(c) any alternative remedy available to the petitioner;

(d) the motives of those in control of the company;

(e) any delay in presenting the petition;

(f) any other relevant factors.

These will now be considered in turn.

4.8 Factors courts take into account

(a) The petitioner's conduct

The petitioner's conduct is one of the factors which the court will take into account in deciding whether the alleged act of the respondent is unfair.[26] It can also affect the nature of the remedy under s.461.[27] The question is whether the court would give only a limited role to the petitioner's conduct when considering unfair prejudice, but take it fully into account when considering what appropriate remedy shall be granted under s.461. The answer to the first point appears to depend on whether the petitioner's conduct happened before or after the respondent's conduct. Where the respondent had unfairly brought about the petitioner's conduct, the tendency appears to be that the court is unlikely to give much weight to that conduct in deciding whether there has been unfair prejudice, although it is certainly something which will affect the remedy later.[28] So in *Re London School of Electronics*,[29] the respondent's conscious and deliberate appropriation of the students of the company, thereby depriving the petitioner of his 25% share of the profits attributable to the students, was held unfairly prejudicial to the petitioner's interest even though the petitioner had also taken with him some 12 students who had previously been with the company. 'His removal of students is certainly something which will have consequences later in the case. It did not in my view have the effect of rendering the prejudicial conduct no longer unfair', concluded Nourse J.

---

26 Nourse J in *Re London School of Electronics* [1986] Ch 211, at 222A; cf *Re R A Noble & Sons* [1983] BCLC 273.

27 Nourse J in *Re London School of Electronics* [1986] Ch 211, at 222A.

28 Ibid., Nourse J at 223D.

29 [1986] Ch 211.

Where the petitioner's conduct was the sole reason for the respondent's conduct or was substantially to blame, then the petitioner's conduct may be a decisive factor.[30] Because of the petitioner's own conduct, the respondent's conduct is not unfair even if it is prejudicial to the petitioner's interest. So where a company has been set up on the basis that the petitioner will make a contribution to the running of its affairs and he fails without cause to do so, the exclusion, though prejudicial, cannot be said to be unfair to the petitioner.[31] To do otherwise would confer a right on the petitioner to be bought out by simply behaving in a way that leaves his fellow shareholders no option but to expel him. So a shareholder/director who by his own conduct has brought about his own exclusion from management cannot complain about the exclusion. Whether he is entitled to any compensation or not depends on whether there is any extrinsic contract of employment with the company.[32] If he is entitled to be compensated then he must be compensated adequately. Failure by the company to do so might be a ground for relief under s.459. He cannot complain about being locked into the company either if the fellow shareholders refuse to buy out his shares. However, if they do decide to buy out his shares, then he has a legitimate expectation that he would be adequately compensated for the fair value of the shares on a discount basis.

While the court is hesitant to consider the petitioner's conduct where it is not the sole reason for the respondent's behaviour, the court is more willing to consider it in deciding what remedy to grant. So in *Re London School of Electronics Ltd.*,[33] although Nourse J thought that as a general rule the date of the order or the actual valuation would be more appropriate than the date of the presentation of the petition or the unfair prejudice, he ordered the petitioner's shares to be valued as at the date of presentation. He thought it would be unfair to the respondents to value the shares as at the date of the order because the respondents had themselves achieved a greater academic standing for the course entirely due to their own efforts and it was 'unlikely that it would have been achieved if the petitioner had remained with the company'.[34] It is, therefore, implicit that the petitioner's conduct affected Nourse J in the order he made.

---

30 See *Re a Company (No. 002470 of 1988) ex p. Nicholas* [1991] BCLC 480. Although the dismissal of the petitioner as a working director was in breach of the original understanding it was not unfairly prejudicial since it was necessary to remove the petitioner, who caused friction and difficulties.

31 See *Re Wondoflex Textiles Pty. Ltd.* [1951] VLR 458, *Re R A Noble & Sons* [1983] BCLC 273.

32 *Southern Foundries v Shirlaw* [1940] AC 701; *Shinlar v Northan* [1960] 2 All ER 239.

33 [1986] Ch 211.

34 *Re London School of Electronics* [1986] Ch 211, at 225A.

(b) Offer made to buy out the petitioner

The articles may have expressly provided that on the occurrence of a specified event, the member prejudiced or affected may be bought out by the remaining members at an agreed price or a fair value to be determined by an independent valuer. Alternatively, where no such provision is made, the remaining members may in fact have decided to make an offer to buy out the members affected at a price offered by them. An offer made under the articles or voluntarily, has always influenced the courts in determining whether the allegedly prejudicial conduct was unfair.

In *Re a Company (No. 004377 of 1986)*,[35] the question was whether the removal of the petitioner from his position as a director, followed by exclusion from further participation in management, constituted unfair prejudice in circumstances in which the company's articles made provision for the petitioner's shares to be transferred on his ceasing to be a director, at a price certified by the auditors as a fair value. Hoffmann J remarked that where there was an irretrievable breakdown in relations between members of a corporate quasi-partnership, the exclusion of a member from management and employment was not *ipso facto* unfairly prejudicial conduct which entitled him to petition under s.459. He went on to state that the question of unfair prejudice:

> '... must depend on whether, if there is to be a parting, it is reasonable that he should leave rather than the other member or members and on the terms he is offered for his shares or in compensation for his loss of employment.'[36]

The learned judge then referred to his own previous decision in *Re a Company (No. 007623 of 1984)*[37] involving a breakdown between members of a corporate quasi-partnership and in which a pension in compensation for loss of employment was given following removal of the petitioner as a director. The articles contained the usual provision allowing the petitioner to offer his shares to other members at a fair value fixed by the auditors. Hoffmann J refused the petitioner's claim under s.459 on the basis that the respondents' conduct had not been unfair. In the present case, Hoffmann J again found there to have been no unfair prejudice:

> 'In these circumstances it seems to me that if the articles provide a method for determining the fair value of a party's shares, a member seeking to sell

35 [1987] 1 WLR 102.
36 Ibid., at 109.
37 [1986] BCLC 362.

his shares on a breakdown of relations with other shareholders should not ordinarily be entitled to complain of unfair conduct if he has made no attempt to use the machinery provided by the articles. I say nothing about cases in which there has been bad faith or plain impropriety in the conduct of the respondents or in which the articles provide for some arbitrary or artificial method of valuation. But a provision that the auditors, or some other independent persons, shall fix a "fair value" for the shares gives the auditors precisely the function which a court would have to perform under s.459.'[38]

The judge then concluded that:

'I am satisfied that, having regard to the articles, the petitioner could have had no legitimate expectation that in the event of breakdown in relations ... they would not be relied upon to require him to sell his shares at fair value. To hold to the contrary would not be to "superimpose equitable considerations" on his rights under the articles but to relieve him from the bargain he made.'[39]

Hoffmann J's approach reveals the danger that the courts might refuse a petition under s.459 in the light of an offer made to purchase the petitioner's shares.[40] Therefore, in so far as the decision of Hoffmann J in *Re a Company (No. 004377 of 1986)* is authority for the proposition that an offer to purchase shares at a fair valuation according to provisions in a company's articles normally precludes a finding of unfair prejudice under s.459, the decision had been criticised by Professor Prentice as one that should not be followed.[41]

Professor Prentice made three major criticisms. First, Hoffmann J's reasoning equated a shareholder forced to leave a company with a voluntary seller. Secondly, his reasoning could lead to the majority being able to oust a minority shareholder as long as the price offered for his shares was in accordance with the provisions in the articles. Lastly, that it would place a shareholder in the company in a worse position than a shareholder in a company with no such provision in its articles.

38 [1987] 1 WLR 102, at 110. See also *Re a Company (No. 006834 of 1988) ex p. Kremer* [1989] BCLC 365, where Hoffmann J again adopted the same approach.

39 [1987] 1 WLR 102, at 111.

40 Such a danger has been illustrated by the decision of Vinelott J in *Re a Company* [1983] 1 WLR 927; [1983] 2 All ER 854 in a petition under the now s.122(1)(g), Insolvency Act 1986.

41 (1988) OJLS 55, at 89-91.

Professor Prentice's criticisms of Hoffmann J's reasoning have in turn been criticised.[42] First, the underlying assumption of the case was that the articles themselves, reflecting the basis upon which the parties joined the company, equated the positions of the forced and voluntary seller. The second and third criticisms argue that as there were ways in which shareholders could order their affairs and protect their own rights, if the parties had not chosen a better protection, why should the law not allow them to accept less protection? If the arrangement between the parties contemplated defeasibility, then so be it.

On the facts, Hoffmann J's decision that there was no unfair prejudice is acceptable, as the alteration to the articles under which the plaintiff was obliged to sell his shares was affected four years before the plaintiff was removed from office and he must have accepted that he could be ousted from the company. As he had then no legitimate expectation that he would not be ousted from office, his exclusion as such was not called into question. The presence of the respondent's offer to purchase at a fair value could only strengthen the respondent's case. Its absence would not however be unfairly prejudicial. Professor Prentice did not seem to have criticised Hoffmann J's decision on the facts. What he, however, criticised was Hoffmann J's dictum that:

> '... if the articles provide a method for determining the fair value of a party's shares, a member seeking to sell his shares on a breakdown of relations with other shareholders should not ordinarily be entitled to complain of unfair conduct if he has made no attempt to use the machinery provided by the articles.'

As the articles commonly contain pre-emption provisions and respondents commonly offer to buy out the petitioner, the extent to which Hoffmann J's dictum represents the law is an important issue which will now be discussed in the light of various circumstances.

(i) *Where the articles contain pre-emption provisions expressly contemplating the purchase of shares by other members from the injured member on the occurrence of some future events, and the articles also provide a machinery for the determination of share price.*

An example of this case is where the pre-emption provisions expressly require a shareholder ceasing to be a director or employee of the company to sell his share to other members. The petitioner cannot complain against the occurrence of the event as prejudicial to his interest, as the occurrence of such

42 A Clark (1989) Co. Law 153.

an event is expressly contemplated and dealt with by the articles and there is no room for any equitable gloss on this provision.[43] Therefore, as there is no unfairly prejudicial conduct, the disputes must be settled in accordance with the machinery provided by the articles. Such was arguably the case in *Re a Company (No. 004377 of 1986)*. The petition under s.459 was struck out arguably not because of the existence of machinery for the determination of share price but because no unfairly prejudicial conduct could be alleged in the first place.

In *Re Castleburn Ltd.*,[44] the articles again contained pre-emption provisions requiring a shareholder ceasing to hold office as a director or employee to give a transfer notice. When the majority shareholders offered to buy the minority's shares at the value certified by the auditors, the minority rejected the offer and petitioned on the ground that the auditor had applied a discount for minority shareholding. Not surprisingly, Judge Baker QC struck out the petition on the ground that there was no allegation of wrongful conduct on the part of the respondents and the dispute was over the terms on which the respondent should buy out the petitioner. The articles in this case directed that the shares were to be valued as between a 'willing vendor' and a 'willing purchaser'. In these circumstances the shares should in general be valued at a discount as the purchaser of those shares will in general have no expectation of participation in management and control. The company's conduct in putting the terms of the articles into effect could not be unfairly prejudicial conduct since it was conduct in conformity with the contract subsisting between the petitioner and the company and the other respondents.

Where the alleged unfairly prejudicial conduct is the valuation of shares by a valuer on a discount basis, then the presence of the pre-emption article is relevant and often given great weight. This is, however, probably subject to the following exceptions where the court may disregard the existence of such a pre-emption provision:

(1) where the articles provide some arbitrary or artificial method of valuation;[45] or

(2) where there has been bad faith or plain impropriety in the conduct of the respondents;[46] or

43 See *Re Postgate & Denby* [1987] BCLC 8.

44 (1989) 5 BCC 652; see also Hoffmann J in *Re a Company (No. 004377 of 1986)* [1987] 1 WLR 102 reaffirmed in *Re a Company (No. 006834 of 1988)* [1989] BCLC 365.

45 Per Hoffmann J in *Re a Company (No. 004377 of 1986)* [1987] 1 WLR 102, at 102b.

46 Ibid., at 102b.

(3) where the valuer was not wholly independent of any connection with the respondent or the transactions of which complaint was made.[47]

Similarly, where there is an arguable case, the pre-emption provision will not prevent a successful petition under the section.[48]

(ii) *Where the articles only provide a common form pre-emption provision requiring a member desiring to transfer shares to offer to sell his shares to his fellow shareholders at a fair value fixed by the auditors. No occurrence of prejudicial conduct is expressly contemplated.*

In this situation, if there is unfairly prejudicial conduct which affects the petitioner qua member, the mere presence of the pre-emption provision should not preclude him from petitioning under s.459, nor should the respondent's offer to buy out the petitioner.[49] The petitioner may, quite properly, want to seek an order other than the purchase order. The court in considering whether to grant such an order, for instance, to restrain the respondent from continuing with the conduct complained of, will have to consider whether the conduct in question is unfairly prejudicial to the petitioner's interests and whether the order sought by the petitioner is appropriate in the circumstances. If the order is appropriate, it should be granted regardless of the pre-emption provision. Even if the only appropriate remedy is the purchase order, being a forced sale, the shares should be valued on a *pro rata* basis. This could only be done by the court on a petition under s.459. If the pre-emption is to be given effect the valuer will very often apply a minority discount.

But if there is no unfairly prejudicial conduct, no petition can be made under s.459. The presence of pre-emption provisions merely provides a contractual mechanism for the valuation of shares, but would not in itself prevent a s.459 petition. But if the respondent refuses to buy out the petitioner when the petitioner tries to invoke the pre-emption provisions, the provisions are relevant in showing that the respondent's refusal is unfairly prejudicial. Thus, Hoffmann J in *Re a Company (No. 007623 of 1984)* said that:

> 'In general it seems to me that if a petitioner is complaining of conduct which would be unfairly prejudicial only if accompanied by a refusal on the part of the majority to buy his shares at a fair price, and the articles

47 Per Morritt J in *Re Boswell (Steels) & Co. Ltd.* (1989) 5 BCC 145, at 151A-B.

48 *Re a Company (No. 00330 of 1991) ex p. Holden* [1991] BCLC 597.

49 *Ex p. Holden* [1991] BCLC 597: the transfer of shares here according to the pre-emption provision would deprive the petitioner of *locus standi* in the s.459 petition, thus order preventing transfer was made.

provide a mechanism for determining such a price, he should not be entitled to petition under [s. 459] until he has invoked or offered to invoke that mechanism and the majority have refused to buy at the price so determined. Certification by the auditors is a swift and inexpensive method of arriving at a price and it has the merit of being the method to which the parties are contractually bound. Where such machinery is available, it seems to me wrong for a shareholder to insist on the same valuation exercise being undertaken by the court at far greater expense.'[50]

He went on:

'In the typical case in which (1) relations between shareholders have broken down without obvious fault on either side (2) the appropriate way to resolve the problem is for one or more shareholders to buy the shares of the other or others and (3) the company's articles provide a means for determining the fair value of those shares, it should not be necessary to resort to [s. 459] unless and until the operation of the articles has failed to provide an adequate solution.'[51]

Hoffmann J reaffirmed this view in *Re a Company (No. 006834 of 1988)* saying:

'The principle to be derived from the cases is that when it is plain that the appropriate solution to a breakdown of relations[52] is for the petitioner to be able to sell his shares at a fair price and the articles contain provisions for determining a price which the respondent is willing to pay or the respondent has offered to submit to an independent determination of a fair price, the presentation or maintenance of a petition under s.459 will ordinarily be an abuse of the process.'[53]

However, in a later case, the matter was left open. In *Re Abbey Leisure Ltd.*,[54] the petitioner prayed for an order under s.122(1)(g) or an order under s.459 as an alternative. The Court of Appeal did not take the opportunity to express its view on the issue whether the petition could have been struck out had the petitioner only claimed relief under s.461 in view of the respondent's offer made in accordance with the pre-emption articles. It left the issue open for some future case in which the point would be clearly in issue.

---

50 [1986] BCLC 362, at 367g-h.
51 Ibid., at 368a-b.
52 Where there is accordingly no unfairly prejudicial conduct.
53 (1989) 5 BCC 218, at 220G-H.
54 [1990] BCC 60 (CA).

However, Balcombe LJ pointed out that under s.459 there was a general inclination towards a *pro rata* basis of valuation as the Court of Appeal decision in *Re Bird Precision Bellows Ltd.*[55] and other first instance cases[56] showed. He said that a careful reading of the judgments in two first instance cases[57] indicated that the offers which it was held unreasonable for the petitioners to refuse were offers to buy them out on a *pro rata* basis. This appears to support the conclusion that if the petitioner had a claim under s.459, it would not be unreasonable for the petitioner to reject an offer made in accordance with the pre-emption provisions.[58] The offer and the pre-emption provisions are simply irrelevant.[59]

It is also clear from *Re Abbey Leisure Ltd.* that the pre-emption provision is irrelevant when the petitioner prays for a winding up order under s.122(1)(g) and as an alternative seeks a remedy under s.459. The case was dealt with on the basis that the petitioner's primary claim was for a winding up order. Hoffmann J struck out the petition on the ground that, under s.125(2) of the Insolvency Act 1986 the petitioner was unreasonable in rejecting an offer made by the respondent in accordance with the articles. The Court of Appeal overruling Hoffmann J's decision held that as the assets of the company consisted of cash, the value of the petitioner's shares (40%) would be the same as the value of the other shareholders' shares (60%) in liquidation. The Court further stated that in a valuation under the pre-emption articles by an independent valuer, as the petitioner ran the risk of being subject to a minority discount, it was not unreasonable for the petitioner to reject the offer by the respondent to purchase his shares at an independent valuation.

However, if it was only alleged that there was no independent means of valuation, then it is appropriate to have regard to the pre-emption provisions. When a fair price is offered for the petitioner's shares in accordance with the pre-emption provisions, unfairness disappears.[60]

---

55 [1986] Ch 658 (CA).
56 Eg *Re a Company (No. 003843 of 1986)* (1987) 3 BCC 624, and *Re a Company (No. 003096 of 1987)* (1988) 4 BCC 80.
57 Ibid.
58 It would only be unreasonable if the offer is to buy out on a *pro rata* basis.
59 See *ex p. Holden* [1991] BCLC 597.
60 See Hoffmann J's dictum in *Re a Company (No. 004377 of 1986)* [1987] 1 WLR 102, reaffirmed in *Re a Company (No. 006834 of 1988)* [1989] BCLC 365.

(iii) *Where there are no pre-emption provisions in the articles, but the respondent nevertheless offers to buy the petitioner's shares at a fair value to be fixed by an independent valuer.*

Where the allegation is that the occurrence of some prejudicial conduct has unfairly prejudiced the petitioner's interest, it seems that a reasonable offer to buy out does not preclude the petitioner from petitioning under the section even if the appropriate remedy in the circumstances is a purchase order. It would generally be wrong in principle to subject a minority shareholder to the discretion of an independent valuer on the issue of a discount for a minority shareholder where it is arguable that no such discount should be applied.[61] It cannot be a sufficient answer to every unfair prejudice petition that the respondents are willing to buy the petitioner's shares at a fair value. The petitioner may have an arguable case to buy out the respondents, or to obtain other types of order against the respondents.[62] Therefore, in determining whether a case of unfair prejudice has been made out, the court should not take into account the reasonable offer already made by the respondent.

It would be different where there is a breakdown of relationships and no one is to blame. Because no s.459 petition could have succeeded in the first place, the reasonable offer made by the other will strengthen the case to strike out the petition.[63] In such a case, fairness requires that the minority should not have to maintain his investment in a company managed by the majority with whom he has fallen out.[64] Similarly, if the petitioner seeks an order that his shares be purchased at a price fixed by the court but no allegation of unfairly prejudicial conduct can be found, the court will in general stay or strike out the petition in view of the respondent's offer to buy out the petitioner at a fair value.[65]

---

61 See *Re Abbey Leisure Ltd.* [1990] BCC 60 (CA), *Re D R Chemicals Ltd.* (1989) 5 BCC 39, at 53-54.

62 Where the petitioner petitions to buy out the respondent or to seek other types of order against the respondent, the court will require the petitioner to show that such an alternative remedy is realistic before allowing the petitioner to proceed. In *Re a Company (No. 003843 of 1986)* [1987] BCLC 562 the petitioners sought orders, *inter alia*, that they be appointed executive directors at substantial salaries. Millett J stayed the petition on the ground that this relief was inappropriate in the circumstances of the case because it would be most unworkable and the petitioners' real wish was proper financial compensation (at 571f-h). In *Re a Company (No. 003096 of 1987)* (1987) 4 BCC 80 where the petitioner sought a liquidation order or alternatively a sale by sealed tender, Peter Gibson J struck out the petition because it was plain and obvious that the petitioners should go (at 93-94).

63 *Re a Company (No. 006834 of 1988)* [1989] BCLC 365.

64 *Re a Company (No. 006834 of 1988)* [1989] BCLC 365.

65 As in *Re a Company (No. 003843 of 1986)* [1987] BCLC 562.

(iv) *Where there are no pre-emption provisions but the respondents offer to buy out the petitioner on a pro rata basis to be valued by an independent valuer.*

In this situation, if the petitioner asks for a purchase order under s.459 for the shares to be valued by the court, it would clearly be an abuse of court procedure,[66] unless it is clear that the valuer is not seen to be independent.

However, if the petitioner seeks some other remedy such as himself to purchase the respondents' shares, then a petition under s.459 should not be stayed or struck out simply because of the offer made by the respondent unless it is clear that it is the petitioner who must go.[67]

(v) *Conclusion*

Viewed in the various situations discussed above, it would appear that the question whether the respondents have made a reasonable offer to the petitioner should not automatically be relevant to the fairness of the respondents' conduct.[68] Whether it is relevant should depend on the particular circumstances of the case. It seems unwise to suggest that Hoffmann J in *Re a Company (No. 007623 of 1984)*[69] has laid down a general principle that a reasonable offer made by respondent will render the otherwise unfairly prejudicial conduct fair. This would assume that whenever there is unfairly prejudicial conduct by the respondent, the only remedy is for the respondent to purchase the petitioner's shares, and that the petitioner is a willing seller. To accept such a general principle would frustrate the whole purpose and existence of s.459 as an effective remedy.

(c) Alternative remedy

One commentator has suggested that a reasonable offer by a respondent to purchase the petitioner's shares or the existence of pre-emption provisions in the articles in effect provide an alternative remedy. Either of these will preclude the petitioner from seeking a remedy under s.459 unless these alternative remedies have been exhausted.[70] It has also been submitted that

---

66 *Re a Company (No. 002567 of 1982)* [1983] BCLC 151, *Re a Company (No. 006834 of 1988)* [1989] BCLC 365.

67 *Re a Company (No. 003843 of 1986)* [1987] BCLC 562, *Re a Company (No. 003096 of 1987)* (1987) 4 BCC 80.

68 But see Robin Hollington, op cit, at 78, para. 4-064.

69 [1986] BCLC 362.

70 Hollington, op cit.

this is not always the case, for the reasons mentioned. Where a petitioner could not have succeeded under s.459, it is in his interest to accept the offer. It seems that the court will stay or strike out the petition not because of the alternative remedy but on the ground that no unfairly prejudicial conduct could have been established. However, where the petitioner could have succeeded under s.459, and the court would order the petitioner to be bought out on a *pro rata* basis, then it seems that the offer should not be relevant unless the respondents have offered to buy on the *pro rata* basis and yet the petitioner refuses such an offer to be valued by independent valuer.

Alternative remedies may also include a common law action for damages and a derivative action. The mere fact that the petitioner may have a common law action based on the same facts as those which found the unfair prejudice action is not a bar to the presentation of the petition.[71] Nor will the fact that a derivative action might lie in respect of the conduct complained of prevent an unfair prejudice petition.[72]

(d) Motive of oppressor

A decision may be taken by the majority at the board or the general meeting which is not for the benefit of the company as a whole or in the best interests of the company but for an improper purpose.[73] Objective observers would generally regard this as unfair.[74] Insofar as alteration of articles is concerned, at common law, the controlling shareholders owe a duty to act *bona fide* for the benefit of the company as a whole. Should a minority shareholder object in a personal action the court may annul the alteration.[75] In a s.459 petition, the motive of the oppressor and the interest of the company as a whole[76] therefore seem relevant here.[77]

---

71 *Re a Company (No. 00477 of 1986)* [1986] BCLC 376.

72 *Re a Company* [1986] BCLC 68, *Re Stewarts (Brixton)* [1985] BCLC 4, *Re a Company (No. 005287 of 1985)* [1986] 1 WLR 281.

73 See eg *Clemens v Clemens Bros. Ltd.* [1976] 2 All ER 268 (resolution to issue shares was passed to dilute the minority's holding); *Brown v British Abrasive Wheel Co. Ltd.* [1919] 1 Ch 290; *Dafen Tinplate Co. Ltd. v Llanelly Steel Co.* [1920] 2 Ch 124 (proposed alterations of article enabling the minority to be bought out compulsorily were found invalid).

74 It has been suggested that the majority's action is unfairly prejudicial if unrelated to company interest: L Crabb; (1982) 3 Co. Law 3, at 4.

75 *Allen v Gold Reefs of West Africa Ltd.* [1900] 1 Ch 656; *Greenhalgh v Arderne Cinemas* [1950] 2 All ER 1120.

76 See also Griffin (1993) Co. Law 83, at 87-88.

77 Motive can be inferred from the consequences of the majority's act on the minority in conjunction with its effect on the company's interest as a whole. If the act is for the benefit of the company as a whole, then the prejudice on the minority is merely incidental, unless some evidence of improper motive can be shown. But if no benefit to the company as a whole can be achieved, then a natural inference is that it is done for an improper motive. Conversely, if the act is done for an improper purpose one may conclude that it is not for the benefit of the company as a whole. Motive and interest of the company thus seem to be interrelated. In *Re a Company ex p. Burr* [1992] BCLC 724, Vinelott J held that in some cases the court might draw the inference that the decision by directors to continue to trade when a company was

However, at common law, the minority has no right or interest to see that other powers of the general meeting are exercised *bona fide* for the benefit of the company as a whole, for the controlling shareholders do not owe fiduciary duties to the company or the other shareholders.[78] Nevertheless, the exercise of these powers may still be prejudicial to a minority's interest or legitimate expectation. For instance, where the minority has a legitimate expectation that the status quo will be maintained, any resolution adopted by the general meeting to ratify the directors' improper allotment of shares to dilute the minority's holding can be prejudicial. In such a situation, in a s.459 petition, the motive of the controlling shareholders and the effect of the resolution on the company's interest can be relevant in determining whether the prejudice is unfair. The court should consider the effect of the resolution on the majority and the minority, bearing in mind the benefit of the company as a going concern as at the time the general meeting action was taken. It should then decide if a reasonable man would regard the majority's conduct as unfairly prejudicial in that light.[79]

As regards directors' exercise of powers, it has earlier been submitted that a member has a legitimate expectation or interest to see that directors will act in accordance with their duties owed to the company including the duty to act for the interest of the company and not for an improper purpose.[80] It has recently been held that the directors' duty to act for proper purposes was a duty owed to shareholders directly and not to the company as such.[81] Thus, their motive and the interest of the company[82] should be relevant. Although at first sight the submission seems irreconcilable with the other fundamental principle of company law, that directors only owe their fiduciary duties to the company and not to the shareholders,[83] as has been explained,[84] the answer is, it is submitted, that under s.459 there is a distinction between 'rights' and 'interests'.[85] Because of the introduction of the word 'interests' into the

---

failing to make a profit was influenced by a desire to remain in office and this could constitute unfairly prejudicial conduct. On the facts, although the company was trading at a loss, it was diversifying into more profitable businesses. Thus, the petition under s.459 was struck out.

78 See Rider [1979] CLJ 148 and *North West Transportation Co. v Beatty* [1887] 12 AC 589; *Burland v Earle* [1902] AC 83; *Regal (Hastings) Ltd. v Gulliver* [1942] 1 All ER 378; *Northern Counties Securities Ltd. v Jackson and Steeple Ltd.* [1974] 1 WLR 1133; *Phillips v Manufacturers' Securities Ltd.* (1917) 116 LJ 290, at 296. But Xuereb ((1985) 6 Co. Law 199, at 199) argued that the principle of *bona fide* for the benefit of the company as a whole can be, should be, and is being extended to the exercise of all general meeting powers. Cf *Clemens v Clemens Bros. Ltd.* [1976] 2 All ER 268 where Foster J said that the controlling shareholders could not exercise their powers as they pleased. The exercise of such power was thought to be subject to equitable consideration.

79 Xuereb (1986) 7 Co. Law 53, at 56.

80 See Chapter 3, para. 3.2(g) above.

81 *Re a Company (No. 005136 of 1986)* [1987] BCLC 82.

82 See Griffin, op cit.

83 *Percival v Wright* [1902] 2 Ch 421. Therefore shareholders qua members do not have a right to see that the board exercises their powers *bona fide* in the best interests of the company. Where there is a breach of such a fiduciary duty it is for the company to sue.

84 See Chapter 3, para. 3.2(g) above.

85 Such a view has been taken by Peter Gibson J in *Re Sam Weller & Sons Ltd.* [1990] BCLC 80.

section, it allows courts to give relief even if strictly speaking the member has no right to complain at common law.[86] Moreover, s.459 does not automatically give a member the right to complain when there is an infringement of his interest; it requires that such an infringement be an unfair one. In contrast, the company as the proper plaintiff can sue directors for breach of fiduciary duties whether the breach is fair or unfair.[87] However, the broad acceptance of s.459 petitions and the difficulty of bringing derivative actions may mean that s.459 will be increasingly used to seek a remedy for the company.[88]

If the submission is correct, even if members have no *right* to demand that the directors will exercise their powers in the best interests of the company, they may nevertheless have a *legitimate expectation* under s.459 to do so. In many cases under s.459, the court has consistently taken into account the interests of the company and the wrongdoer's motive. For example, where it was known that some of the shareholders were unable to take up a rights issue offered to all shareholders *pro rata* without good commercial or financial reason, this was thought capable of being unfairly prejudicial.[89] This was so because it was made for an improper purpose (to dilute the minority's shareholding), although the minority had no right to complain under the rule in *Foss v Harbottle*.[90] The fact that an allotment is for an improper purpose and not in the best interests of the company may then be taken into account to see if it is unfairly prejudicial. *Re Cumana*[91] seems also to illustrate just such a principle.[92] It has further been suggested that unfair prejudice can be discerned not only as a result of the application of the 'equitable considerations' enunciated in the *Westbourne Galleries* case;[93] it may also arise in the case of non-partnership companies from an application of the principle in *Allen v*

86 In *Re a Company* [1983] 1 WLR 927; [1983] 2 All ER 854 (a petition for winding up order under s.222(f) of the 1948 Act), Vinelott J saw 'considerable force' in the submission by counsel for the respondents that the phrase 'unfairly prejudicial to the interest of some part of the members' in s.75 of the 1948 Act admitted the contention that where there is 'unfair exclusion from the management of the affairs of the company, the interest of the minority shareholder under the agreement, express or implied, that he will be allowed to participate and to be paid remuneration is affected, though his strict rights as a shareholder may not be' (at 859). Such a view was later affirmed by Hoffmann J in *Re a Company (No. 008699 of 1985)* [1986] BCLC 382.

87 Eg *Regal (Hastings) v Gulliver* [1942] 1 All ER 378.

88 See Companies Act 1985, s.461(2)(c).

89 See Harman J in *Re a Company (No. 002612 of 1984)* (1984) 1 BCC 99, 262; Vinelott J in *Re Cumana (1986)* 2 BCC 99, 453, affirmed by Court of Appeal (1986) 2 BCC 99, 495; *Re D R Chemicals* (1989) 5 BCC 39.

90 *Bamford v Bamford* [1970] Ch 212; *Hogg v Cramphorn Ltd.* [1967] Ch 254.

91 (1986) 2 BCC 99, 453; affirmed by Court of Appeal (1986) 2 BCC 99, 495.

92 See too *Re D R Chemicals* (1989) 5 BCC 39.

93 [1973] AC 360.

Gold Reefs of West Africa Ltd.,[94] viz., the majority's prejudicial action is unfair if unrelated to the company's interest.[95] Would it make any difference if it was *bona fide* in the company's interest to make a rights issue but to do so would have the effect of diluting the minority's shareholding? Provided there is no evidence of malice, mere discrimination may not be decisive, and the act may therefore not be unfairly prejudicial. In *Re a Company (No. 007623 of 1984)*,[96] the petitioner complained, *inter alia*, of a proposed rights issue which he did not have the resources to take up. Hoffmann J found that the directors were acting reasonably in what they considered to be the interests of the company:

> 'In this case, however, it seems to me that the petitioner, if he lacks the resources or inclination to contribute *pari passu* to the company, could protect his interests by offering to sell his existing holding to the majority. Indeed, if the company needs funds and he does not want to pay his share, it seems to me only fair that he should offer to sell out.'[97]

However, Hoffmann J added:

> 'Nevertheless, I do not think that the *bona fides* of the decision or the fact that the petitioner was offered shares on the same terms as other shareholders necessarily means that the rights issue could not have been unfairly prejudicial to his interests. If the majority know that the petitioner does not have the money to take up his rights and the offer is made at par when the shares are plainly worth a great deal more than par as part of a majority holding (but very little as a minority holding), it seems to me arguable that carrying through the transaction in that form could, viewed objectively, constitute unfairly prejudicial conduct.'[98]

It seems, therefore, that if it is in the company's interest to issue shares and it is not for an improper purpose, the prejudice is not unfair. This seems to be quite consistent with the test of unfairness laid down in *Re Bovey Hotel Ventures Ltd.*[99] which is an objective one. A reasonable bystander would be more likely to think that a decision, though prejudicial to the minority, is not unfairly so if it is *bona fide* in the interest of the company and without an improper purpose.

94 [1900] 1 Ch 656.
95 Crabb (1982) 3 Co. Law 3, at 4.
96 [1986] BCLC 362.
97 Ibid., 367 a-c.
98 Ibid., at 367 a-c.
99 Unreported, 31 July 1981.

The difficulty here is what is the meaning of the phrase '*bona fide* for the benefit of the company as a whole' or '*bona fide* in the best interests of the company'? In the context of alteration of articles of association, the phrase '*bona fide* for the benefit of the company as a whole' was first laid down by Lindley M.R. in *Allen v Gold Reefs of West Africa Ltd.*[100] Later cases have sought to elucidate the meaning of the phrase. Eventually, in *Greenhalgh v Arderne Cinemas Ltd.*, Lord Evershed attempted a more refined analysis of its meaning:

> 'It is now plain that '*bona fide* for the company as a whole' means not two things but one thing. It means that the shareholder must proceed on what, in his honest opinion, is for the benefit of the company as a whole. Secondly, the phrase, 'the company as a whole' does not (at any rate in such a case as the present) mean the company as a commercial entity as distinct from the corporators: it means the corporators as a general body. That is to say, the case may be taken of an individual hypothetical member and it may be asked whether what is proposed is, in the honest opinion of those who voted in its favour, for that person's benefit.'[101]

Lord Evershed's attempt notionally to distinguish 'the company as a commercial entity' from 'the corporators as a general body' does not, however, seem to have cleared the doubts on the meaning of the phrase. Where the interests of the majority and the minority are in conflict it is difficult to see what common 'benefit' they share as 'corporators' other than that they share in the company as a 'commercial entity'.[102] Following the passage quoted above, Lord Evershed went on to say that 'the matter can, in practice, be more accurately and precisely stated ... by saying that a special resolution of this kind would be liable to be impeached if the effect of it were to discriminate between majority shareholders and minority shareholders, so as to give the former an advantage of which the latter were deprived'.[103] Judicial response to this is unclear, however, as Foster J in *Clemens v Clemens*[104] has since interpreted and applied this passage on a wider and more generous basis than is supportable by the *Greenhalgh* dicta.[105] It is, however, clear that evidence of malice and discrimination could help prove that the

100 [1900] 1 Ch 656, at 671.
101 [1951] Ch 286, at 291 (CA).
102 But see Griffin (1993) Co. Law 83, who suggests that the 'benefit of the company' means 'the benefit of the whole membership' and not 'the benefit to the company as a commercial entity' (at 87, note 43).
103 [1951] Ch 286, at 291.
104 [1976] 2 All ER 268.
105 In *Greenhalgh*, the alteration was valid even though it did not allow all shareholders the freedom to sell their shares to outsiders. Mere discrimination was not sufficient since Lord Evershed did not require the majority to 'dissociate themselves altogether from their prospects'.

articles were not altered '*bona fide* for the benefit of the company as a whole'.[106] If the act was directed against the plaintiff specifically with malicious motive, it ceases to be *bona fide* at once.[107] Discrimination by the majority against the minority may also be relevant, though not conclusive. It has been suggested that the test is whether a reasonable man in good faith would conclude that a measure which is discriminatory against the minority is nevertheless for the benefit of the company as a whole.[108] The possibility of benefit accruing to the company must be sufficiently real to satisfy the test. An alteration of articles empowering the majority to compel any member to sell his shares at a price to be fixed from time to time by the directors to a person (whether a member or not) determined by the directors was not for the benefit of the company as a whole.[109] Peterson J in *Dafen Tinplate Co. Ltd. v Llannelly Steel Co.*[110] also suggested that any reduction of the amount of dividend which would otherwise be due to a shareholder would be a form of discrimination not in any way related to the company's benefit.[111] It would, therefore, seem that, although reducing a dividend in general does benefit a company, discriminatory reduction is unrelated to the company's benefit since this simply transfers the minority's stake in the company to the majority.[112] On the other hand, the elimination of a competitor from the company,[113] or an obstructive shareholder-director from the board,[114] the abolition of a restriction on the majority's right to transfer its shares,[115] or the creation of a lien over the plaintiff's shares to cover all his debts to the company,[116] have been held capable of being for the benefit of the company as a whole despite discrimination against the minority.

It appears that the directors' duty to act *bona fide* in the best interests of the company has a slightly different meaning. Professors Boyle & Birds[117] suggest that while the 'interests of the company' may now include the interests of the company's employees and in some cases the interests of its creditors, it otherwise means the interests of the company as a *commercial entity*, to be judged in most cases by reference to the interests of present and

---

106 Boyle & Birds' *Company Law*, 2nd ed., at 65.
107 Sterndale MR in *Sidebottom v Kershaw, Leese* [1920] 1 Ch 154, at 168 and Warrington LJ at 172.
108 Boyle & Birds' *Company Law*, 2nd ed., at 66.
109 *Dafen Tinplate Co. Ltd. v Llanelly Steel Co.* [1920] 2 Ch 124.
110 [1920] 2 Ch 124.
111 Ibid., at 141.
112 Boyle & Birds' *Company Law*, 2nd ed., at 67.
113 *Sidebottom v Kershaw, Leese* [1920] 1 Ch 154: the court could not agree that there was any *mala fide* or dishonest intention to get rid of a shareholder who was also a competitor of the company.
114 *Shuttleworth v Cox* [1927] 2 KB 9: there was no 'trace of any vindictiveness or wrong motive'.
115 *Greenhalgh v Arderne Cinemas* [1951] Ch 286.
116 *Allen v Gold Reefs of West Africa Ltd.* [1900] Ch 656.
117 Boyle & Birds' *Company Law*, 2nd ed., at 593. Farrar's Company Law, 3rd ed. at 384, however, suggests that it means the interests of the corporators as a general body (citing Evershed MR's dicta in *Greenhalgh v Arderne Cinemas* [1951] Ch 286, at 291).

future shareholders alone. Whatever is the meaning of the phrase, motive is clearly relevant here, for Latham CJ said[118] that before the exercise of a discretionary power by directors will be interfered with by the court, it must be proved by the complaining party that they have acted for an improper motive. Equally, discrimination would seem relevant.

(e) Delay in petitioning

It is clear from Peter Gibson J's judgment in *Re D R Chemicals Ltd.*[119] that laches may bar relief on a s.459 petition. However, the delay in bringing petition must have been inexcusable. In *Re D R Chemicals Ltd.*, the respondents argued that the delay of some two and a half years between the time when the petitioner first knew of the allotment and the presentation of the petition rendered it inequitable for the petitioner to be allowed to obtain relief. It was found that the delay was not inexcusable, for during a good deal of that period the petitioner through his solicitors and accountants was quite reasonably attempting to discover exactly what had occurred in relation to the allotment and was not receiving prompt answers from the respondents.[120]

(f) Other relevant factors

In *Jesner v Jarrad Properties Ltd.*,[121] it was held that the interest of the shareholders of a company were prejudiced by interest free loans by the company to another company. However, it was not unfair to the petitioners because the company had had a long history of interest free intercompany loans. In *Re a Company (No. 002470 of 1988) ex p. Nicholas*,[122] although the withholding of money owed to a subsidiary company by a parent company that exercised financial control over it was conduct prejudicial to the members of the subsidiary, it was not unfairly so because the parent company withheld the payments in order to secure its own survival. There was not enough money to go round but it was sufficient to keep the creditors of the parent company at bay. If payments to its subsidiary were not withheld, it would have collapsed, bringing its subsidiary down with it. The attempt to keep the group afloat was therefore a reasonable business judgment in the circumstances and was not unfairly prejudicial.

118 *Mills v Mills* (1938) 60 CLR 150.

119 (1989) 5 BCC 39, sub nom *Re a Company (No. 005134 of 1986) ex p. Harries* [1989] BCLC 383.

120 Ibid., at 53.

121 [1992] BCC 807.

122 [1992] BCC 895.

4.9 Conclusion

It seems clear that in a s.459 petition, the fundamental test is whether the petitioner has been unfairly treated. The test of unfairness has been deliberately left undefined so that it can be flexibly applied in various circumstances. All relevant factors will be taken into account and at the end of the day it is a fine judicial balancing exercise which will determine the outcome of a case. The factors referred to above merely serve to illustrate how such an exercise may be conducted. These judicial factors also show that s.459 provides a far more effective and flexible way of dealing with unfair conduct by the majority against the minority than the old 'oppressive conduct' approach under s.210 of the 1948 Act and the common law approach under the exceptions to the rule in *Foss v Harbottle*.

Chapter 5

The Application of Section 459

As the concept of unfair prejudice is potentially very wide, to attempt to lay down a general definition would restrict the proper application of the remedy. The courts have rightly refused to place any 'gloss'[1] on the very wide discretion conferred on them by the section. Nonetheless, it is difficult to predict how the courts will exercise their discretion in applying the test without referring to decided cases.

Having considered the abstract concepts of interests, prejudice and unfairness, and the test of unfairness, the practical circumstances where unfair prejudice petitions may arise will now be analysed in greater detail.

5.1 Exclusion from management

A company, public or private, may by ordinary resolution remove a director before the expiration of his period of office, notwithstanding provisions in its articles of association, or in any agreement between it and him, but subject to any claim in damages he might have.[2] Where the excluded director has no legitimate expectation to be involved in the management of the company, such an exclusion is not prejudicial to the director's interest qua member, and so he cannot complain under s.459.[3] Where a member has a legitimate expectation to be involved in the management of a company, and in particular to be employed with a salary, as in most of the quasi-partnership cases, his exclusion from management is certainly prejudicial to his interest as a member.[4]

There remains the question whether such an exclusion is *per se* unfairly prejudicial. Where there is a breakdown of relations between joint venturers, the departure of one party is usually the only possible and sensible outcome.[5] Whether there is unfairly prejudicial conduct will depend on whether it is reasonable that X departs rather than Y, and on the terms of that parting.[6] It is

---

1 [1986] BCLC 382, at 388 per Hoffmann J.
2 Section 303, Companies Act 1985.
3 Neither can he sue under s.14, CA 1985 (*Eley v Positive Government Security Life Assurance Co.* (1876) 1 Ex D 88) nor claim that it is a variation of class right (*Cumbrian Newspapers Group Ltd. v Cumberland and Westmorland Herald Newspapers and Printing Co. Ltd.* [1987] Ch 1).
4 See Chapter 3, para. 3.2(a) above.
5 *Re a Company (No. 007623 of 1986)* [1986] BCLC 362.
6 *Re a Company (No. 004377 of 1986)* [1987] 1 WLR 102; [1987] BCLC 94.

necessary to analyse the evidence in detail and decide whether the excluded party was partly to blame for the result (eg the petitioner's disinterest in the company's affairs). In this situation, the court is willing to take into account the petitioner's conduct prior to the alleged unfair prejudice. This could be a decisive factor to tip the scale in favour of the respondents and make their conduct not unfair even though prejudicial to the petitioner's interest.[7] On the other hand, if the petitioner is excluded from management in that after an altercation with the majority, the latter run the company business without reference to the petitioner, the exclusion can be unfairly prejudicial.[8]

Where there is an irretrievable breakdown of relationship without obvious fault on either side, it had been held that it could not be oppressive under the old s.210.[9] Under s.459, it has been said that the only solution was to part company.[10] If one of them asks the other to leave the business, the former cannot automatically be regarded as having acted in a manner unfairly prejudicial to the interests of the latter. It must depend on whether it is reasonable that one should leave rather than the other and, even more important, on the terms on which he is asked to go.[11] In this respect, proper valuation of shares is crucial.[12]

5.2 Breach of directors' duties

Directors are said to be in a fiduciary position and hence are not entitled to profit from that position, unless otherwise expressly provided. Where they do so, they are generally liable to account for the profit.[13] Directors also owe a duty to exercise their powers *bona fide* in the interest of the company and not for a collateral purpose.[14]

Directors' duties are generally owed to the company[15] and a breach of duty is a wrong done to the company[16] unless the articles provide otherwise.

7 *Re R A Noble & Sons (Clothing) Ltd.* [1983] BCLC 273, at 288i-289a, 292a-b.
8 *Re Ghyll Beck Driving Range Ltd.* [1993] BCLC 1126 at 1131f.
9 *Elder v Elder & Watson* (1952) SC 49 (petitioner excluded from office as a result of a series of hostile disputes which developed among the shareholders, in the course of which the shareholders took sides).
10 *Re a Company (No. 007623 of 1986)* [1986] BCLC 362.
11 Ibid., at 366 a-c.
12 See Chapter 7, para. 7.2 below.
13 *Regal (Hastings) v Gulliver* [1942] 1 All ER 378; *Cook v Deeks* [1916] 1 AC 554.
14 *Re Smith & Fawcett* [1942] Ch 304.
15 *Percival v Wright* [1902] 2 Ch 421. But see *Re a Company (No. 005136 of 1986)* [1987] BCLC 82.
16 Members do not have a personal right not to have the value of their shares reduced by the wrongdoing of the directors where that wrongdoing has caused damage to the company and the shareholders' loss is only consequential to that: *Prudential Assurance v Newman (No. 2)* [1982] Ch 204.

The proper plaintiff is the company and where the directors are in control of the company, an action by the company against the directors is improbable. At common law, the shareholders' only remedy is to bring a derivative action under the fraud on minority exception to the rule in *Foss v Harbottle*. However, the difficulties that the shareholders will encounter in bringing a derivative action are well known.[17]

There do not, however, appear to be such problems under s.459. It has been submitted[18] that shareholders have a legitimate expectation that the directors will not be in breach of their duties. It is clear from the cases that the deliberate diversion of the company's business by those in control of the company to another business owned by them is unfairly prejudicial to the shareholders who have no interest in the new business.[19] It is not necessary to show that those in control had acted in bad faith, for it is sufficient if a reasonable bystander would regard the consequences of their conduct as having unfairly prejudiced the petitioner's interest.[20] So, in *Re Cumana Ltd.*,[21] the Court of Appeal agreed with Vinelott J's finding that the deliberate diversion of the company's business into another company, without good commercial reason, was unfairly prejudicial to the minority's interests.

Using assets of the company unscrupulously for one's personal benefit and for the benefit of family and friends can also be unfairly prejudicial. In *Re Elgindata Ltd.*,[22] the respondent bought a Porsche as a 'company car' at a cost of £41, 595 at a time when the company was making a loss. He also used company's money to buy a Ford Escort used only occasionally by him and his children. Otherwise, the car stood idly in the company's car park and other company staff were not permitted to use it. He charged the cost of refurbishment on his own flat to the company's accounts. He used the company's money to entertain his friends, to pay for holidays for himself and his family and to pay for other personal expenditure. Although there was no allegation of dishonesty on the respondent's part, the totality of the evidence of such conduct was held to constitute unfair prejudice. Warner J found that even though the conduct did not seriously jeopardise or diminish the value of the shares in the company, it was, nevertheless, unfairly prejudicial because by its very nature the misapplication of a company's assets by those in control of

17 See Chapter 1, para. 1.4 above and Sealy, Problem of Standing, Pleading and Proof in Corporation Litigation, in *Company Law in Change* (ed Pettet, 1987).

18 See Chapter 3, para. 3.2(g) above.

19 See *Scottish Co-operative Wholesale v Meyer* [1959] AC 324; *Re Stewarts (Brixton) Ltd.* [1985] BCLC 4; *Re Cumana Ltd.* (1986) 2 BCC 99, 495; *Re London School of Electronics* [1986] Ch 211; *Re XYZ Ltd.* [1987] 1 WLR 102.

20 Slade LJ in *Re Bovey Hotel Ventures Ltd.* (unreported, 31 July 1981).

21 [1986] BCLC 430.

22 [1991] BCLC 959, at 1001-1003. See Goo (1993) JBL 283.

its affairs for their own benefit is unfairly prejudicial to the interests of minority shareholders.

The application of s.459 extends to all kinds of breach of director's duties, not just to cases of diversion of business. So, in one case, a breach of directors' fiduciary duties not to mislead shareholders when making statements supporting one of two rival take-over bids was regarded as capable of establishing unfair prejudice.[23] In another case, where the petitioners were fraudulently induced to sell their shares in a private company to a small public company, it was also regarded as capable of establishing a case under s.459.[24]

In *Re Hailey Group Ltd.*[25] an employee gave a month's notice of resignation and renounced all the shares to which he was entitled to one of the respondents for a sum of £40, 000 paid by the company alleged to be an *ex gratia* payment.[26] The deputy judge found that the payment was a consideration for the renunciation and was a *prima facie* breach of s.151(1) of the Companies Act 1985 and a clear breach of duty on the respondent's part.[27] This was held to be unfairly prejudicial to that part of the members who could not benefit from the renunciation.[28] The deputy judge also found evidence to the effect that certain payments by the company to its working shareholders was illegal, being in breach of s.152(2) of the Companies Act 1985, and was a misuse of the powers of those involved.[29] This too was presumably unfairly prejudicial.[30]

It would appear that *Regal (Hastings) v Gulliver*[31] could well be dealt with more easily and more satisfactorily under s.459. In *Regal (Hastings) v Gulliver*, directors had obtained their profits by reason of , and in the course of, the execution of their office as directors of Regal in selling off the company. They had utilised the position and knowledge possessed by them by virtue of their office as directors to enter into the transaction. They were, thus, liable to the purchaser of the company to account at common law, notwithstanding that they had acted *bona fide* throughout. Their liability did not depend on fraud or absence of *bona fide*. The decision has been much

23 *Re a Company (No. 008699 of 1985)* (1986) 2 BCC 99, 024.

24 *Re a Company (No. 00477 of 1986)* (1986) 2 BCC 99, 171.

25 [1993] BCLC 459.

26 Ibid., at 464g-h.

27 Ibid., 464i-465c.

28 Ibid., at 465d.

29 Ibid., at 471b.

30 Ibid., at 471f.

31 [1942] 1 All ER 378.

32 See Gower's, *Principles of Modern Company Law* (5th ed. 1992) at 566.

criticised[32] and on occasions distinguished.[33] Under s.459, the shareholders would have had a legitimate expectation that the directors would not benefit from their position. However the breach of the expectation was probably not unfair because there was no detriment to the shareholders, who in fact benefited, as the company as a whole only did a successful deal because the directors participated in the investment. It would therefore appear that it was not unfairly prejudicial for the directors to keep their profits as a result of the position and knowledge they possessed. On the contrary, it would seem that the purchaser's claim was itself unjust and unmeritorious given that they had received an unexpected windfall.[34] As s.459 also does not depend on bad faith or the absence of good faith, the fact that the directors had acted *bona fide* throughout would not be a bar for relief under s.459.

Where an act of the board is not a fraud on the minority, the act is ratifiable. If duly ratified by the general meeting, the minority has no derivative action under an exception to the rule in *Foss v Harbottle*, as the members in general meeting can vote for their own personal interests.[35] As far as s.459 is concerned, as we have seen, ratifying prejudicial acts of directors can be prejudicial to the minority too. And it has been suggested that 'if a reasonable man would consider the action to be to the detriment of the company or would consider that it could confer no benefit upon the company, the action is unfair'.[36] Thus, even if the directors' breach of duty is duly ratified, the minority can still petition under s.459, provided it can be shown that its interest or legitimate expectation has been prejudiced and that the prejudice is unfair.[37]

As regards negligence and inefficiency in management by directors, as we have seen, although the Jenkins Committee intended that the reformed statutory remedy might be used in this regard,[38] the court decided otherwise under the old s.210. In *Re Five Minute Car Wash Service Ltd.*,[39] the petitioner, a minority shareholder, claimed that the company had lost £200,000 in five years largely because of the acts and omissions of Evison, the managing director and chairman. He made some fifteen allegations against the

33 See *Peso Silver Mines v Cropper* (1966) 58 DLR (2d) 1; *Island Export Finance Ltd. v Umunna* [1986] BCLC 460.

34 See [1967] 2 AC 134, at 157, *per* Lord Porter; Lowry, 'Regal (Hastings) Fifty Years On: Breaking the Bonds of the Ancient Regime' (1994) NILQ 1.

35 *Hogg v Cramphorn* [1967] Ch 254. But see *Clemens v Clemens Bros. Ltd.* [1976] 2 All ER 268 (resolution could be set aside where it was oppressive to the minority shareholders).

36 Crabb (1982) 3 Co. Law 3, at 8.

37 See *Re Kenyon Swansea Ltd.* [1987] BCLC 514. Even if the unfairly prejudicial conduct has been put right retrospectively it was still unfairly prejudicial.

38 Cmnd. 1749 (1962) paras. 207-8.

39 [1966] 1 All ER 242.

respondent including: the non-payment of accounts to the point where writs were received weekly; the company's good name had been ruined; the sale of car-washing vouchers at below cost price; the estrangement of petrol companies; the failure to remove inefficient staff; the acquisition of equipment and machines without proper tests; and the failure to observe the Factories Act. Buckley J held that the mere fact that a member of a company had lost confidence in the manner in which the company's affairs were conducted did not lead to the conclusion that he was oppressed, nor could resentment at being outvoted, or mere dissatisfaction with or disapproval of the conduct of the company's affairs, whether on grounds relating to policy or to efficiency, however well founded.[40] Buckley J found that the respondent was unwise, inefficient and careless in the performance of his duties as managing director and chairman of the board of the company. He said the respondent had not acted unscrupulously, unfairly, or with any lack of probity towards the petitioner or any other member of the company. Neither had he overridden or disregarded the wishes of the board of directors. His conduct could not be characterised as harsh or burdensome or wrongful towards any member of the company. The court, therefore, held that such conduct was not oppressive under the old s.210.

In *Five Minute Car Wash* the petitioner alleged that by failing to remove Evison, the managing director, the majority shareholder had condoned Evison's oppressive conduct. Buckley J thought that such an omission could only be oppressive if it was 'designed to achieve some unfair advantage' over the oppressed minority.[41] A rather wide approach to omission was adopted in *Re H R Harmer*[42] where it was thought that intentional wrongdoing was not a necessary part of oppressive conduct, although 'what is done consciously strikes with a sharper edge.'

How would the *Five Minute Car Wash* case be decided today under s.459? A director clearly owes a duty of care and skill to the company and the members arguably have a legitimate expectation that a director will act with due care in the running of the company's business. The problem is in establishing unfairness. The court should be able to hold that serious mismanagement which causes real economic harm to the company's business (and therefore to the value of the members' interests) could be unfairly prejudicial to the interests of shareholders.[43] But, as Warner J pointed out, there are two main difficulties

40 Ibid., at 247.
41 [1966] 1 All ER 242, at 247I.
42 [1958] 3 All ER 689, at 710c.
43 Gore-Browne on Companies (44th ed. 1986) Vol 2, at 28.021 also suggests that the terminology in s.459(1) referring to 'any actual or proposed act or omission of the company including an act or omission on its behalf' should be of assistance too.

which the courts are ill-qualified to resolve.[44] First, there will be cases where there is disagreement between petitioners and respondents as to whether a particular managerial decision was commercially appropriate or justifiable. He added that there can be no unfairness to the petitioners if the respondents take a different, albeit incompetent, view on such matters. Secondly, a shareholder acquires shares knowing that their value depends to a certain extent on managerial competence. He takes the risk that the management may prove not to be of the highest quality. Thus, it is perhaps not surprising that the court will normally be very reluctant to accept that incompetent managerial decisions can amount to unfairly prejudicial conduct.[45] However, the possibility of a s.459 petition against serious mismanagement of a company's business is not completely ruled out.[46] One example of a case where the court might nonetheless find that there was unfair prejudice to a minority shareholder would be one where the majority shareholders, for reasons of their own, persisted in retaining a demonstrably incompetent member of their family in charge of the management of the company's business.[47] In *Re Elgindata Ltd.*,[48] on the facts, the respondent was found to have neglected the management of the company's business. There were also instances of bad management on his part. His management lacked vigour and purposefulness. However, Warner J held that it was prejudicial to the petitioner's interests but not unfairly so; it was of a kind for which the petitioner took the risk when he invested in the company.[49] When serious mismanagement is *unfairly* prejudicial must therefore depend on the precise facts of each case.

One commentator has suggested that 'if a reasonable man would consider the action to be to the detriment of the company or would consider that it could confer no benefit upon the company, the action is unfair'.[50] Another has said, 'the new standard is plainly intended to be a more objective one which is concerned with running the company, even if it is done in the best of faith, in a way which is clearly unfair in its consequences to the complaining shareholder'.[51] Apart from the benefit of the company, other factors, such as the complaining shareholders' encouragement or acquiescence or whether the director has acted unscrupulously or dishonestly, may be relevant. The director in *Re Five Minute Car Wash* did not act 'unscrupulously, unfairly or with any

44 *Re Elgindata Ltd.* [1991] BCLC 959, at 993.
45 See Peter Gibson J in *Re Sam Weller & Sons Ltd.* [1990] BCLC 80, at 89.
46 Warner J in *Re Elgindata* [1991] BCLC 959, at 993i.
47 Ibid., at 994d.
48 [1991] BCLC 959. See Goo (1993) JBL 283; Griffin (1992) 108 LQR 389; Stapledon (1993) 14 Co. Law 94.
49 Ibid., at 1000i.
50 Crabb (1982) 3 Co. Law 3, at 8.
51 Boyle (1981) 1 Co. Law 280, at 281.

lack of probity'. Although he had held more than half the issued shares at the time of the alleged misconduct, more shares were later allotted to other shareholders which took away his control. This showed that before allotment the petitioners had so far acquiesced in his running of the company's business. He had not 'overborne or disregarded the wishes of the board of directors'. Thus, on the facts, perhaps the director's mismanagement and negligence may still not constitute unfair prejudice. To quote Warner J, it was conduct 'of a kind of which the petitioner took the risk when he invested in the company'.

5.3 Excessive remuneration

The payment of excessive remuneration to directors, to the detriment of the members, was one of the examples of conduct which the Cohen Committee intended to be dealt with under s.210 of the 1948 Act. Where controlling directors pay themselves above the going rate, it is clearly prejudicial to the financial interests of those members who are not directors. It may be unfairly prejudicial if the salaries are grossly in excess of any reasonable return for their services in conducting the affairs of the company. The difficulty is, however, to ask the court to embark on the task of inquiring into the reasonableness of the remuneration. The courts have a natural disinclination to find remuneration excessive and will not, generally, interfere with matters which require the commercial judgment of the board. At common law, where the company pays remuneration to its directors under an express power, such as Article 82 of Table A, the court will not inquire into the reasonableness of the remuneration even if it is paid out of capital (as opposed to divisible profits) and the power of a solvent company to pay such remuneration is not subject to any *bona fide* test.[52] In *Smith v Croft*,[53] Walton J rejected the plaintiff's contention that the directors' salaries were excessive and warned that in certain areas of business, such as the entertainment business, salaries were justifiable though far in excess of what could be earned in other professions.

A similar restrictive approach had been taken with regard to the old s.210. In *Re Jermyn Street Turkish Baths Ltd.*,[54] it was said that if a director of a company were to draw remuneration to which he was not legally entitled or in excess of the remuneration to which he was legally entitled, this might no

52 *Re Halt Garage* [1982] 3 All ER 1016. As the court is more prepared to scrutinise the reasonableness of directors' remuneration under s.459, the remuneration paid in *Re Halt Garage* could now be subject to an unfair prejudice petition. However the result may be the same as Oliver J held that, on the facts, having regard to the company's turnover, the amounts in question were not patently excessive or unreasonable.

53 [1986] 1 WLR 580.

54 [1971] 1 WLR 1042, CA. Pennycuick J thought the remuneration paid was grossly excessive and oppressive to the petitioners ([1970] 1 WLR 1194).

doubt found misfeasance proceedings or some other kind of relief, but it would not of itself amount to oppression. As unfair prejudice is wider than oppression, this case could well be decided differently today under s.459.

It has been suggested[55] that under s.459 if it can be shown that the directors have pursued a deliberate policy of not paying dividends and instead paying salaries related to profit rather than services rendered, or, it may be added, that the directors have made a disguised gift to themselves, it could be said that the remuneration paid is unfairly prejudicial. Thus, in *Re Cumana*[56] where the respondent was alleged to have received, during a period of 14 months, in the region of £160, 000 to £356, 000 by way of bonus and £190, 000 by way of pension contributions, Vinelott J found that the remuneration paid was plainly in excess of anything the respondent had earned and was so large as to be unfairly prejudicial to the petitioner. The Court of Appeal agreed.

More recently, Vinelott J pointed out that there must be sufficient evidence to show that the directors are paid in the aggregate more than the company would have had to pay to secure suitable replacements or that the level of remuneration was out of line with that paid to executive directors of other companies of comparable size and turnover.[57]

5.4 Inadequate dividends

In the absence of anything to the contrary in the articles,[58] a company cannot be compelled to declare a dividend, and no action can be brought for its recovery until it has been declared.[59] This applies to preference shareholders as well as to ordinary shareholders.[60] However, such a failure to declare or to pay adequate dividends, or dividends at all, could sometimes be the basis of an allegation of unfair prejudice as members have a financial interest in the business of the company.[61] A policy of low dividend payments can amount to 'unfair prejudice'.[62] As we have seen earlier,[63] the fact that it prejudices all members equally will not bar a petition under s.459 today.

---

55 Robin Hollington, *Minority Shareholders' Rights*, Sweet & Maxwell, 1990, at 66.

56 (1986) 2 BCC 99, 485; [1986] BCLC 430, CA.

57 *Re a Company ex p. Burr* [1992] BCLC 724, at 735f.

58 Articles commonly require a declaration of dividend in general meeting by ordinary resolution following a recommendation by the directors: see Article 102, Table A.

59 *Bond v Barrow Haematite Steel Co.* [1902] 1 Ch 353.

60 *Buenos Ayres Great Southern Railways Co. Ltd. v Preston* [1947] Ch 384, [1947] 1 All ER 729.

61 See Chapter 3, para. 3.2 (c) above.

62 *Re a Company (No. 00823 of 1987) The Times* 26 July 1989; *Re Sam Weller & Sons Ltd.* [1990] BCLC 80.

63 See Chapter 4, para. 4.6 above.

Peter Gibson J, however, made it clear in *Re Sam Weller & Sons Ltd.*[64] that he did not intend to suggest that a shareholder who did not receive an income from the company except by way of dividend was always entitled to complain whenever the company was controlled by persons who did derive an income from the company and when profits were not fully distributed by way of dividend. He said that the court would view with great caution allegations of unfair prejudice on this ground. Therefore, it would seem that failure to declare dividends alone may not *per se* be unfair unless it is adopted by the company as a long term policy without good commercial reasons. Factors such as whether it is in the interest of the company to retain dividends, as the directors recommended, will also be taken into account.[65]

Failure to pay a dividend after it had been declared can still be unfairly prejudicial. For instance, those in control of the affairs of a company may arrange for their own dividends to be paid promptly while delaying the payment of dividends to minority shareholders.[66]

5.5 Take-over situations

On the subject of take-over bids, the most important controls are set out in the City Code on Takeovers and Mergers administered by the City Panel. Section 459 may, however, be of assistance to dissentient shareholders in a take-over bid in the following three circumstances, which will now be considered in turn.

(i) Misleading information or advice

Whether directors owe a duty to shareholders personally in a case of a take-over bid is not clear cut. There have been cases where directors do owe duties to individual shareholders if there is a close enough nexus between the actions of the directors and the individual interest of the shareholders.[67] In *Heron International v Grade*,[68] the directors of the target company were faced with two competing bids. Under the articles, the board had the power to choose the bidder to whom shares could be transferred. Hoffmann J held that

---

64 [1990] BCLC 80.

65 The Draft Fifth EC Directive on Company Law, Article 49, would require compulsory distribution of at least 5% of profits in each financial year to a statutory reserve until that reserve amounts to not less than 10% of the subscribed capital.

66 Per Warner J in *Re Elgindata Ltd.* [1991] BCLC 959, at 991.

67 *Allen v Hyatt* (1914) 30 TLR 444; *Coleman v Myers* [1977] 2 NZLR 225; *Gething v Kilner* [1972] 1 WLR 337; cf *Percival v Wright* [1902] 2 Ch 421.

68 [1983] BCLC 244.

the directors must not exercise their powers in such a way as to prevent the members from obtaining the best price for their shares. They owed a duty to the current shareholders to obtain for them the opportunity to accept or reject the best price reasonably obtainable. This case must, however, be read in the light of the powers the board had to choose the bidder to whom the shares could be transferred and the fact that they had chosen the lower bidder. There they had deprived the shareholders of the company of the opportunity of accepting the higher bid and breached the duties owed to the shareholders. The board is not inevitably under a positive duty to the shareholders to recommend, and take all steps within its power to facilitate, whichever is the highest offer unless there is a close nexus between them. So, if the directors are not involved in the negotiations, no such duties are owed to the shareholders personally.

As to contested take-over battles in the case of companies listed on the Stock Exchange, the position is more complicated and it is a fair guess that the courts are not keen to enter the fray especially on an interlocutory basis.

These cases could, however, be decided under s.459 more easily. In *Re a Company (No. 008699 of 1985)*,[69] a failure by directors to advise shareholders impartially in regard to two competing take-over bids (in one of which they were themselves interested) was held capable of constituting unfairly prejudicial conduct. It was unfair conduct because it affected the shareholders' right to sell their shares to a higher bidder and it affected them qua member because one of the members' interests was in being able to sell their shares at the best price.[70]

Hoffmann J could not accept the proposition that the board must inevitably be under a positive duty to recommend, and take all steps within their power to facilitate, whichever was the highest offer.[71] But he said:

> 'I think that if the board chooses to give advice on the matter, fairness requires that such advice should be factually accurate and given with a view to enabling the shareholders ... to sell, if they so wish, at the best price.'[72]

It is submitted that although the board is not generally under a *positive duty to recommend, and take all steps within their power to facilitate,*

69 [1986] BCLC 382.
70 Ibid., at 387b.
71 Ibid., at 389a.
72 Ibid., at 388c-d.

whichever is the higher offer,[73] they are still required, though not more than, *to give the shareholders sufficient information and advice* to enable them to reach a properly informed decision, *and to refrain from giving misleading information or advice or exercising their fiduciary powers in a way which would prevent or inhibit shareholders from choosing the better price*, whether they choose to advise the shareholders to accept whichever is the highest offer or not. A shareholder in an offeree company, as a member, has a legitimate expectation to be given sufficient and accurate factual information about the offer, though not their opinion on whichever is the higher offer, in order to make a properly informed decision in a take-over bid. His interest may be unfairly prejudiced if he or his fellow shareholders are misled by insufficient or inaccurate information or advice into accepting an offer.

(ii) Compulsory acquisition under s.429, Companies Act 1985.

If the offeror achieves a 90% (in value) acceptance figure within four months of the date of the offer, he can serve a notice on those who have not accepted the offer within two months of achieving the 90% threshold that he desires to acquire their shares. The 90% threshold applies to each class of shares separately, so that each class is the subject of a separate offer for this purpose.[74] Provided that the notice has been validly served, the offeror 'shall be entitled and bound to acquire' compulsorily the non-acceptor's shares on the terms of the offer.[75]

This compulsory purchase power, like any other powers, can naturally be abused by the majority shareholders who hold 90% of shares of the offeree company in an artificially created sham take-over, for instance by selling their shares to a newly formed company wholly owned by them.[76] Under s.430C(1), within six weeks of receiving a notice of intent to acquire, any non-acceptor can apply to the court for an order preventing the compulsory acquisition or specifying different acquisition terms. The court will only make such an order if it is satisfied that the scheme is unfair to the general body of shareholders in the transferor company. Where not less than nine-tenths of the shareholders in the transferor company approve the scheme or accept the offer, the offer is normally taken, *prima facie*, to be a proper one, and it is up to the dissentients to show to the court why their shares should not be

---

73 Unless there is a close link between the board and the shareholders to give rise to a positive duty as in *Coleman v Myers* [1977] 2 NZLR 225.

74 Section 429(1), (2), (3) of the Companies Act 1985.

75 Section 430(2) of the Companies Act 1985.

76 See eg *Re Bugle Press Ltd.* [1961] Ch 270, CA.

acquired by the transferee company.[77] In the absence of very strong grounds, the court will not set up its own view of the fairness of the scheme in opposition to so very large a majority of the shareholders who are concerned.[78] The court will, however, take into account the current stock market price of those shares as cogent, though not conclusive, evidence of their true value to determine whether the offer is a fair one.[79] The test of fairness is whether the offer is fair to the offerees as a body and not whether it is fair to a particular shareholder in the peculiar circumstances of his own case.[80] It is not enough to prove that the scheme is open to criticism or capable of improvement.[81] Orders for costs or expenses may be made against an applicant if it is improper or vexatious.[82] However, the mere fact that the overwhelming majority of shareholders have accepted the offer as fair does not establish that an action alleging that it is unfair is vexatious.[83]

However, if the dissentient shareholders showed that in substance the transferee company is the same as the majority holding in the transferor company, the onus is on the majority to satisfy the court that the scheme is one which the minority ought reasonably to be compelled to fall in with. In *Re Bugle Press Ltd.*,[84] there were three shareholders, J and S who each held 4,500 shares, and the applicant who held 1, 000 shares. J and S formed a company in which they held all the shares and then offered to acquire the whole of the shares of Bugle Press Ltd. at a price of £10 per share. The applicant refused to sell. In the Court of Appeal, Harman LJ said,

> 'This is a barefaced attempt to evade that fundamental rule of company law which forbids the majority of shareholders, unless the articles so provide, to expropriate a minority. It will be all too simple if all you had to do was to form a £2 company and sell to it your shares and then force the outsider to comply ... [The minority shareholders have simply to show] that the transferee company was nothing but a little hut built round his two co-shareholders ... and the whole thing is seen to be a hollow sham. It was then for the transferee company to show that nevertheless there was some good reason why the scheme should be allowed to go on [(eg that the minority shareholders were acting in a manner highly damaging to the interests of the company)] ... The

77 Maugham J in *Re Hoare & Co. Ltd.* (1933) 150 LT 374.
78 Ibid.
79 Plowman J in *Re Grierson, Oldham & Adams Ltd.* [1968] Ch 17; [1967] 1 WLR 385; [1967] 1 All ER 192 (Ch).
80 Ibid.
81 Ibid.
82 Companies Act 1985, s.430C(4).
83 *Re Britoil* [1990] BCC 70, CA.
84 [1960] 3 WLR 956.

minority shareholder has nothing to knock down, he has only to shout and the walls of Jericho fall flat.'[85]

A compulsory acquisition pursuant to s.429 may still be unfairly prejudicial to the minority shareholders as s.459 does not import any requirement of impropriety. The difficulty is to show unfairness. Maugham J pointed out in *Re Hoare & Co. Ltd.*[86] that where nine-tenths of shareholders have accepted the offer, it is difficult to see that the compulsory purchase is unfairly prejudicial. However, the burden of showing unfairness in s.459 is unlikely to be more heavy than that in s.429. There is normally a heavy burden of proof on the dissentient under s.429[87] and there is a *prima facie* presumption that the scheme is a fair one. A substantial failure to comply with the provisions of the City Code could be a major factor negating any assumption that the offer was fair.[88] It is, however, not enough that the materials put before the shareholders are inadequate to enable them to form a just conclusion as to the acceptance or refusal of the offer.[89] In Professor Gower's words 'it seems clear that the court's discretion under s.429, save in very exceptional circumstances, merely ensures that the necessary formalities have been complied with'.[90] And it has been criticised as a very ineffective protection for minorities.[91] This is because our court procedure is ill-fitted to enable the courts to pass judgment on the economic merits of schemes. The courts are naturally reluctant to substitute their opinion for those reached by a large majority of the members. The traditional attitude of respecting rule of the majority is still very much alive in this area.

The difficulty is that the courts are primarily concerned with the formal legal rights of the parties. Provided that these rights are not infringed, it is difficult for them to intervene effectively, however inequitable the results may be. It may be, however, that s.459 can provide a better safeguard against unfair schemes. As the section requires the 'interests' not the 'rights' of a shareholder to be 'unfairly' prejudiced, it enables the courts to look at the wider equitable consideration and to embark on the task of looking into the fairness of the scheme, and not just the propriety of it.

---

85 [1960] 3 WLR 956, at 964. This case was followed by the Supreme Court of Canada in *Esso Standard (Inter-America) Inc. v J W Enterprises* [1963] SCR 144, 37 DLR (2nd) 598. Judson J said that the nine-tenths threshold must be independently held.

86 (1933) 150 LT 374.

87 *Re Sussex Brick Co. Ltd.* [1961] Ch 289n.

88 *Re Chez Nico (Restaurants)* [1991] BCC 736.

89 *Re Evertite Locknuts Ltd.* [1945] Ch 220.

90 Gower's *Principles of Modern Company Law*, 4th ed., at 717.

91 See Gower's *Principles of Modern Company Law*, 4th ed., at 715.

Under s.459, it appears, by analogy, from the reasoning of Hoffmann J in *Re a Company (No. 008699 of 1985)*,[92] that if the dissentient could show that his fellow shareholders are misled into accepting the offer (or no sufficient information or advice has been given to them so as to enable them to make a properly informed decision), and as a result he is wrongfully subjected to the power of compulsory purchase, he could ask the court to refuse the compulsory purchase order. Alternatively, the minority can seek an order for their shares to be bought out at a fair value as if they are not minority shareholders according to the principle in *Re Bird Precision Bellows*,[93] on the ground that it is a forced sale. This is much more advantageous to the minority, as under s.429 it is not unfair to offer a minority shareholder the value of what he possesses, ie. a minority shareholding.[94] Cases like *Re Bugle Press Ltd.* would still be decided in the same way as a sham scheme is clearly unfairly prejudicial to the minority shareholders' interest.

(iii) Breach of City Code

The provisions of the City Code set out a code of conduct which has been laid down by responsible and experienced persons in the City as being fair and reasonable conduct in relation to companies which have obtained the benefit of a public quotation on the Stock Exchange.[95]

The Code has been quoted and used as a guide to good commercial practice in an area where the court has a discretion.[96] Where a director of a public company chose to flout the City Code or to ignore the City Panel's directions thus leading to the withdrawal of the company's Stock Exchange quotation, the courts have taken this as strong evidence in favour of granting a winding up petition on the just and equitable ground.[97] A substantial failure to comply with the provisions of the City Code was taken to be a major factor negating any assumption that an offer made in pursuant to s.429 was fair.[98] By analogy, it could also be strong evidence showing conduct unfairly prejudicial to the interests of the shareholders because, as members, they have an interest to be able to sell their share at the best price.[99] A withdrawal of the company's

92 [1986] BCLC 382.
93 [1986] 2 WLR 158, CA.
94 Plowman J in *Re Grierson, Oldham & Adams Ltd.* [1968] Ch 17.
95 *Per* Dillon J in *Re St Piran Ltd.* [1981] 3 All ER 270, at 277b.
96 Lord Denning MR, Roskill LJ and Lawton LJ in *Dunford & Elliott Ltd. v Johnson & Firth Brown Ltd.* [1977] 1 Lloyd's Rep 505, at 510, 515, 516 CA.
97 *Re St Piran Ltd.* [1981] 3 All ER 270.
98 *Re Chez Nico (Restaurants)* [1991] BCC 736.
99 Hoffmann J said (*Re a Company (No. 008699 of 1985)* [1986] BCLC 382 at 389g) that the provision of the City Code on Take-overs and Mergers was a helpful guide to the City's view on fairness, but the detailed provisions of the Code did not necessarily coincide with the requirements of fairness for the purposes of s.459.

Stock Exchange quotation will have the effect of jeopardising the value of their shares. Furthermore, Street CJ in *Ampol Petroleum v R W Miller (Holdings) Ltd.* suggested that 'persons buying shares in listed companies are entitled to expect directors faithfully to abide by Stock Exchange rules'.[100]

The suspension of Polly Peck's Stock Exchange Quotation serves as a good example in this context. The company's quotation was suspended on 20 September 1990 when its largest shareholder, Mr Nadir, tabled a conditional buy-out proposal on 12 August and then withdrew it five days later causing an investigation by the Stock Exchange's insider dealing group and the Serious Fraud Office. The shares lost more than half their value in a few hours of suspension and continued to fall. The conduct of Mr. Nadir infringing the City Code and causing the value of the companies' shares to be diminished may be clearly unfairly prejudicial to the interest of other shareholders in the company. Minority shareholders who have suffered may, in theory, be able to bring a petition under s.459 against the wrongdoing directors for an order to buy out their now worthless shares, to be valued as at the date of unfairly prejudicial conduct.

This principle would also seem to apply to companies which have enjoyed quotation on the Unlisted Securities Market which, though not governed by the City Code, are subject to General Permission issued by the Department of Trade and Industries under the Financial Services Act 1986.[101]

5.6 Alteration of articles

As we have seen, an alteration of articles is not invalid merely on the ground that it affected the existing rights of shareholders adversely, even resulting in their *de facto* expropriation. However, such power must be exercised not only in the manner required by law, but also *bona fide* for the benefit of the company as a whole, and it must not be exceeded.[102] These conditions are always implied, and seldom, if ever, expressed. Thus, the shareholders have an interest to see that the powers will be so exercised and the fact that those powers have not been so exercised is a relevant factor to be taken into account in deciding whether the matter complained of is *unfairly* prejudicial.

However, the wide jurisdiction of s.459 not only covers cases where the alteration is not in the interest of the company, but also cases where even if the

100 [1972] 2 NSWLR 850, at 882.

101 Financial Services Act 1986 (Investment Advertisements) (Exemptions) (No. 2) Order 1988, SI 1988 No. 716, Article 4 and the schedule.

102 *Allen v Gold Reefs of West Africa Ltd.* [1900] 1 Ch 656.

alteration is *bone fide* in the interest of the company, either the members' other interests are nevertheless unfairly affected or the benefit to the company is so negligible and unnecessary that no reasonable man would consider the prejudice fair. Thus, although a common law action might not succeed because the resolution could be said to have been passed *bona fide* for the benefit of the company as a whole, a remedy might be available under s.459. Much, however, depends on the question of the unfairness that the alteration has inflicted on the minority.

In *Allen v Gold Reefs of West Africa Ltd.*,[103] the alteration of articles, which gave the company a lien on fully paid shares in respect of debts owed by members, was held to be made *bona fide* for the benefit of the company as a whole. The fact that the complaining minority shareholder was the only person practically affected at the time by the alteration, though raising suspicion as to the *bona fides* of the company, did not affect the validity of the alteration. The altered articles were intended to apply to all holders of fully paid shares and the complaining shareholder happened to be the only holder of fully paid up shares who at the time was in arrears of calls.[104] The position may still be the same under s.459. Such an article is perhaps not unfairly prejudicial to the complaining shareholder because it is only fair that the company should be able to have a lien over shareholders' shares as security for debts owed by them to the company. The alteration extended the existing articles, which conferred a lien on partly paid shares, to all fully paid shares equally.

Similarly, the alteration in *Shuttleworth v Cox*[105] may not be unfairly prejudicial. A director, S, on 22 occasions within 22 months failed to account for the company's money he received, but he was not disqualified from office by any one of the six events specified under the existing articles. The articles were accordingly altered by adding a seventh event disqualifying a director, namely, a request in writing signed by all the other directors that he should resign. Such a request was made to S. The alteration was held valid for it was for the benefit of the company as a whole. Such an alteration is potentially unfairly prejudicial depending on the circumstances in which the altered article is used. On the facts of *Shuttleworth*, even if S has a legitimate expectation that he would not be excluded from the board the request would not be unfairly prejudicial because of his own conduct and the benefit that the expulsion would bring to the company. However, if there had been no gross misconduct on S's part but mere mismanagement due to his inexperience, although the expulsion may be in the interest of the company, it may still be unfairly prejudicial.

---

103 [1900] 1 Ch 656.
104 *Per* Lindley MR [1900] 1 Ch 656, at 675.
105 [1927] 2 KB 9.

Neither would the alteration in *Sidebottom v Kershaw, Leese*[106] appear to be unfairly prejudicial on its facts. There, the articles were altered to require any shareholder who competed with company's business to transfer his shares, at their fair value, to nominees of directors. It was held to be *bona fide* for the benefit of the company as a whole. It would not be unfairly prejudicial for 'it is for the benefit of the company that they should not be obliged to have amongst them as members persons who are competing with them in business and who may get knowledge from their membership which would enable them to compete better'.[107] However, it may be unfairly prejudicial if the likelihood of the minority shareholder competing with the company is so minimal that no reasonable man would consider it fair to exclude the minority shareholder from the company.

The best example of alteration of articles held *bona fide* for the benefit of the company and yet likely to be unfairly prejudicial to minority shareholders is, perhaps, the case of *Greenhalgh v Arderne Cinemas.*[108] Here, the pre-emption articles were altered so as to permit a transfer to any person with the sanction of an ordinary resolution. This was held *bona fide* and valid even though the minority lost their rights of pre-emption. Although the alteration was thought *bona fide* for the benefit of the company as a whole, it may, nevertheless, have been unfairly prejudicial as in practice the minority not only lost the right of pre-emption, but also did not obtain the same advantage conferred on the majority by the new articles. The effect of the alteration was not similar to that in *Allen v Gold Reefs of West Africa Ltd.* which would apply to all holders of fully paid share regardless of the whim of the majority. In *Greenhalgh*, the minority could only have the same advantage as the majority if the majority joined them in voting for an ordinary resolution. The loss of rights of pre-emption and the practical advantage that they had been deprived of by a simple alteration of articles must have been unfair to the minority.

In *Re Ringtower*,[109] Peter Gibson J accepted the contention that a special resolution validly passed according to the tests in *Greenhalgh* could nevertheless amount to unfair prejudice.[110]

---

106 [1920] 1 Ch 154.

107 *Per* Lord Sterndale MR [1920] 1 Ch 154, at 166, CA.

108 [1950] 2 All ER 1120.

109 (1989) 5 BCC 82.

110 (1989) 5 BCC 82, at 102. In the case, the alteration was, however, found not unfairly prejudicial because it was not alleged that it was motivated by malice or not acting *bona fide* and there was never any intention to discriminate on the part of the respondents. The alteration was prejudicial but not unfairly so.

5.7 Miscellaneous

(a) Variation of class rights

If a company has only one class of shares, and the rights attached to those shares are contained in the company's articles, they may be altered by special resolution under s.9 of the Companies Act 1980 and if contained in the company's memorandum, under s.17 of the Act. If there is more than one class,[111] the variation can only be made in accordance with s.125. Section 127, however, provides that the holders of no less than 15% of the issued shares of the class affected, if they did not consent to or vote in favour of the variation, may apply to the court to have the variation cancelled. The court may, if satisfied that the variation would unfairly prejudice the shareholders of the class represented by the applicant, disallow the variation; if not so satisfied, it must confirm it. There is no reported use of the section. It is interesting to note that the concept of 'unfair prejudice' is shared by both sections.[112] It thus appears that the matter could be resolved on a petition under s.459. However, a holding of 15% of shares of the class in question is not necessary and the wider range of remedies under s.461 means that s.459 is perhaps more attractive.

(b) Autocratic behaviour and disregard of proper procedure

In *Re H R Harmer Ltd.*,[113] the father, who was the founder of the firm, made a gift of the majority of shares to his sons, but retained voting control in the general meeting. He continued to run the business as if it were his own and to disregard the wishes of his sons, who were shareholders and co-directors. He committed the company to business ventures without obtaining proper authorisation and procured the appointment of directors who submissively did his bidding. As a result of his autocratic and unbusinesslike behaviour, it became impossible for the company to be carried on successfully. Roxburgh J. held that a case of oppression under s.210 of the 1948 Act had been made out. It was irrelevant that the misconduct was not for financial gain but simply due to the father's overwhelming desire for power and control.

---

111 Rights or benefits either annexed to particular shares or though not so attached were none the less conferred on the beneficiary in the capacity of member or shareholder of the company: *Cumbrian Newspapers Group Ltd. v Cumberland & Westmorland Herald Newspaper & Printing Co. Ltd.* [1987] Ch 1; [1986] 2 All ER 816.

112 The concept of 'unfair prejudice' is also used in s.27 of Insolvency Act 1986.

113 [1958] 3 All ER 689.

Jenkin LJ held that the section was wide enough to cover oppression by anyone who was taking part in the conduct of the affairs of the company, whether *de facto* or *de jure*, and that the word 'oppressive' must be given its ordinary meaning as adopted by Viscount Simonds.[114] The decision would perhaps be the same under s.459. Because there was an understanding between them that the father was to retain control by means of his predominant votes in the general meeting there was no way of preventing the father from voting in the general meeting. But the father could not exercise his control irregularly by doing what he thought fit without reference to the board or in defiance of the board's decisions or proper procedure. To do so would probably amount to unfair prejudice.

(c) Decisions to continue trading at a loss

See Chapter 3, para 3.2(h) above.

(d) Failure to provide information requested

A member has a right and expectation to receive sufficient information required by law to be made available to him. Thus, he may examine the accounting records of the company and may obtain an order for the inspection of books of account.[115] However, it is clear that a member's right in this regard is rather limited. For example, he is not entitled to know the basis of a valuation or the identity of the valuer; it is sufficient that he is told what the valuation is.[116] Extracts of report made by the company's auditors incorporating valuations of the shares on different bases are likewise not strictly available to a member.[117] Therefore, failure to supply any information requested may only be unfairly prejudicial if the information is one which the members are entitled to receive and it is necessary in order to establish some impropriety or impartiality.[118]

(e) Lack of probity

As a quasi-partnership company is one based very much on a personal relationship between shareholders, involving mutual confidence, it is not

114 'Burdensome, harsh and wrongful' in *Scottish Co-operative Wholesale Society Ltd. v Meyer* [1959] AC 324, at 342.
115 *Murray's Judicial Factor v Murray & Sons* [1993] BCLC 1437 at 1451d. See also Palmer's *Company Law* (25th ed.) Vol II 9-104; *McCusker v McRae* (1966) SC 253.
116 *Murray's Judicial Factor v Murray & Sons*, ibid., at 1451f.
117 Ibid., at 1451g.
118 Ibid., at 1451h, 1455d-g, 1457g-h.

surprising that Vinelott J has recently held in *Re Ghyll Beck Driving Range Ltd.*[119] that if there is sufficient evidence to show that, after the initial breakdown of relationship, the majority cannot now be trusted to deal with the petitioner fairly, the majority can be asked to buy out the petitioner under s.459. Evidence such as:

(i) the majority's dishonest attempt to escape making their contribution to the joint venture;

(ii) a majority's fabricated evidence of a board meeting to deceive the petitioner;

(iii) the majority's use of sham board meetings as a pretext for removing the petitioner as a director on the ground that he had failed to attend such meetings;

(iv) the fact that the interest paid to the petitioner on his loan since the breakdown in relations was considerably less than the interest paid to the majority on their loans and that the records showed no clear basis on which the calculations were made or the period for which they were made,

(are all sufficient to show that the majority can no longer be trusted.)[120]

119 [1993] BCLC 1126 at 1134a-b.
120 Ibid., at 1131g-1134a.

Chapter 6

Procedural Aspects

Many petitions under s.459 have in recent years involved procedural matters rather than the substantive law of unfair prejudice. It would therefore be useful to examine these cases here. It should however be emphasised that it is beyond the scope of this book to discuss all procedural matters relating to a s.459 petition in detail.

6.1 The Courts

For the purposes of Part XVII of the 1985 Act, 'the court', in relation to a company, means the court having jurisdiction to wind up the company.[1] The High Court has such jurisdiction provided the company is registered in England and Wales.[2] The County Court of the district in which the company's registered office is situated also has concurrent jurisdiction if the company's paid-up (or credited as paid up) share capital does not exceed £120, 000.[3] Procedure in the County Court is similar to that in the High Court and a County Court which has such jurisdiction has all the powers of the High Court.[4] However, in practice, practitioners prefer to use the High Court and, for this reason, this chapter will only examine the relevant procedural aspects of a s.459 petition in the High Court.

Petitions in the High Court may be made in the Royal Court of Justice, London, or in any Chancery district registry (Birmingham, Bristol, Cardiff, Leeds, Liverpool, Manchester, Newcastle-upon-Tyne and Preston).[5] All petitions in the High Court are assigned to, and proceed in, the Companies Court which is part of the Chancery Division.

6.2 Procedural provisions

Actions by shareholders on the grounds of unfairly prejudicial conduct are by way of petition under Part XVII of the Companies Act 1985. The procedure

1 Section 744 of the Companies Act 1985.
2 Section 117(1) of the Insolvency Act 1986.
3 Section 117(2) of the Insolvency Act 1986.
4 Section 117(5) of the Insolvency Act 1986.
5 RSC 1965, Ord 102, rr 2(4), 3(2) and 4(2) and ChD Practice Direction (9) White Book Supplement, para. 824.

for petition presented on or after 29 December 1986 is governed by the Companies (Unfair Prejudice Applications) Proceedings Rules 1986.[6] Except in so far as they are inconsistent with the 1985 Act and the 1986 Rules, the Rules of the Supreme Court and the practice of the High Court apply to proceedings under Part XVII of the Act in the High Court, and the Rules and practice of the County Court apply to such proceedings in a County Court.[7]

The petition is entitled[8] in the same way as an originating summons and must be made in the prescribed form set out in the Schedule to the 1986 Rules.[9] The petition is addressed to the appropriate court. This is then followed by the name and address of the petitioner. The respondent's name and address only appear in a footnote. It then sets out the details of the company of which the petitioner is a member: the full name of the company, the date of incorporation, the address of the registered office, the nominal capital of the company, its divided shares, and the nominal value of each share, the paid up capital, and the number of shares held by the petitioner. The petitioner must state if the shares he holds have been registered in his name or have been transferred or transmitted to him by operation of law. The petition also sets out the principal objects for which the company was established, apart from those stated in the memorandum of association of the company. It then sets out the grounds on which the petition is presented, in consecutively numbered paragraphs, in a manner similar to a statement of claim. It tends to include detailed background of the affairs of the company leading to the alleged unfairly prejudicial conduct. This can run to numerous pages. The petition then concludes with a prayer for the relief he wants. Petitioners commonly ask for an order to buy out the respondents or to be bought out by them. They also often ask for a just and winding up order in the alternative. The prescribed form also contains a prayer for such other order which the court may think fit.

The petitioner in the prescribed form must be presented to the Registrar of the Companies Court, or to the district registrar with sufficient copies for court filing and service. No affidavit is required at this stage. The Court will then fix a hearing for a day (called 'the return day') on which the petitioner and any respondent (including the company) shall attend before the registrar in chambers for directions to be given in relation to the procedure on the petition.[10] On fixing the return day, the court will return sealed copies of the

6 See SI 1986 No. 2000. For petition made before 29 December 1986, see the Companies (Winding-up) Rules 1949 (SI 1949 No. 330).
7 The Companies (Unfair Prejudice Applications) Proceedings Rules 1986, r 2(2).
8 See Appendix 2.
9 The Companies (Unfair Prejudice Applications) Proceedings Rules 1986, r 3(1). See Appendix 1.
10 Ibid., r 3(3).

petition to the petitioner for service. Each of the sealed copies of the petition is endorsed with the return day and the time of hearing.[11]

The petition must serve a sealed copy of the petition on the company and every respondent named in the petition at least 14 days before the return day.[12] No acknowledgment of service is required. The respondents may simply appear at the hearing on the return day. A petition is as much a litigious procedure as any other. Thus, interrogatories and discovery may be made by an application by summons before the registrar of the Companies Court.

On the return day, or at any time after it, the court shall give such directions as it thinks appropriate on the following matters:

(a) service of the petition on any person, whether in connection with the time, date and place of a further hearing, or for any other purpose;
(b) whether particulars of claim and defence are to be delivered, and generally as to the procedure on the petition;
(c) whether, and if so by what means, the petition is to be advertised;
(d) the manner in which any evidence is to be adduced at any hearing before the judge and in particular (but without prejudice to the generality of the above) as to
    (i) the taking of evidence wholly or in part by affidavit or orally
    (ii) the cross-examination of any deponents to affidavits
    (iii) the matters to be dealt with in evidence;
(e) any other matter affecting the procedure on the petition or in connection with the hearing and disposal of the petition.[13]

The Registrar is, under this new procedure, given wide powers to direct the manner in which the petition should be proceeded, including powers to direct the service and advertisement of the petition and the manner in which any evidence is to be adduced at subsequent hearings.

When an order has been made by the court under Part XVII of the 1985 Act, the petitioner and every other person who has appeared at the hearing must leave at the court all the documents required for enabling the order to be carried out.[14] Unless it is necessary in the particular circumstances of the case, no further hearing will be fixed for any person to settle the order. The court

---

11 Ibid., r 3(4).
12 Ibid., r 4.
13 Ibid., r 5.
14 Ibid., r 6(1).

may give directions as to whether the order should be advertised, and if so the manner and time of advertisement.[15]

6.3 Parties to the s.459 petition

Every person who is intended to be affected by the order the court may make must be joined as a party. The company is always joined as a nominal party to a s.459 petition. This is important because an order made by the court under s.461 may affect the rights of the company. Vinelott J has further stated that in a small private company every member ought, as a matter of practice, to be joined in the petition, as their rights may also be affected.[16] This is so even if there was no evidence that they had taken part in the affairs of the company or that the wrongdoer had acted in accordance with their directions. But if the rights of the members would not be affected by any order made by the court it may be appropriate not to join them in the petition.[17]

Today, under Ord 15, r 6(1), 'no cause or matter shall be defeated by reason of the misjoinder or nonjoinder of any party; and the court may in any cause or matter determine the issues and questions in dispute so far as they affect the rights and interests of the persons who are parties to the cause or matter'. Furthermore, at any stage of the proceedings in any cause or matter, the court may on such terms as it thinks just, and either of its own motion or on application, order any person who has been improperly or unnecessarily made a party, or who has for any reason ceased to be a proper or necessary party, to cease to be a party.[18] The court may also order any person to be joined as a party who ought to have been joined as a party or whose presence before the court is necessary to ensure that all matters in dispute in the cause or matter may be effectually and completely determined and adjudicated upon.[19] The court may also order any person to be joined as a party if, as between that person and any party to the cause or matter, there exists a question or issue arising out of, or relating to, or connected with, any relief or remedy claimed in the cause or matter which, in the opinion of the court, it would be just and convenient to determine as between him and that party as well as between the parties to the cause or matter; but no person shall be added as a plaintiff without his consent signified in writing or in such other manner as may be authorised.[20]

15 Ibid., r 6(3).
16 *Re a Company (No. 007281 of 1986)* [1987] BCLC 593.
17 Ibid.
18 RSC Ord 15 r 6(2).
19 r 6(2).
20 r 6(4).

In *Re BSB Holdings Ltd.*,[21] the petitioners, London Merchant Securities plc (LMS) joined the company BSB Holdings Ltd. (BSB) in which LMS was a minority shareholder, and BSB's formerly wholly owned subsidiary, British Sky Broadcasting Ltd. (B Sky B) in a s.459 petition. The allegations in the petition arose out of the financing of a satellite broadcasting business originally carried on by BSB which was later transferred to B Sky B (then wholly owned by BSB). That business was then merged with that of Sky Television, allegedly in breach of various agreements and arrangements to which LMS was a party. LMS alleged that the effect of the merger was that the business which initially belonged to BSB had been diverted to some of its shareholders. LMS sought relief for various shareholders in BSB to transfer B Sky B shares to other members of BSB, alternatively to transfer B Sky B shares and loan stock to LMS. No direct relief was sought against B Sky B. B Sky B applied to strike out or stay LMS's petition as against it on the grounds that in the circumstances it was improper to make it a respondent or to serve the petition on it. B Sky B argued that it was made a respondent improperly, simply for the purpose of obtaining an order for discovery.

Vinelott J held that as B Sky B was directly concerned in the transaction, and the allegation involved the manipulation of the affairs of B Sky B, the presence of B Sky B was necessary to ensure that all matters in dispute were determined. There was an issue between LMS and B Sky B relating to the relief sought in the petition within the meaning of RSC, Ord 15, r 6(2)(b)(i) and (ii).

A former member may be joined as a party if relief is sought against him.[22] Where the relief sought is for the petitioner to buy out the shares previously owned by the wrongdoing former members, the former members are not the proper parties to the relief sought. The proper parties are the shareholders in whom the shares in question are now vested and with whom the court is primarily concerned.[23]

Where a petition is brought against the majority without joining the company because the dispute does not really involve the company, the directors should not resolve to commit it to participate in the proceedings. If the directors commit the company to the proceedings, they may render themselves personally liable for any costs which it incurred.[24]

---

21 [1992] BCC 915.
22 *Re a Company* [1986] BCLC 68, 71e-f.
23 *Re Baltic Real Estate Ltd.* [1992] BCC 629.
24 *Re a Company (No. 001126 of 1992)* [1993] BCC 325.

6.4 Service out of jurisdiction

A petition may be served out of the jurisdiction in appropriate cases. Under the traditional rule,[25] in order for a petition to be served out of jurisdiction, leave must be granted.[26] Leave will only be granted if, first, the case clearly falls within one of the grounds set out in Ord 11, r 1(1); secondly, the petitioner has a good arguable case on the merits; and thirdly, the discretion should be exercised to allow service out of jurisdiction.[27]

In *Re Baltic Real Estate Ltd.*,[28] the petitioner held 510 of the 1, 000 shares in the company. The other 490 shares were allotted to the second and third respondents who immediately thereafter transferred those shares to the fourth and fifth respondents. The transfer was recited in a subsequent shareholders' agreement between the petitioner, the second and the third respondents, and the company. The allegation of unfairly prejudicial conduct was made against the second and third respondents, but the petitioner sought leave to serve the petition on the fourth and fifth respondents out of jurisdiction. Leave was refused on the ground that the petitioner had failed to show that r 1(1)(d)(i) applied. Under r 1(1)(d)(i), a petition may be served out of jurisdiction with leave if 'the claim is brought to enforce, rescind, dissolve, annul or otherwise affect a contract, or to recover damages or obtain other relief in respect of the breach of a contract which was made within the jurisdiction'. The shareholders' agreement was part of the background of the matter, but was too remote to treat it as 'affected' by the petition. Knox J thought that 'affect' in r 1(1)(d) required some direct effect on the relevant contract.

6.5 Petition to strike out or stay proceedings

Very frequently, after a petition for an order under Part XVII of the 1985 Act is made (or a petition to wind up a company under the just and equitable grounds), an application is made to strike out or stay the proceedings. On an application under RSC Ord 18, r 19(1),[29] 'the court may at any stage of the proceedings order to be struck out or amended any pleading or the indorsement of any writ in the action, or anything in any pleading or in the indorsement, on the ground that (a) it discloses no reasonable cause of action or defence, as the case may be; or (b) it is scandalous, frivolous or vexatious;

25 That is where the defendant is abroad in a non-EC country(see the Brussels Convention 1968) or non-EFTA country (European Free Trade Association) (see Lugano Convention 1988).

26 *Re Harrods (Buenos Aires) Ltd.* [1991] BCLC 666, CA reversing Harman J's judgment in the High Court ([1991] BCLC 69). Application for leave to appeal to House of Lords was granted.

27 See Cheshire and North's *Private International Law*, 12th ed. 1992, at 191.

28 [1992] BCC 629.

29 Ord 18, r 19(1) applies to a petition: r 19(3).

or (c) it may prejudice, embarrass or delay the fair trial of the action; or it is otherwise an abuse of the process of the court; and may order the action to be stayed or dismissed or judgment to be entered, as the case may be'. Alternatively, the application to strike out may be made to the court under its inherent jurisdiction. The same principles apply to County Court actions.[30] An application to strike out is usually made by summons to the Master or by motion to the judge in the High Court. In the County Court, the application is made by notice of application to the District judge.

An application for striking out will only succeed in plain and obvious cases.[31] In *Re a Company ex p. Burr*,[32] the petitioner sought a winding up order or a purchase order under s.459. An application to strike out the petition was allowed because the petitioner failed to adduce any evidence which, if accepted at the trial, would support the allegations in the petition and justify the relief sought. Vinelott J, thus, concluded:

> 'The petitioner's case in substance is that something might be revealed on discovery in the course of cross-examination of the directors that could be relied on as justifying the petition. That is not a proper ground for presenting a petition. The damaging effect which the presentation of the petition may have on the business of a company, even if it is not advertised, has often been the subject of judicial comment. A petition should not be presented unless it can be supported by evidence which, if accepted at the trial, would found a claim for relief.'[33]

Striking out applications may be made not only in cases where there is no substantial evidence to support the petitioner's case, but also where the relief sought by the petitioner is inappropriate. Thus, it is common to find that in a winding up petition under s.122(1)(g) of the Insolvency Act 1986, the respondent often seeks to strike out the petition on the ground that other more appropriate remedies are available under s.459.[34] It is equally common to find that s.459 is used as an alternative to just and equitable winding up order in an action under s.122(1)(g),[35] or winding up to be used as an alternative to an order sought under s.459.[36] The principles discussed above apply equally to these cases and will be discussed in more detail below.[37]

---

30 CCR Ord 13, r 5(1).
31 *Williams & Humbert Ltd. v W & H Trade Marks (Jersey) Ltd.* [1986] AC 368, HL.
32 [1992] BCLC 724.
33 Ibid., at 736.
34 Eg *Re a Company (No. 003096 of 1987)* (1988) 4 BCC 80 and *Re a Company (No. 001363 of 1988)* (1989) 5 BCC 18.
35 Eg *Re Abbey Leisure Ltd.* (1989) 5 BCC 183 and *Re a Company (No. 00314 of 1989) ex p. Estate Acquisition and Development Ltd. and Others* [1991] BCLC 154.
36 Eg *Vujnovich & Anor v Vujnovich* (1989) 5 BCC 740, PC; *Re a Company (No. 002470 of 1988) ex p. Nicholas* [1991] BCLC 480; *Re J E Cade & Son Ltd.* [1991] BCLC 213.
37 See 6.9 below.

6.6 Advertisement of petition

On return day, or at any time after it, the court may give directions as to whether, and if so by what means, the petition is to be advertised.[38] When an order has been made, and if the court considers that the order should be advertised, it may also give directions as to the manner and time of advertisement.[39] Similar power exists in cases of winding up applications under s.122(1)(g) of the Insolvency Act 1986:[40] it was held[41] that in the context of r 4.23(I)(c) of the Insolvency Rules 1986[42] the meaning of the word 'advertised' included 'notified'. Accordingly, where the registrar has ordered that there should be no advertisement of the s.459 and s.122(1)(g) winding up petition, a letter from the petitioner's solicitors to the company's bank informing them of the existence of the winding up proceedings was in breach, even if unintentionally, of the registrar's order.[43]

6.7 Interlocutory orders

(a) Injunction

Scott J has pointed out[44] that s.461(1) contains a statutory requirement that the petition is well founded before an order under a s.459 petition can be made. The court cannot be satisfied that the petition is well founded until it has been satisfied that 'the company's affairs are being or have been conducted in a manner which is unfairly prejudicial to the interests of some part of the members including at least himself ...' (see s.459(1)). The court has no jurisdiction to make an order (interlocutory or final) on the petition until the statutory criterion set out in s.461(1) has been satisfied. That criterion will not be satisfied until the hearing of the petition.

However, as already mentioned, the Rules of the Supreme Court and the practice of the High Court apply to proceedings under Part XVII of the Act in the High Court unless they are inconsistent with the Act and the Companies (Unfair Prejudice Applications) Proceedings Rules 1986. The High Court has the power under s.37(1) of the Supreme Court Act 1981 to make interlocutory

38 The Companies (Unfair Prejudice Applications) Proceedings Rules 1986 (SI 1986 No. 2000), r 5(c).
39 Ibid., r 6(3).
40 Insolvency Rules 1986 (SI 1986 No. 1925), r 4.23(I)(c).
41 *Re a Company (No. 00687 of 1991)* [1992] BCLC 133.
42 SI 1986 No. 1925.
43 *Re a Company (No. 00687 of 1991)* [1992] BCLC 133.
44 *Re a Company (No. 004175 of 1986)* [1987] BCLC 574, at 577e-f.

(or final) orders by way of injunction or the appointment of a receiver 'in all cases in which it appears to the court to be just and convenient to do so.' Application for an interlocutory injunction can be made to the High Court under RSC Ord 29. The applicant needs to show an arguable case first. He then has to show that the balance of convenience favours the granting of an injunction. In considering the balance of convenience, the court must consider the adequacy of damages, to the applicant and respondent respectively, in the event that the injunction is granted or refused.[45]

There is nothing in the 1985 Act and the 1986 Rules which expressly prevents the court from making interlocutory orders. Does the 1985 Act impliedly rule out the court's jurisdiction under s.37 of the 1981 Act because no order can be made until the court is satisfied that the petition is well founded? In the few decided first instance decisions where interlocutory orders were granted or rejected, only in *Re a Company (No. 00596 of 1986)*[46] was the order sought under s.37 of the 1981 Act. This has made it somewhat difficult to see the distinction seemingly made by Scott J between the jurisdiction of the court to grant interlocutory orders under the 1981 Act and the lack of jurisdiction under s.459. From the cases to be discussed below it appears that, despite Scott J's dictum cited above, the court's jurisdiction to grant interlocutory order under s.37 of the 1981 Act is not inconsistent with s.459. It appears that where interlocutory orders are sought the court needs only to be satisfied that a *prima facie* case is proved. So the court may make an interlocutory order under the wide jurisdiction of s.461, for example, so as to regulate the conduct of the company's affairs in the future.

When an interlocutory order is sought in a s.459 petition, although one cannot literally apply the rules in *American Cyanamid v Ethicon Ltd.*[47] since s.461 does not provide for an award of damages at common law, a factor which the court takes into account in determining the question of convenience, as the section nevertheless allows the court to order various forms of financial compensation, the rules in *American Cyanamid* can be applied by analogy.[48]

Thus, in *Re Postgate & Denby (Agencies) Ltd.*,[49] where the petitioner could not establish that there were special circumstances which gave rise to a legitimate expectation that the directors would not exercise their powers in a

---

45 *American Cyanamid v Ethicon* [1975] AC 396. For a more detailed account see Odgers on High Court Pleading and Practice, 23rd ed. 1991, at 78-84.
46 [1987] BCLC 133.
47 [1975] AC 396.
48 See Hoffmann J in *Re Postgate & Denby (Agencies) Ltd.* [1987] BCLC 8, at 15d.
49 [1987] BCLC 8.

particular way, the interlocutory relief sought was not granted. Hoffmann J went on to say that even if there was an arguable case, the petitioner could not show that it was just and convenient that an injunction should be granted. There was evidence that if an injunction was granted there was a risk of causing irreparable harm to the company and its shareholders as a whole. If, however, the injunction was refused and on the hearing of the petition the transaction proved to have been unfairly prejudicial to the petitioner, he could be fully compensated by orders which enabled him to receive the value his shares would have had if the transaction had not taken place. An injunction was therefore refused.

Where the factors which would tip the balance of convenience one way or the other appear to be equally balanced, then it would be appropriate to preserve the status quo pending trial by granting an injunction.[50] Thus, in *Re a Company (No. 002612 of 1984)*,[51] Harman J having concluded that there was an arguable case that jurisdiction existed under s.75 to restrain a proposed *pari passu* rights issue, said that:

> 'In cases of litigation under s.75 [of the 1980 Act] it is most desirable that the position of the company be not altered or disturbed more than is absolutely essential, between the presentation and the hearing of the petition. The existing share structure, the existing contractual rights, the present service contracts and so forth, should in my judgment be maintained as they are pending the determination of the litigation. There might be circumstances where change was essential, but if possible the existing position should be preserved. In my judgment, that is a factor which in these matters arising under contributories patterns is particularly powerful and has more than the normal 'Cyanamid' force in favour of preserving the status quo, since it is the very nature of this matter that the status quo must affect the remedy which may be available.'[52]

In *Re Malaga Investment Ltd.*,[53] an interlocutory order was granted when a *prima facie* case for preserving the status quo was established although the *American Cyanamid* case was not referred to. The petitioners were substantial shareholders in Bremner plc. They were prevented from voting at an extraordinary general meeting by virtue of an unopposed application by other members to the court which resulted in the disenfranchisement of the petitioners. The petitioners then applied under s.459 for an order preventing

50 [1975] AC 396, at 409.
51 [1985] BCLC 80.
52 Ibid., at 82i-83c.
53 (1987) SLT 603.

the issue of further shares in the company and preventing the disposal of assets of the company pending the holding of a further extraordinary general meeting.

Lord Jauncey having considered the history of events and the reasons alleged for the delay which elapsed between the petitioners' requisition and the holding of the meeting, concluded that the petitioners had made out a *prima facie* case for maintaining the status quo both as to shareholding and property of Bremner pending the holding of a meeting at which the petitioners could exercise their voting right. The order sought was ordered accordingly.

As the court in making interlocutory orders in the cases discussed above did not refer to s.37 of the 1981 Act, it is not entirely clear whether the court's jurisdiction to make such orders flows from s.461. It may well be that an independent jurisdiction is developing under s.461 to grant interlocutory orders on an analogous application of the rules in *American Cyanamid.*

(b) Appointment of a receiver

Where there is a dispute between the majority and minority in a company as to the manner in which the company is being run, the court can on request make an interlocutory order under s.37 of the Supreme Court Act 1981 to appoint a receiver at an early stage to run the affairs of the company pending the outcome of the final hearing. Where the company is effectively a quasi-partnership, the court will act upon principles similar to those which will be applied in a partnership dispute. Such a course implies no judgment on the merits of the petition, but is taken to preserve the status quo. Where there is evidence that the respondents are not managing the affairs of the company in the interests of all, a receiver may be appointed.[54] Once a receiver is appointed, the powers of the board of directors will be suspended until the receiver is later discharged.

(c) Interim payment order

Although the court is given wide power to make 'such order as it thinks fit for giving relief in respect of the matters complained of' under s.461(1), Scott J held in *Re a Company (No. 004175 of 1986)*[55] that where a petition was brought under s.459(1), the court had no jurisdiction to make an interim

54 *Re a Company (No. 00596 of 1986)* [1987] BCLC 133.
55 [1987] 1 WLR 585.

payment order. The company was established with an issued share capital of £100, 000, the petitioner holding 30%, the balance being held by two others. The company was run as a quasi-partnership, and there came a time when the petitioner was told he was no longer wanted. An offer was made to purchase the petitioner's shareholding for £45, 000. The offer was rejected, the petitioner having had the company independently valued at about £600, 000. The petitioner moved for an interim payment order of £40, 000. Dismissing the application, Scott J held that:

> 'A power for the court to anticipate a purchase order made pursuant to s.461(2)(d) and, before the statutory criterion has been shown to be satisfied, to make an interim order for payment on account of the purchase price, would require in my judgment to be spelled out by clear words of statutory authority. There is none ... Under s.459(1) and s.461(1) and (2), the court may have jurisdiction to order payment to be made by the respondents to the petitioner. But that jurisdiction will not, in my judgment, arise until the specified statutory criterion has been satisfied. Until then the court does not, in my judgment, have jurisdiction to make any order for payment, whether interim or final.'[56]

Scott J also dismissed the argument that an interim payment order could be made under s.37 of the 1981 Act and RSC Ord 29 because an order under s.461(2)(d) even if given at trial, was only an order for the purchase of shares and would only entitle the petitioner to money when, but not until, he tenders the share certificates against the purchase money. It could not therefore be said to be a 'judgment against the defendant for a substantial sum of money'. Scott J's decision is however inconsistent with the Court of Appeal's view in *British Holdings plc v Quadrex*.[57] There it was held that if the court is satisfied, *inter alia*, that if the action proceeded to trial, the plaintiff would obtain judgment for substantial damages, then it could make an order for interim payment.[58] Thus, it seems clear that even if the court has no jurisdiction to make such orders under s.459-461, the same result could be achieved under its general jurisdiction under Ord 29.

However, if it was plain that at the end of the day the petitioners would obtain an order for the purchase of their shares, for example, if the respondent has conceded that the company's affairs had been conducted in a manner which was unfairly prejudicial to the petitioner's interest, and the parties have agreed that the court should order the company or the respondent to purchase the petitioner's shares at a certain price, then the court may grant an interim

56 Ibid., at 589H, 590D.
57 [1989] 3 All ER 492.
58 *Ibid.*, at 509b.

payment order in a s.459 petition.[59] The court will have no such jurisdiction, however, where the same court has given the plaintiff unconditional leave to defend under Ord 14.[60]

6.8 Discovery of documents

Under RSC Ord 24, r 3:

> ' ... the court may order any party to a cause or matter .. to make and serve on any party a list of the documents which are or have been in his possession, custody or power relating to any matter in question in the cause or matter ...'.

A party to the proceeding may however object to producing for inspection certain documents protected by legal professional privilege.[61] Communications between lawyer and client made for the purpose of giving and receiving legal advice about any matter, whether or not litigation was contemplated at the time, are privileged. Where a company is joined as a party to a s.459 petition the issue is the extent to which legal documents received by the company in previous litigation or prior to any litigation can be discovered by the petitioner in his petition against the respondents. As the company is a party to the petition, legal documents in its 'possession, custody or power' relating to any matter in the petition should be discoverable under r 3. The question is, can the company claim legal professional privilege? The general rule is that the shareholders of a company are entitled to discovery of legal documents which arose in the course of the administration of the company; but if the documents were not for that purpose, but were for the company's own defence in litigation against itself by the shareholders, the company is protected by legal professional privilege[62]

In *Re Hydrosan Ltd.*,[63] the company had paid the respondent's solicitors' bills incurred in defending a first s.459 petition. The petitioner argued in a second s.459 petition that this was a wrongful application of the company's

---

59 *Ferguson v Maclennan Salmon Co. Ltd.* [1990] BCC 702 (Court of Session, Inner House).

60 *British Holdings plc v Quadrex* [1989] 3 All ER 492. See also *Shanning International v George Wimpey International* [1988] 3 All ER 475, same decision was reached by a court of three judges and followed by *British Holdings plc*. In *Ricci Burns Ltd. v Toole* [1989] 3 All ER 478, exactly the opposite conclusion was reached by a two judge Court of Appeal and not followed by *British Holding plc*. *Ricci* is therefore deemed overruled: *Young v Bristol Aeroplane* [1944] KB 718.

61 *Greenough v Gaskell* (1833) 1 My & K 98.

62 *Woodhouse & Co. Ltd. v Woodhouse* (1914) 30 TLR 559; *W Dennis and Sons Ltd. v West Norfolk Farmers' Manure and Chemicals Co-operative Co. Ltd.* [1943] Ch 220; *Re Hydrosan Ltd.* [1991] BCC 19.

63 [1991] BCC 19.

funds.[64] In the course of the petition, he applied for discovery of the earlier solicitors' bills. Harman J held that they were discoverable. This was because the first petition, in which the documents were created, was in its true nature, a petition brought against those in control of the company rather than against the company itself. If, on the contrary, documents are created in the course of proceedings, other than such a s.459 petition (for instance, claim brought by a person in Chancery proceedings against the company for wrongful dismissal), the claim is truly against the company, and the documents will be protected.

In *Re Hydrosan Ltd.*,[65] the petitioner also sought discovery of documents relating to a rights issue proposed by the company. It is a settled rule that all communications between a solicitor and a client upon a subject which may lead to litigation should be privileged.[66] On the facts, Harman J found that the date of issue of a notice and circular convening the EGM was a date from which the possibility of litigation could be contemplated. Thus, documents created before that date were documents concerning the administration of the company and thus could be discovered. But documents created after the date could not be discovered. As the documents relating to the rights issue were created before that date, they were held discoverable.

The decision in *Re Hydrosan Ltd.* is essential to make s.459 an effective shareholder remedy. Following the decision in *Re Hydrosan Ltd.*, as a s.459 petition is often a dispute between shareholders, relevant legal documents will be discoverable by the petitioner. If it were otherwise, a petitioner in a s.459 petition would have to face the same difficulty a minority shareholder faces in getting detailed internal information to show a *prima facie* case for derivative action.[67]

Where the document is not in the possession of the company but in its subsidiary's possession, discovery may be possible if there is sufficient control by the company to justify the lifting of the corporate veil by the court.[68]

---

64 See also *Re A & BC Chewing Gum Ltd.* [1975] 1 WLR 579, at 592; *Re Crossmore Electrical and Civil Engineering Ltd.* (1989) 5 BCC 37, at 38G.

65 [1991] BCC 19.

66 *Greenough v Gaskell* (1833) 1 My & K 98.

67 See Chapter 1, para. 1.4(vi) above. It appears that minority shareholder in a derivative action, who is in truth bringing an action on behalf of the company though technically against the company, will be able to get access to documents in the company's possession once a derivative action is allowed. In this respect a minority shareholder in a derivative action would have been better off had the decision in *Re Hydrosan Ltd.* been otherwise.

68 *Re Tecnion Investments Ltd.* [1985] BCLC 434, CA. See also *Lonrho v Shell Petroleum Co. Ltd.* [1980] 1 WLR 627.

6.9 Section 459 of the Companies Act 1985 and s.122(1)(g) of the Insolvency Act 1986

As we have seen,[69] there was a close relationship between s.210 of the Companies Act 1948 and what is now s.122(1)(g) of the Insolvency Act 1986. The petitioner had to show that it was just and equitable to wind up the company but to do so would be unfairly prejudicial to him. Thus, the two sections were linked together with s.210 as an alternative. Although s.459 has now abandoned the requirement of just and equitable winding up, the practice of using s.459 and s.122(1)(g) together continues. Therefore, s.459 is commonly used as an alternative to just and equitable winding up order in an action under s.122(1)(g).[70] It is equally common for a petitioner under s.459 to add as an alternative a prayer for the winding up of the company.[71] Furthermore, as s.459 often provides a better solution, it has an effect on the chances of success of a petition seeking a just and equitable winding up order. Therefore, it is common to find that in a winding up petition under s.122(1)(g) of the Insolvency Act 1986, the respondent often seeks to strike out the petition on the ground that other more appropriate remedies are available under s.459.[72] The relationship between s.459 and s.122(1)(g) has come to be considered by the court.

(a) Striking out a s.122(1)(g) petition

A petitioner may simply petition for the 'sledge-hammer' remedy under s.122(1)(g) that the company should be wound up on the ground that it is just and equitable to do so. The respondent often then applies for the winding up petition to be struck out or stayed on the ground that, under s.125(2) of the 1986 Act, the petitioner is unreasonably refusing to pursue some other form of relief (eg an order under s.459) or to accept some other remedy (eg an offer from the respondent to buy out the petitioner). To succeed in a stay or striking out application, the respondent needs to show that it is plain and obvious from the beginning that the petitioner has an alternative remedy but has unreasonably refused to pursue it. But if there is a risk that the alternative remedy may not be sufficient, then the application to strike out the winding up petition may be rejected. Thus, in *Re Abbey Leisure Ltd.*[73] where there was a

69 See Chapter 1, paras. 1.1 and 1.7 above.

70 Eg *Re Abbey Leisure Ltd.* (1989) 5 BCC 183 and *Re a Company (No. 00314 of 1989) ex p. Estate Acquisition and Development Ltd. and Others* [1991] BCLC 154.

71 Eg *Vujnovich & Anor v Vujnovich* (1989) 5 BCC 740, PC; *Re a Company (No. 002470 of 1988) ex p. Nicholas* [1991] BCLC 480.

72 Eg *Re a Company (No. 003096 of 1987)*(1988) 4 BCC 80 and *Re a Company (No. 001363 of 1988)* (1989) 5 BCC 18.

73 [1990] BCC 60.

risk of a discount being applied to the valuation of the petitioner's interest in the company by an independent accountant, the Court of Appeal refused to strike out a petition for just and equitable winding up. This is because, as Warner J pointed out in *Re a Company (No. 001363 of 1988)*, 'at the hearing of the [winding up] petition the judge may, on the full facts when they are found, hold that it would be unreasonable to grant him the remedy of a winding up and that he should pursue his remedy under s.459, but it is a very strong thing to say, on the application to strike out, that it is plain and obvious that a petitioner is behaving unreasonably in seeking a winding up order'.[74] It is submitted that this approach is correct because unless and until all the facts are found by the trial judge, the court cannot be sure that in an application to strike out the winding up petition a suitable alternative remedy is or will be available and that it is unreasonable for the petitioner not to pursue it. Until the issues are well defined and have been considered by the court, a shareholder who can satisfy the criteria laid down by the House of Lords in *Re Westbourne Galleries*[75] has a *prima facie* right to petition for winding up under s.122(1)(g).

(b) Using s.459 as an alternative in s.122(1)(g) petition

A petitioner may attempt to gain some tactical advantage by choosing to petition for a just and equitable winding up in the first place, but failing that as an alternative, seek an order under s.459.[76] Or he may later seek to amend the winding up petition to include, as an alternative to a winding up order, relief under s.459. This tactical move may pressurise the respondent into making a favourable settlement with the petitioner. If the respondent is not threatened by the winding up order into submission and the petitioner fails to get a winding up order, he may still get an order in the alternative under s.459. To deny the petitioner this tactical advantage, the respondent may immediately ask the court to strike out or to stay the winding up petition. In this case the principles discussed in para (a) above apply. Alternatively, the respondent may wait until the main hearing and ask the court to refuse a winding up order at the hearing. Here the court will have to evaluate the case for a winding up order against the merits of other alternative remedies. Where a suitable alternative remedy can be found, a winding up order is likely to be denied, if only because of its potential destruction of an otherwise viable business. Thus, unless the petitioner can show why it is reasonable for him not to pray for an order under s.459 in the first place, the petitioner should not adopt these tactical moves and should petition solely for an order under s.459.

---

74 (1989) 5 BCC 18, at 25D-F.

75 [1973] AC 360.

76 Eg *Re a Company (No. 00314 of 1989) ex p. Estate Acquisition and Development Ltd. and Others* [1991] BCLC 154.

However, the fact that s.459 is a potential alternative remedy does not prevent a winding up order being granted. They are two quite distinct remedies. In a winding up petition, it is not necessary to show that the petitioner has been unfairly prejudiced. In some cases, there may be no unfair prejudice but it is nevertheless just and equitable that the company should be wound up. One such case is *Re R A Noble & Sons (Clothing) Ltd.*[77] where a winding up order was made because there was a substantial destruction of mutual confidence in the personal relationship even though the petition under s.459 failed. More recently, in *Jesner & Anor v Jarrad Properties Ltd. & Ors*,[78] the Inner House of the Court of Session allowed an order to be made that a company be wound up on the ground that it was just and equitable to do so under s.122(1)(g) notwithstanding that the petitioner was not entitled to a share purchase order on the ground of unfair prejudice under s.459.

In fact, in the case of exclusion of the petitioner from management as a result of irretrievable breakdown of relationship in a quasi-partnership company, where the respondent is not to blame for this, the exclusion is not *unfairly* prejudicial to the petitioner. If no reasonable offer has been made by the respondent or the petitioner has not unreasonably refused to accept the offer, it seems easier to satisfy s.122(1)(g) and s.125 of the Insolvency Act 1986. Where there is a risk that the petitioner will not obtain a sufficient alternative remedy, a winding up order can be made.[79]

(c) Section 122(1)(g) as an alternative to a s.459 order

It is also common to find cases where a petitioner chooses to petition under s.459 in the first instance, but also pray for a just and equitable winding up order should his s.459 petition fails. If he cannot obtain a remedy under s.459, he would rather see that the company is wound up. At the hearing, the court will first determine if the alleged unfair prejudice can be established and if it is established, what order can be made under s.461 of Companies Act 1985. Where the petitioner fails to establish a case under s.459, the court will proceed to determine whether the company should nevertheless be wound up on the just and equitable ground. As we have seen, the courts in *Re R A Noble & Sons (Clothing) Ltd.* and *Jesner & Anor v Jarrad Properties Ltd. & Ors* did order the company to be wound up despite the fact that there was no unfair prejudice.

---

77 [1983] BCLC 273.
78 *The Times*, 26 October 1992.
79 Eg *Re Abbey Leisure Ltd.* [1990] BCC 60 and *Re a Company (No. 001363 of 1988)* (1989) 5 BCC 18.

The problem caused by this type of petition is that if the court ultimately grants a winding up order, any disposition of the company's property, and any transfer of shares, or alteration in the status of the company's members, made after the commencement of the winding up is, unless the court otherwise orders, void.[80] The winding up is deemed to have commenced at the time of the presentation of the petition.[81] As a result, when a prayer for the winding up is included as an alternative in a s.459 petition, the company's business will be paralysed, in view of the potential winding up order that may be granted by the court, usually to the prejudice of all concerned. Accordingly, in a recent Practice Direction,[82] attention is drawn to the undesirability of including as a matter of course a prayer for winding up as an alternative to relief under s.459. It should be included only if that is the relief which the petitioner prefers or if it is considered that it may be the only relief to which he is entitled. This is an attempt to discourage the use of an alternative prayer for winding up as a tactical device to put pressure on the company and its controllers.[83] Where such a prayer is included the petitioner is required to state in advance whether he consents or objects to a s.127 order in the standard form. This orders that, notwithstanding the presentation of the petition, payments made into or out of the company's bank accounts or dispositions of the property of the company, made, for proper value, in the ordinary course of the business of the company,[84] between the date of presentation of the petition and the date of judgment or further order in the mean time shall not be void by virtue of s.127 of the Insolvency Act 1986 in the event of a winding up order being ordered.[85]

If he consents to a s.127 order in the standard or modified form, the petitioner could still ask for a winding up order as an alternative in a s.459 petition[86] and the registrar will normally make a s.127 order in such form

80 Section 127 of the Insolvency Act 1986.

81 Section 129 of the Insolvency Act 1986.

82 Practice Direction (winding up: petition by contributory) (Ch 1/90) [1990] BCLC 452 dated 22 February 1990.

83 Sealy & Milman, *Annotated Guide to the 1986 Insolvency Legislation*, 3rd ed. 1991, at 157.

84 The bank with whom the company has an account may not know and not able to ascertain whether the making of payments from the company's account was in the ordinary course of business. To preserve the bank's position, Harman J in *Re a Company (No. 00687 of 1991)* [1992] BCLC 133 agreed that a proviso that 'the bank should be under no obligation to verify for itself whether any transaction through the company's bank accounts is in the ordinary course of business, or that it represents full market value for the relevant transaction' should be added to the standard s.127 order. He added that the proviso should become a usual part of the standard s.127 order for the future. In *Re Crossmore Electrical and Civil Engineering Ltd.* (1989) 5 BCC 37, it was held that costs of unfair prejudice petition were not costs incurred in the ordinary course of business, but costs of defending a creditor's petition for winding up were.

85 Practice Direction [1990] BCLC 452.

86 A recent example of such a petition is *Re a Company (No. 00687 of 1991)* [1992] BCLC 133.

without further inquiry.[87] Failure to comply with the practice direction and any omission as to the applicability of the s.127 order is 'quite a bad error'.[88]

(d) Conclusion

Section 459 clearly has an impact on the operation of s.122(1)(g). Where remedies other than a winding up including relief under s.459 are available and more appropriate in the circumstances, they should first be sought. A shareholder should not as a matter of course use a winding up petition as a tactical device to pressurise the respondent. Neither should he seek a remedy under s.459 as an alternative to winding up without very good reason. This is because if his petition for a remedy under s.459 as an alternative is likely to be successful, his winding up petition is likely to be struck out. If a s.459 order is unlikely, there is no point in petitioning for one in the alternative. Where the chances of the petitioner getting a remedy under s.459 are good, a straightforward petition under s.459 should be presented and it should not be presented in the alternative. The position is different if a s.459 order is available but it is reasonable not to pursue it. Ironically, what the petitioner may do, however, despite the Practice Direction, is to seek a winding up order in the alternative in the s.459 petition in the event that a remedy under s.459 is refused provided that he agrees to a s.127 order whether in the standard or modified form. It would therefore appear that, in the future, most petitions are likely to be in the form of a straightforward s.459 petition. Alternatively, where the criteria in *Westbourne Galleries* case can readily be satisfied, the petitioner may petition under s.459 with a prayer for a winding up order in the alternative. Winding up as a remedy where shareholders come to blows will always be a remedy of last resort.

6.10 Indemnity as to costs

Two issues need to be mentioned here. The first is the extent to which a petitioner under s.459 can be indemnified by the company for the costs of his litigation. It is a general principle of company law that the company's money

---

87 Paragraph 5 of the Practice Direction. Section 125(2) of Insolvency Act 1986 would not prevent the petitioner from seeking a winding up order as an alternative provided that it would be just and equitable to make such an order: eg *Vujnovich & Anor v Vujnovich* [1990] BCLC 227, PC. The mere availability of a s.459 petition would not make it unreasonable for a petitioner to seek a winding up order: *Re a Company (No. 001363 of 1988) ex p. S-P* [1989] BCLC 579.

88 *Re Whitechurch Insurance Consultants Ltd.* [1993] BCLC 1359 at 1361 c.

should not be expended on disputes between the shareholders.[89] As mentioned earlier, one of the greatest obstacles to minority shareholder litigation is the enormous costs which it entails. Although the position in a derivative action was eased somewhat following the decision of the Court of Appeal in *Wallersteiner v Moir (No. 2)*,[90] recent case law has shown a reluctance to allow minority shareholders to be indemnified.[91] In a s.459 petition, the company is normally a nominal party. In substance, the dispute is between the shareholders.[92] The jurisdiction to make orders under s.459 for the indemnification of shares as to costs is limited to those cases where the company is the true plaintiff and the shareholder is suing on behalf of the company.[93] This accords with the principle applicable in a derivative action. But the policy considerations against granting an indemnity order have seemingly been applied here more rigorously. In *Re a Company (No. 005136 of 1986)*,[94] an unfair prejudice petition was made to restrain a proposed issue of new shares which would alter the balance of votes in the company. The petitioner also applied for an interlocutory order that the company indemnify him for the costs of the petition. Hoffmann J refused the application. He said that the petitioner's complaint was, in substance, not that a wrong had been done to the company but that a wrong had been done to him as an individual shareholder. The alleged breach of directors' fiduciary duties might in theory be a breach of duty owed to the company, but in substance was an infringement of a member's contractual rights under the company's articles.[95] This liberal view in regarding breach of director's duties as a wrong done to a member personally has unfortunately worked to the petitioner's disadvantage. As it stands, minority shareholders in a similar situation will either have to face the difficulty of proving fraud on the minority with a hope of getting a *Wallersteiner* order, or to petition under s.459 out of his own pocket for a wrong which traditionally has been regarded as a wrong done to the company. It may be more satisfactory if Hoffmann J had taken the view that as this is a wrong done both to the company and to the member personally, a petition is allowed under s.459 and costs could be indemnified if the petitioner had acted in good faith and reasonably in petitioning.

89 *Pickering v Stephenson* (1872) LR 14 Eq 322; *Re Crossmore Electrical and Civil Engineering Ltd.* (1989) 5 BCC 37; *Re Kenyon Swansea Ltd.* [1987] BCLC 514, at 521; *Re Elgindata Ltd.* [1991] BCLC 959, at 1008; *Re Milgate Developments Ltd.* [1991] BCC 24; *Canniford v Smith, Financial Times*, December 21, 1990; *Re a Company (No. 004502 of 1988), ex p. Johnson* [1992] BCLC 701.

90 [1975] 2 QB 373.

91 See *Smith v Croft* [1986] 2 All ER 551.

92 *Re Crossmore Electrical and Civil Engineering Ltd.* (1989) 5 BCC 37, at 38.

93 *Re a Company (No. 005136 of 1986)* [1987] BCLC 82.

94 [1987] BCLC 82.

95 Ibid., at 84g.

It is, however, clear from Hoffmann J's judgment that where the petition is in substance to protect the interests of the company, for example, to restrain a transaction which is disadvantageous to the company,[96] then the petitioner might be entitled to such an order for indemnification under Part XVII of the 1985 Act. As a prerequisite, the petitioner must also be unfairly prejudiced qua member. It is hoped that the court will take a more liberal approach in construing whether the act complained of is both a wrong done to the company and to the members personally.

At common law, a *Wallersteiner* order will not be made if the shareholder's action is not a derivative one. But if the result of the case is beneficial to members generally, an order for costs may be made on a common fund basis.[97] This common law principle has been extended to a s.459 petition by Hoffmann J who made it clear that a petitioner who brought a personal action would not necessarily in the end recover no more than costs on the standard basis if he won or even had to pay costs if he lost; the court had a discretion to give a shareholder who brought a member's personal action his costs out of the company's assets on a common fund basis as in *Marx v Estates & General Investments Ltd.*[98]

A more liberal approach should be adopted in dealing with the issue of costs. The primary purpose of s.459 is to remedy the mischief of the rule in *Foss v Harbottle*. If a petitioner who genuinely seeks to remedy a wrong done to the company under the section cannot get an indemnity order or has to take the risk of costs at least until the stage when the issue of unfair prejudice is determined, a derivative action will be more attractive, assuming that the difficulties of establishing fraud on the minority can be overcome. This would frustrate the primary objective of s.459.

The second issue involves a more general point on the extent to which a successful litigant can get the costs from the unsuccessful party. The issue was considered by the Court of Appeal in *Re Elgindata Ltd.*[99] recently. The principles were laid down in Nourse LJ's unanimous judgment. He held that the general rule was that a successful party was entitled to his costs notwithstanding that he might have failed on some issues. But if his failure had caused a significant increase in the length of the proceedings he could be deprived of the whole or a part of his costs. Furthermore, where the successful party raised issues or allegations improperly or unreasonably, the court could

96 Ibid., at 85a-c.
97 *Marx v Estates & General Investments Ltd.* [1975] 3 All ER 1064; [1976] 1 WLR 380.
98 [1987] BCLC 82, at 85e.
99 *The Times*, 18 June 1992.

not only deprive him of his costs but might order him to pay the whole or part of the unsuccessful party's costs, but not otherwise.

6.11 Security for costs

It may sometimes happen that the respondent is confident in defeating the petitioner's claim, but is worried that the petitioner may not be able to meet the order for costs. An impecunious petitioner may begin a petition calculated to cause inconvenience and annoyance to the respondent, even though he has very little prospect of success. The respondent frequently applies to strike out or to stay the petition. The respondent may, however, want to apply for security for costs under RSC Ord 23[100] before he makes a striking out application. This will ensure that when he eventually wins the case, the order for costs made by the court against the petitioner will be met. When the order for security for costs is made, it will also temporarily halt the proceedings until the petitioner complies with the order.

The respondent may apply for security for costs where the petitioner is ordinarily resident out of the jurisdiction, or where the petitioner is a nominal party who is petitioning (not in a representative capacity) for the benefit of some other person and that there is reason to believe that he will be unable to pay the costs of the respondent if ordered to do so, or where the petitioner has changed his address during the course of the proceedings with a view to evading the consequences of the litigation.[101] The petitioner may also apply for security for costs where the petitioner's address is not stated in the petition or is incorrectly stated therein, unless the court is satisfied that the omission or mis-statement was made innocently and without intention to deceive.[102] Where the petitioner is a limited company, the court having jurisdiction in the matter may, if it appears by credible testimony that there is reason to believe that the company will be unable to pay the defendant's costs if successful in his defence, require sufficient security to be given for those costs, and may stay all proceedings until the security is given.[103]

100 Or Ord 13, r 8, CCR in the County Court. RSC Ord 23 enables the court to make order for the security for costs against *plaintiff to an action or other proceedings* in the High Court. It would appear that a petitioner under s.459 is a plaintiff for the purposes of Ord 23: cf *Re Unisoft Group Ltd.* [1992] BCC 494; affirmed *Re Unisoft Group Ltd. (No. 1)* [1993] BCLC 1292, at 1294 g, CA.

101 RSC Ord 23, r 1(1).

102 Ibid., r 1(1), (2).

103 Section 726(1) Companies Act 1985. It was held in *Re Unisoft Group Ltd.* [1992] BCC 494 that a limited company which presented a s.459 petition was a 'plaintiff in an action or other legal proceeding' within the meaning of s.726(1) and the court, therefore, had jurisdiction to order security for costs; affirmed by the Court of Appeal on appeal [1993] BCLC 1292, at 1294 h.

6.12 Interest prior to judgment

Where the petitioner has been granted a purchase order one interesting issue is whether the amount payable under the order ought to bear interest from a date to be fixed by the court before judgment. Such a submission was made in *Re Bird Precision Bellows*[104] where Nourse J had little difficulty in rejecting it because the consent order in that case did not specifically provide that the price should bear interest. As regards cases where the court makes a purchase order in the absence of consent, it is also difficult to see how interest can be granted for a period prior to the date on which the award of purchase moneys is made. Until that date no principle sum is due and therefore no interest can be due either. Nourse J left open the question as to whether the plaintiff could be compensated for 'loss of the use of the purchase moneys during a period when they ought to have been in hand'. In principle the court does have this option given the wide jurisdiction under s.461 to do as it thinks fit. Compensation for the loss of the use of the purchase moneys should be the norm whether the respondent has operated the company in the period as between the date of consent order and the date of purchase order at a loss or not; it is the putative use to which the petitioner could have put the purchase money that is important.[105] Where there has been unfairly prejudicial conduct over a period of time throughout which the petitioner constantly asked to be bought out, subsequently bringing a s.459 petition only in the face of the respondent's refusal to do so, the court may be willing to make such compensation. Equally, where the unfair prejudice has partly deprived the petitioner of income over a long period, for example where the respondents have excluded the petitioner from any return on his shares during that period, it would appear fair that interest should be awarded over that period.

6.13 Escape clauses

An order made under s.461(2)(d) can be made subject to terms. It can contain an 'escape clause' to deal with the contingency that the respondent against whom a purchase order has been made is unable to raise the finance for the purpose. However, it is not mandatory for such an escape clause to be included. The problem arose specifically in *Re Cumana Ltd.*[106] where the respondent having been found guilty of unfairly prejudicial conduct, was ordered to buy the petitioner's shares for £925, 000. He appealed to the Court of Appeal on the ground that the trial judge should have appreciated the difficulties in raising such a sum and should have included a provision (an

---

104 [1984] 2 WLR 869.
105 Prentice (1988) OJLS 55, at 87.
106 [1986] BCLC 430.

escape clause) which would enable the court to make some other order if, despite the best endeavours of the respondent, he was unable to raise the purchase money. Lawton LJ categorically rejected this argument as wrong in principle. The fact that the wrongdoer was impecunious did not automatically require the court to include an escape clause in the purchase order and there was no reason why judgment should not be given against him. Nicholls LJ agreed, pointing out the difficulties in formulating and implementing an appropriate escape clause, and that such a clause might give rise to further litigation with the parties disagreeing over its scope and effect. On the facts, the court was also not satisfied that the unfairly prejudicial conduct here could have been remedied by an order other than compelling the respondent to purchase the petitioner's shares. Nicholls LJ thought that it was no longer sensible or just for the petitioner to remain in the company controlled and run by the respondent, and above all, mutual trust and confidence had been destroyed. As the petition arose only because of the respondent's unscrupulous attempt to deprive the petitioner of his benefit by improper allotments, he could not argue that the relief ordered against him was too harsh.

Chapter 7

Remedies

It is now necessary to examine the remedies available in a s.459 petition. Building onto the foundation laid down in s.210 of the Companies Act 1948, the court is now given extremely wide power under s.461(1) to make such order as it thinks fit. In seeking an order, the petitioner should bear in mind the guiding principle that an order will only be made if it is appropriate 'for giving relief in respect of the matters complained of'.[1] In *Re a Company (No. 008126 of 1989)*,[2] after the petition was presented, the company went into administrative receivership. The petition, as presented, asked for an order to buy out the majority, but sought an order for the majority shareholders to buy his shares after the appointment of administrative receiver. The order sought was refused, even though the affairs of the company had been conducted by the majority in a manner which was unfairly prejudicial to the petitioner. This was because the appointment of the administrative receiver rendered a purchase order inappropriate 'for giving relief in respect of the matters complained of'. The appointment had enabled the company to be properly run, so far as it was running at all.

The generality of subsection (1) is one of the twin pillars of the minority shareholders' protection under Part XVII of the 1985 Act along with the concept of 'unfair prejudice' in s.459. Its scope is in no way limited by the more specific order a court may make under subsection (2).

7.1 Final orders

As already mentioned, under s.461(1) the court may make such order as it thinks fit for giving relief in respect of the matters complained of. Under s.461(2) the court may:

'(a) regulate the conduct of the company's affairs in the future,

(b) require the company to restrain from doing or continuing an act complained of by the petitioner or to do an act which the petitioner has complained it has omitted to do,

---

1 *Re JE Cade & Son Ltd.* [1992] BCLC 213, at 223. The remedy should also be specified in the petition.

2 (1992) BCC 542.

(c) authorise civil proceedings to be brought in the name and on behalf of the company by such person or persons and on such terms as the court may direct.'

Subsection (2)(c) would enable the court to order civil proceedings to be brought on behalf of the company against persons who are not a party to the proceedings. Where the company has been joined in the s.459 petition, by the end of the hearing of the petition, the very wide powers conferred on the court under s.461 will enable it to make a final order. It would, therefore, appear that the court would not make a s.461(2)(c) order because nothing more could be achieved by further proceedings.[3] Where, however, the company is not originally joined as a party to the petition, the court cannot make orders in favour of the company. This subsection is intended to enable a remedy to be sought for the company[4] and may well render derivative actions obsolete.

Finally, s.461(2)(d) most importantly empowers the court to:

'Provide for the purchase of the shares of any members of the company by other members or by the company itself and, in the case of a purchase by the company itself, the reduction of the company's capital accordingly.'

The court can also order the company not to make any, or any specified, alteration in the memorandum or articles, and the company does not then have power without leave of the court to make any such alteration in breach of that order: s.461(3).

In the vast majority of cases, orders are normally made against the company and its present members. In appropriate circumstances, an order may be made against a former member who was guilty of unfairly prejudicial conduct but has since ceased to be a member at the time of the petition provided he is joined in the petition.[5]

The most commonly sought and the most practical remedy is usually an order for the purchase of the petitioner's shares, either by the company or by another member. It has the advantage of realising the value of the petitioner's shares without winding up the company. It is particularly appropriate where it would be unfair for the petitioner to be 'locked in' as minority in the company and there is no practicable way of regulating the future conduct of the company's affairs.[6]

3 *Re Elgindata Ltd.* [1991] BCLC 959, at 961.
4 See Cmnd. 1749, para. 206.
5 *Re a Company* [1986] BCLC 68, at 71e-f.
6 *Re Elgindata Ltd.* [1991] BCLC 959, at 1005.

It is common for the court to order the respondent to buy out the petitioner. Exceptionally, in some cases, the petitioner may be allowed to purchase some or all of the other members' shares. This seems to be a matter of what the petitioner requests and of judicial policy. The court tends to adopt a pragmatic and common sense approach, bearing in mind that the order granted must be appropriate for giving relief in respect of the matters complained of. A major concern seems to be the long term interest of the company as a going concern. Thus, the court will be less willing to allow the majority shareholders to be bought out by the petitioner unless it is absolutely appropriate to do so. A compulsory acquisition order of a majority shareholder's interest by a minority shareholder was made in *Re a Company (No. 00789 of 1987) ex p. Shooter*[7] where the respondent was clearly unfit to manage the company in accordance with the formalities and requirements of company law.

It is inconceivable that the court will order the respondents to be bought out by the petitioner where the petitioner only holds a very small percentage of the shares in the company, or where the petitioner is himself an admitted wrongdoer, and it is plain and obvious that the petitioner ought to be bought out. Similarly, the court will not put the petitioners in a position where they will acquire some further shares, thereby creating the condition for further conflict when, by common sense, there has been an irretrievable breakdown between the parties.[8]

It has to be very unusual for the court to order a majority shareholder actively concerned in the management of the company to sell his shares to a minority shareholder whose contribution to the company's growth measured in both time and degree of responsibility has been relatively small. This is particularly so where the majority is willing and able to buy out the minority at a fair price.[9] It is not clear what would be the position if both the petitioner and the respondent are financially unable to buy out the other. This is not uncommon in a period of recession when many companies are in difficult financial positions. An order for the company itself to buy out the petitioner's shares may not be financially possible. Although the court may give orders other than share purchase orders to give relief, where there is also a breakdown of relationships it would be impracticable to order the respondent not to act in an unfairly prejudicial manner. It would be interesting to see if the

7 [1990] BCLC 384, *sub nom Nuneaton Borough AFC Ltd.* (1989) 5 BCC 792. See Lowry (1992) JBL 186.

8 *Re Ringtower Holding plc* (1989) 5 BCC 82, at 103. Here, in view of the breakdown of relations, the smallness of their holdings (5.5 %), the opposition of the respondents including some senior managers, and the absence of the petitioners from the company for 18 months, the petitioners were not allowed to buy out the respondents.

9 *Re a Company (No. 006834 of 1988)* (1989) 5 BCC 218, at 220H-221A.

court would force one party to seek financial assistance from other sources to buy out the other.[10]

Where, after the petition was presented, the creditor had appointed an administrative receiver, the appointment will render any other order inappropriate.[11] This is because any order other than a purchase order is intended to ensure that the company can be properly run, so far as it is running at all, and this can be achieved after the appointment of an administrative receiver.[12] Mr Richard Sykes QC sitting as a deputy judge of the High Court in *Re Hailey Group Ltd.* however conceded that there might be circumstances in which, despite the appointment of an administrative receiver (or administrator or liquidator) before the hearing of the petition, it would be appropriate to order the respondents to purchase the petitioner's shares. For example, where the unfairly prejudicial conduct had prevented the petitioner from selling his shares at a proper price prior to the onset of insolvency, or where the substantive relief sought at a time where the company was solvent was a purchase order.[13] It would appear that where no administrative receiver is appointed by the creditor, the court may, by its own motion, appoint a receiver to run the affairs of the company on terms.[14]

In appropriate circumstances, the court may give orders other than share purchase orders. In *McGuinness & Anor, Petitioners*,[15] the directors of a public company were ordered to convene an extraordinary general meeting on a specified date and to appoint a firm of accountants as independent scrutineers. In *Re H R Harmer*,[16] the company was ordered under s.210 of the Companies Act 1948 to appoint the respondent (the autocratic father who was the founder of the company) as the president for life without real powers and he must not interfere with the company's business and must respect the decision of the board. There is no reason why a similar remedy for the future regulation of the company's affairs could not be ordered under s.459.

7.2 Valuation of shares

Where the order is for the purchase of the shares of any members of the company by other members or by the company itself, the question of

10 See *Re Cumana* [1986] BCLC 430, despite evidence that respondent was impecunious, a purchase order was made against him.
11 *Re Hailey Group Ltd.* [1993] BCLC 458.
12 Ibid., at 472h-473e.
13 Ibid., at 473e-g.
14 See Chapter 6 para. 6.7(b) above.
15 [1988] BCLC 673.
16 [1958] 3 All ER 689.

valuation of shares arises. This is a matter which requires expert evidence by accountants and other experts and reference to specialised books on this subject is essential.[17] A wide range of factors are taken into account: the company's net asset value and profits, the nature of the business and the period of its operation.[18] But above all, two important legal criteria need to be known to the valuer: the basis on which the valuation must be carried out and the precise date of valuation. The statute contains no provisions expressly made for the principles of valuation to be applied by the court. The matters are left to the discretion of the court.

Where a shareholder freely elects to sell his shares, as the control of a company has always been regarded as of paramount importance, it is established that in the valuation of shares, the valuer is entitled to take the 'control factor' into account and value the minority shares on a discount basis.[19] The following figures compiled by an expert clearly demonstrate the value of 'control'on the value of different holdings in a small private company.[20]

Value of	100%	shareholding:	£100, 000
Value of	51%	shareholding:	48, 000
Value of	50%	shareholding:	35, 000
Value of	20%	shareholding:	5, 000
Value of	10%	shareholding:	1, 000

It is, therefore, important to know whether the minority shares ought to be valued on a *pro rata* basis or a discount basis when the price of a minority holding of shares has to be fixed pursuant to an order under s.461.

17 Eastaway and Booth, *Practical Share Valuation* (2nd ed.).

18 For an example of valuation of shares see *Re Ghyll Beck Driving Range Ltd.* [1993] BCLC 1126, at 1134g-1138a.

19 *Short v Treasury Comrs* [1948] AC 534; *Gold Coast Selection Trust v Humphrey* [1948] AC 459, at 473.

20 R M Walters [1977] Brit Tax Rev 34, at 44. Reproduced in Sealy, *Cases and Materials on Company Law*, 5th ed., at 457.

(a) Basis of valuation

(i) Pro rata

In *Re Bird Precision Bellows*, Nourse J said that the overriding requirement under s.461(2)(d) is that the 'price fixed by the court must be fair'.[21] 'A fair price would be ... the value which the shares would have had at the date of the petition, if there had been no oppression'.[22] Fairness 'can never be conclusively judged in regard to a particular case until the facts are known'.[23] Subject to this important reservation, and his observation that there was no rule of universal application when a purchase order was made under s.461 for valuing minority holdings in private companies, Nourse J held that there was a general rule in a case where the company was at the material time a quasi-partnership and the purchase order was made either where (1) the unfairly prejudicial conduct on the part of the majority had resulted in the purchase order or (2) where there had been an agreement for the price to be determined by the court without any admission as to such conduct. The general rule is that the fair basis of valuation in a quasi-partnership case is to fix the price *pro rata* according to the value of the shares as a whole and without any discount for minority holding.[24] As the sale will normally have been forced upon the minority shareholder, it would be 'most unfair that the minority shareholder should be bought out on the fictional basis applicable to a free election to sell his shares in accordance with the company's articles of association or indeed on any other basis which involves a discounted price'.[25] Similarly, such a general rule applies to a case where the order provides for the purchase of the shares of the delinquent majority. It would be most unfair that the majority should receive a price which involves an element of premium. This general rule is to be welcomed, bearing in mind that its application depends on the facts of the particular case. It also provides the majority with an incentive to seek an agreed sale with the minority which will inevitably contain an element of discount or premium, as the case may be, which is not allowed by the court.[26] It also enhances the bargaining power of

---

21 [1984] 2 WLR 869, at 876E.

22 Per Lord Denning in *Scottish Co-operative Wholesale Society Ltd. v Meyer* [1958] 3 All ER 66, at 89; [1959] AC 324, at 369.

23 *Re Bird Precision Bellows* [1984] 2 WLR 869, at 876E

24 Nourse J also suggested that even without unfairly prejudicial conduct, in general, *pro rata* basis is the fair basis of valuation in a quasi-partnership case: [1984] 2 WLR 869, at 878E. On this, the author has his doubts.

25 [1984] 2 WLR 869 at 877D. A recent example of *pro rata* approach is *Re Ghyll Beck Driving Range Ltd.* [1993] BCLC 1126. The company was a joint venture of four with equal contributions. The total value of the company's shares was estimated at £160, 000. On a successful petition for the majority to buy out the petitioner, the petitioner was held entitled to £40, 000 for his shares.

26 Prentice (1986) 102 LQR 179 and (1988) OJLS 55, at 84.

the minority, the victim of unfairly prejudicial conduct, to settle the dispute out of court.

(ii) Discount basis

Nourse J did not, however, rule out the application of the 'discount rule' in appropriate cases. Without expressing a concluded view, he suggested that if the petitioner had:

> '... acquired shares from another at a price which is discounted because they represent a minority, it is self-evident that there cannot be any universal or even a general rule that he should be bought out under [s. 459] on a more favourable basis, even in a case where his predecessor has been a quasi-partner in a quasi-partnership. He might himself have acquired the shares purely for the investment and played no part in the affairs of the company. In that event it might well be fair - I do not know - that he should be bought out [on a discount basis].'[27]

It is therefore clear that where the petitioners have acquired the shares purely for investment and not as quasi-partners, a discount would most likely be applied to the valuation.[28] Where, however, the petitioners have acquired shares at a discounted price, but have since participated in the management as a quasi-partner in pursuance of a common understanding or agreement with the other quasi-partners, then the 'no discount rule' should apply when later the petitioners are forced to be bought out. The mere fact that they have previously acquired the shares at a discounted price should not enable the respondents as wrongdoers to take the advantage of a discounted valuation.

Where Nourse J's general rules do not apply, then the presumption seems to be that in the absence of any special features, fairness requires that the value of the petitioner's shares must reflect the fact that his holding is only a minority holding.[29] In *Re D R Chemicals*,[30] as the petitioner had elected to

---

27 *Re Bird Precision Bellows* [1984] 2 WLR 869, at 878A-C.

28 See *Re Elgindata Ltd.* [1991] BCLC 959, at 1007f-i: shares to be valued on a discount basis. There was, however, a letter signed by the respondent agreeing not to sell or transfer a controlling interest in the company without the sanction of a special resolution. Warner J, therefore, said that if valuation experts agreed that the effect of the letter was to make such a discount inappropriate, the valuation will be on a *pro rata* basis.

29 For example, where there was evidence that the petitioner had acquired the shares prior to the alleged unfairly prejudicial conduct at a discount to reflect his minority holding, or where it was inappropriate after the petitioner's election to remain a minority shareholder for some years after expulsion to treat the company as being in any sense a quasi-partnership company. See *Re D R Chemicals* (1989) 5 BCC 39.

30 (1989) 5 BCC 39.

remain a minority shareholder and did not petition immediately after his expulsion, Peter Gibson J thought that it was only fair that he should be bought out on a discount basis.

The court's wide discretion to determine the basis of share valuation only exists under s.461. Thus, *Re Bird Precision Bellows* was distinguished in *Howie & Ors v Cramford*,[31] a case which did not involve an unfair prejudice petition. Under a shareholder agreement, the respondent's shares were to be offered to the other members of the company who would then have to pay for such shares at a 'fair market price'. Vinelott J held that where a fair market price was to be paid, it was the fair price which the share would fetch in the open market between a willing vendor and a willing purchaser. In *Howie's* case, a discount should be applied. As it was not a s.459 petition, the judge did not have the wide discretion to apply the 'no discount rule'. On an unfair prejudice petition, the court would have had a discretion to apply the 'no discount rule' even if a provision in the articles of association had provided that the shares were to be bought out at a fair market price. This case illustrates the distinction between the application of contractual pre-emption and the wide discretion under s.461 in the context of valuation of shares.

It is also self-evident that where the conduct complained of under s.459 is not unfairly prejudicial and the petitioner sought to be bought out by the respondent in accordance with the articles which directed that the shares were to be valued as between a willing vendor and a willing purchaser, then the court has no jurisdiction to apply 'no discount rule'.[32] Indeed, such a petition will be struck out on an application by the respondent on the ground that it is an abuse of the process of the court. Provided the articles are themselves fair, the company's conduct in conformity with the articles could not be unfairly prejudicial. So, where the auditor is called upon to value the shares at a fair price or fair market price, and no unfairly prejudicial conduct is shown, he is entitled to fix a value which reflects the percentage holding of the shares on a discount basis. If the valuer makes a mistake, that does not constitute unfairly prejudicial conduct by the company, and the petitioner is advised to attack the valuation without resort to petitioning under s.459.[33]

(iii) Pragmatic approach

A rather different approach has been taken by Hoffmann J in *Re a Company (No. 007623 of 1984)*.[34] It will be recalled that there was no unfair prejudice in

---

31 [1990] BCC 330.

32 *Re Castleburn Ltd.* (1989) 5 BCC 652; *Re a Company (No. 006834 of 1988)* (1989) 5 BCC 218.

33 *Re a Company (No. 004377 of 1986)* [1987] 1 WLR 102, at 111C; *Re Castleburn Ltd.* (1989) 5 BCC 652, at 664E.

34 [1986] BCLC 362.

that case. But Hoffmann J went on to say that he would nevertheless be willing to apply some discount for a minority holding if there had been unfair prejudice.

> 'A fair value must ... reflect the potential value of the shares to both vendor and purchaser. It was common ground that an outsider would not be willing to pay more than a nominal sum for the petitioner's shares. It was also clear that he would not, on a winding up, obtain his proportionate part of anything like the value of the company calculated on the basis of its previous earnings.'[35]

On the other hand, as the petitioner went into the company on the understanding that he would be employed and paid a salary and that this would be the principal way in which he would share in its profitability, Hoffmann J thought that a fair value for his shares must reflect the fact that this expectation had been frustrated.[36]

This case shows that the 'no discount rule' does not apply automatically even if there is unfair prejudice. It all depends on the circumstances of the case. The 'no discount rule' is no more than a guide in determining a fair price. The ultimate criterion is that fair valuation must be made on the assumption that the unfairly prejudicial conduct has not occurred. Had the unfairly prejudicial conduct not occurred here, the fair value that the petitioner would have received for his minority holding would not be more than a nominal sum. A fair value should, therefore, reflect this. But since he would have been employed and paid a salary had unfair prejudice not occurred, this too should be reflected in the valuation. This approach is undoubtedly more flexible and realistic.[37] Damages in effect are being awarded for constructive dismissal through the back door of share valuation - the petitioner's legitimate expectation in the earnings from employment is compensated. But the outcome of this approach is much more unpredictable.

(b) Factors affecting the basis of valuation

The whole framework of the section is to confer on the court a very wide discretion to do what is fair and equitable in order to put right and cure for the future the unfair prejudice which the petitioner has suffered. The court's discretion does not stop short when it comes to the terms of the order for purchase in the manner in which the price is to be assessed, or indeed the

35 Ibid., at 369b.
36 Ibid., at 369c.
37 Hollington, *Minority Shareholders' Rights*, 1990, at 80 para. 4-070.

terms of any orders the court may make. As we have seen, the court has to consider whether there has been unfair prejudice to the petitioner and how it had taken place under s.459. The inquiry into the merits is more fundamental than merely considering the basis of the valuation of the shares. Unless unfair prejudice is proved, the court is simply being asked to undertake a sort of arbitration *in vacuo*, which it has no jurisdiction to do.[38] Having considered the merits as he is required to do, it is unreasonable then to require the judge to put that entirely out of his mind when it comes to the question of the terms of the orders. The fact that there has been an agreed sale or consent order without admitting that unfairly prejudicial conduct has taken place will not avail the respondents to expect or require the court not to inquire into the merits and take full account of them to determine the value of the shares. This can prevent the respondent from gaining a tactical advantage which he does not deserve.[39] It is therefore clear that in considering the terms of the purchase order, the factors that the court takes into account in determining 'unfairness' are as much relevant here though different weight may be given to each of them in this context. Among others, two factors need to be mentioned here.

(i) The Petitioner's conduct

The conduct of the petitioner should be taken into consideration in setting the price. For example, where a shareholder deserves his exclusion, the 'no discount rule' will not be applied. He who has been partially responsible for his own plight could be taken to have 'made a constructive election to sever his connection with the company'.[40] Similarly, in *Re D R Chemicals*, as the petitioner did not petition immediately, it was thought fair to apply the 'discount rule'.[41]

(ii) Minimum price

What is the effect of any provision in the company's articles which stipulates the price which a transferring shareholder is to be paid for his shares in a

---

38 This approach is different from that taken by the court where an interlocutory order which does not involve interim payment is sought.

39 In fact, there are dangers in consenting to purchase the petitioner's shares at a price to be fixed by the court without any admission of unfairly prejudicial conduct towards the petitioners, see eg *Re Bird Precision Bellows* [1986] Ch 658, CA. There is little to be gained from the respondent's point of view in agreeing to that type of purchase order. It is, on the contrary, very much to the petitioner's advantage. If the respondent wants to avoid this sort of examination by the court, it is necessary to remove the matter entirely from the court by agreement; for example, he might agree to purchase without admitting unfair prejudice at a price to be determined by arbitration or by two valuers and an umpire.

40 *Re Bird Precision Bellows* [1984] 2 WLR 869, at 877H, 878E.

41 (1989) 5 BCC 39, at 54.

transaction between a willing vendor and a willing purchaser? In *Re Bird Precision Bellows*,[42] Oliver LJ, without expressing a concluded view, indicated a willingness to look at the articles of association in assessing the fairness of the price set by the court under s.461(2)(d), and stated that he would not order purchase at a price below that otherwise obtainable under the articles. Consistent with the court's wide discretion under s.461(1), the provision of a valuation basis in the articles of association can at most operate to set a floor but not a ceiling on the price. This is particularly desirable where the articles artificially depreciate the purchase price, so as to enable the court to determine a price which exceeds that provided in the articles of association. To do otherwise would encourage the majority shareholder to lay down an artificial pricing mechanism in the articles well in advance. Thus, although such a provision can be taken into account on the grounds that it obviously reflects the basis on which the petitioner was involved in the company's affairs, it cannot be a deciding factor.

(c) Date of valuation

There are three probable principal categories of date for valuation: the dates prior to the petition, the date of the petition, and the date of the order. The date of valuation chosen by the court may substantially affect the valuation awarded for the petitioner's shares. The value of the shares may have been jeopardised or diminished considerably as a result of the unfair prejudice. On the other hand, it may have increased after the date of the petition as a result of the respondent's increased efforts in running the company despite unfairly prejudicial conduct towards the petitioner.[43] The court has refused to lay down a rigid rule as to the proper date for the valuation of shares. It is a matter for the exercise of the trial judge's discretion, bearing in mind the overriding requirement that the valuation must be fair on the particular facts.

(i) General rules

(a) Date of the petition

In *Re a Company (No 002612 of 1984)*,[44] Vinelott J seems to have taken the view that the correct starting point is generally the date of the petition:

---

42 [1985] 3 All ER 523, at 534a.
43 Eg *Re London School of Electronics* [1986] Ch 211.
44 Court of Appeal's decision reported as *Re Cumana Ltd* [1986] BCLC 430.

'I would at least incline to the view that the date of the petition is the correct starting point, the valuation, of course, being adjusted to take account of unfair conduct which has depreciated the value of the shares as in *Meyer*, and that a departure from this date must be justified on the ground of some special circumstances. The date of petition is the date on which the petitioner elects to treat the unfair conduct of the majority as in effect destroying the basis on which he agreed to continue to be a shareholder and to look to his shares for his proper reward from participation in a joint undertaking.'[45]

(b) Dates prior to the petition

The Court of Appeal in *Re Cumana Ltd* upheld Vinelott J's approach.[46] Lawton LJ, however, re-emphasised the one special circumstance which Vinelott J pointed out as would justify taking a date earlier than that of the petition at which to value the share; that is where the unfairly prejudicial conduct has in some way affected the share value. Emphasising that the fixing of the date for valuation was a matter for the trial judge's discretion, his Lordship said:

'If, for example, there is before the court evidence that the majority shareholder deliberately took steps to depreciate the value of shares in anticipation of a petition being presented, it would be permissible to value the shares at a date before such action was taken.'[47]

The back-dating of a valuation was ordered in *Re OC (Transport) Services Ltd.*[48] where the court held that the valuation should be at a date on which the shares, which allowed another company to come in as a substantial shareholder, were allotted. It would be wrong to value the shares at the date of the petition as the value of the company's shares by then may have been affected by its association with its new shareholder.

(c) Date of the order

Another important principle which may determine the proper date for valuation is that the date chosen should not allow a petitioner to benefit from any contribution for the benefit of the company attributable exclusively to the

45 2 BCC 99, 453, at 99, 492-99, 493.
46 [1986] BCLC 430 at 436a.
47 [1986] BCLC 430 at 436c.
48 [1984] BCLC 251; (1984) 1 BCC 99, 068.

efforts of the respondents. Likewise, the respondent should not benefit from any contribution made to the company by the petitioner which is only reflected in the company's balance sheet after the petitioner's departure. Thus, in *Re London School of Electronics Ltd.*,[49] Nourse J ruled that, *prima facie*, an interest in a going concern ought to be valued at the date of the order for purchase. However, on the facts, the date of the order was held unacceptable because by that time the company's profits had increased substantially, wholly through the efforts of the respondents.[50]

(ii) Process of elimination

Sometimes the date is arrived at by a process of elimination, with other possibilities being ruled out as unfair. Thus, in *Re London School of Electronics Ltd.*,[51] the date of order was ruled out as unfair for the reasons mentioned above. So too was the date of unfair prejudice, because the profits to be earned from the misappropriation of the students (the unfairly prejudicial conduct) would not arise until later. To value the shares on the date of unfair prejudice would give too low a figure and so the date of the petition was chosen.

The date of the order has rarely been used by the court despite Nourse J's observation. The overriding requirement that the valuation should be fair on the particular facts and the likelihood that the parties' positions would have changed means that the dates prior to the petition or the date of the petition will find more favour with the courts in most cases.[52] However, in *Re D R Chemicals Ltd.*,[53] the date of order was accepted by Peter Gibson J. The date on which the respondents first offered to buy out the petitioner was not a fair valuation date as the unfair prejudice did not occur until a year later. He said that the petitioner acting entirely within his rights and not unreasonably, had remained a minority holder and only now was he seeking an order requiring the respondents to purchase his shares; accordingly, logic and fairness dictated that the valuation should be at the date of the order. He added that this

---

49 [1986] Ch 211.

50 [1985] BCLC 273. In *Re Elgindata Ltd.* [1991] BCLC 959, at 1007, the date of order was chosen because the company's accounts would only be adjusted in respect of money wrongly charged to the company at that date.

51 [1984] Ch 419.

52 See Hannigan (1987) 8 BLR 21, at 22. Prentice ((1986) LQR 179, at 185) suggests that it will only be in rare cases that the date of exclusion would be the appropriate valuation date and in most cases probably the most appropriate date is the date of order. Among other reasons, he suggests that it is because the company will retain the benefit of the petitioner's investment and any valuation should reflect this. This is certainly true where the company is a going concern and the positions of the parties have not been substantially altered.

53 (1989) BCC 39.

conclusion was strongly supported by the fact that a petitioner under s.459 was unable to obtain an order for interest running from a date before the purchase order was made.[54] He, however, pointed out that in some cases its particular circumstances might require a date earlier than the date of the order, such as where there had been a sea change in the company's business since the petitioner last associated himself in any way with the company.

54 See *Re Bird Precision Bellows Ltd.* [1984] Ch 419, at 437; approved on appeal by the Court of Appeal [1986] Ch 658.

Chapter 8

Conclusions

Until 1980 minority shareholders' rights were relatively limited at common law, mainly as a result of the rule in *Foss v Harbottle* and judicial reluctance to be involved in commercial judgments and the lack of judicial creativity in interpreting s.210 of the Companies Act 1948. Many procedural hurdles were invented to turn away minority shareholders who sought relief even where the merits of their cases may have justified judicial intervention.

Although s.210 was introduced in 1948, giving a wide discretionary statutory remedy for aggrieved minority shareholders, persistent failure by the judges to take the opportunity for intervention rendered s.210 of the Companies Act 1948 a substantial failure. So it had to be scrapped and re-drafted. The full potential of this new remedy could then be exploited with the enactment of s.75 of the Companies Act 1980 (now s.459 of the Companies Act 1985). Although s.459 has replaced the restrictive ground of 'oppression' with a more flexible test of 'unfair prejudice', and has removed many procedural obstacles, in its early years the remedy was not without difficulties. At one stage it seemed that the notorious 'qua member' requirement would restrict the effectiveness of the section. However that threat appears to have now been eliminated, with judges being prepared to look into the equitable considerations of each case, particularly in the case of small private companies. A more realistic approach of giving effect to shareholders' 'legitimate expectation' was thus adopted.

Conduct which affected all members was thought not to be a ground for petition under the section. Parliament has however amended the section making it clear that unfair prejudice to the members as a whole is actionable. This would in theory open the way for s.459 petitions arising out of complaints of miserly dividend payments. Although the court has in principle accepted this possibility, the traditional reluctance of the judges in interfering with what are essentially business policy decisions is likely to remain a formidable obstacle in such cases.

On the other hand, the Court of Appeal's approval that the test for unfair prejudice is result-based rather than motive-based, and the ruling that the petitioner does not have to come to the court with 'clean hands' would encourage successful application of the section.

It is clear that compliance with the provisions of the Companies Act or articles of association would not guarantee immunity from suit under s.459. It also appears that shareholders in a quasi-partnership company who are excluded from management are more likely to obtain relief and to have a bigger say in the adminstration of the company's affairs. In other areas, the section has essentially provided a code of conduct which requires fairness and evenhandedness in the running of the company. For instance, individual shareholders may seek redress against directors notwithstanding that the directors owe their duties to the company and not to the members. The range of conduct covered by the section is almost unlimited. The flexibility of the relief offered has made the section the most attractive solution for a wide range of shareholders' disputes.

The section has an impact on the development of company law as a whole. It has provided means of circumventing the rule in *Foss v Harbottle* and its difficulties as a minority member may now seek a direct remedy for himself and with a greater chance of success. Documents in the company's possession are in most cases discoverable. It also offers more appropriate and flexible relief than a just and equitable winding up order. It has rendered the debate on the extent of the personal right conferred by s.14 of the Companies Act 1985 less important as it protects interests and legitimate expectations in addition to rights strictly conferred qua member by s.14. It makes it unnecessary to invoke the much criticised case of *Clemens v Clemens Bros. Ltd.* in future.

Another consequence of the liberal application of s.459 may be that greater detail will now be inserted into the articles, or a separate shareholder agreement entered into, in an attempt to define exhaustively the parties' relationship, in order to prevent the court from taking into account any equitable consideration. This may reduce the scope for s.459 petition even though it may not eliminate its application altogether for it applies to all companies.[1]

There are however some worrying aspects. An equitable owner of shares who has not been registered as a member is prevented from seeking relief under the section. The important phrase 'act of the company' appears ill-defined. Cases showing the application of s.459 in public companies remain scanty. Many propositions in this book in that respect remain speculative although in theory such companies are not excluded from its scope. And it seems clear that relief for exclusion from management in such companies remains difficult to obtain.

1 Hannigan (1988) LMCLQ 60, at 81.

Protection for shareholders in public companies will be improved if the Draft EEC Fifth Directive is adopted. Under Article 16 holders of 10% of the subscribed capital may seek relief for 'damage sustained by the company as a result of breaches of duty by members of those organs in carrying out their functions' (Article 14). It should however be noted that the success of Article 16, even if adopted, depends on the shareholders' ability to reach the requisite 10% threshold which can be a real difficulty in a large public company with numerous shareholders. Furthermore, the Directive may not be applicable in cases of exclusion from management. With the future of the Draft Fifth Directive still uncertain and the restrictive approach taken by the Court of Appeal in the *Prudential* case, shareholders in such companies should in the meantime be given the same protection under s.459. Their ability to sell their shares may ease the problem somewhat but should not be the only answer. Parliament has now clearly intended that the section should be applied in statutory water companies (s.459(3)). It is hoped that the court will likewise apply the section to other public companies.

Another worry is that although there has been judicial willingness to make the section a success since its enactment in 1980, there has been one example of extreme judicial caution. Hoffmann J[2] has shown reluctance to permit reliance on s.459 in cases where the articles provide a pre-emption provision and the respondent has offered to buy out the petitioner in accordance with such provision. It is hoped that Balcombe LJ's *obiter* in *Re Abbey Leisure Ltd.*[3] that it might be equitable in the appropriate case to ignore buy-out provisions in the articles under s.122(1)(g), would persuade the court to take a similar view with regard to a s.459 petition. It is also hoped that the view taken in *ex p. Holden* that pre-emption provision should not *per se* prevent a successful petition under s.459 will be preferred in future.

It should also be noted that the vast majority of decisions under the section are first instance decisions of a small coterie of few judges. Furthermore, many judicial statements are merely *obiter dicta.* There are few Court of Appeal decisions and none from the House of Lords at the time of writing.[4] Palmer's *In Company*[5] has warned of the danger of a possible reactionary decision from a higher court neutralising the advances that have been made in the past decade.

---

2 Who, with respect, deserves credit for introducing the wider concept of 'legitimate expectation' into s.459 to overcome the qua member restriction.

3 See para. 3.8(b).

4 The House of Lord's decision in *Scottish Co-operative Wholesale Society v Meyer* [1959] AC 324 relates to the old s.210.

5 Issue 2, February 1991, at 3.

In conclusion, s.459 has generally provided many minority shareholders with effective relief against unfairly prejudicial conduct never previously available. Its flexibility has rendered the section a substantial success. The many negotiated buy-outs that never reach the courts, though not quantifiable, must probably be a major part of this success. Though the court's wide jurisdiction and discretion has to be carefully controlled lest it be used as a means of oppression in the hands of the minority, it is hoped that the court will not be too over cautious in its application and will continue to give appropriate relief to minority shareholders.

Appendix 1

SCHEDULE
RULE 3

Petition on Ground that Members Unfairly Prejudiced

(a) Insert title of court	To (a)...............................
(b) Insert full name(s) and address(es) of petitioner	The petition of (b)...............................
(c) Insert full name of company (d) Insert date	1. (c)................................ (hereinafter called 'the company' was incorporated on (d)..............................under the Companies Act(s) 19.........
(e) Insert address of registered office	2. The registered office of the company is at (e)... 3. The nominal capital of the company is £.......... divided into .... shares of £.......... each. The amount of the capital paid up or credited as paid up is £.......... The petitioner(s) is/are the holders of .... shares of £....... each.
(f) Delete as applicable	Such shares at the date of the petition (f) [are registered in the name(s) of the petitioner(s)] [have been transferred or transmitted to the petitioner(s) by operation of law]. 4. The principal objects for which the company was established are as follows: .... and other objects stated in the memorandum of association of the company.
(g) Set out the grounds on which the petition is presented	5.(g)... ....
	In these circumstances your petitioner submits that the affairs of the company are being conducted in a manner which is unfairly prejudicial to the interests of (f) [some part of the members (including your petitioner)] [your petitioner] or (f) [The act or omission] [the proposed act or omission] referred to in part 5 above (f) [is] [would be]

unfairly prejudicial to the interests of (f) [some part of the members (including your petitioner)] [your petitioner].

(h) Here set out the nature of relief sought

The petitioner therefore prays as follows (h)

....

....

or

that such other order may be made as the court thinks fit.

Note

It is intended to serve this petition on:

....

....

Endorsement

This petition having been presented to the court on ...., let all parties attend before the Registrar in Chambers on:

Date...

Time...

Place...

for directions to be given

The solicitor(s) for the petitioner is/are:

Name...

Address...

....

Tel No...

Reference...

(j) Delete if London Agents not instructed

(j) Whose London Agents are:

Name...

Address...

....

Tel No...

Reference...

Appendix 2 (fictitious)

IN THE HIGH COURT OF JUSTICE **No. 001234 of 1993**

CHANCERY DIVISION

IN THE MATTER of Benny & Co Limited
AND IN THE MATTER of the Companies Act 1985
BETWEEN

JANE ELIZABETH SMITH

Petitioner

and

(1) SIMON WILLIAM MITCHELL
(2) KIM RICHARD LANE
(3) VICTORIA JUDITH DIXON

Respondents

TO Her Majesty's High Court of Justice

The petition of Jane Elizabeth Smith of 145 Pennington Road, Exeter EX4 6RD

1. Benny & Co Limited (hereinafter called 'the Company') was incorporated on 15th of August 1967 under the Companies Act 1948.
2. The registered office of the Company is at 12 High Street, Exeter EX4 6DJ.
3. The nominal capital of the Company is £20,000 divided into 20,000 shares of £1 each. The amount of the capital paid up or credited as paid up is £15,000. The petitioner is the holder of 2,000 shares of £1 each. Such shares at the date of this petition are registered in the name of the petitioner.
4. The principal objects for which the Company was established are to carry out business as a fashion retailer and other objects stated in the memorandum of association of the company.
5. The respondents Simon William Mitchell and Kim Richard Lane were the original directors of the Company. On incorporation the company had a nominal capital of £100 divided into 100 shares of £1 each, the respondents Simon William Mitchell and Kim Richard Lane being at that time the holders of 50 shares each.
6. From time to time the nominal capital of the Company was increased by resolutions passed by the Company in general meeting, and further shares were allotted by the directors.

7. By a written contract of employment dated 14th of October 1975 (hereinafter 'the employment contract') the petitioner was employed by the Company as a fashion designer. At that time the Company had 10 employees.
8. Subsequently the business of the Company expanded at a considerable rate, and by April 1984 the Company employed 35 staff and in the year ending 31st May 1984 had a turnover of £3,975,343 and pre-tax profits of £54,783.
9. The success of the company was largely due to the hard work and designing skill of the petitioner. In recognition of this, the petitioner was appointed a director of the Company at the annual general meeting of the Company held on 3rd of April 1984. The other directors of the Company at that time were the respondents Simon William Mitchell, Kim Richard Lane and Victoria Judith Dixon, the wife of the respondent Simon William Mitchell.
10. At a meeting of the board of directors also held on 3rd of April 1984, the petitioner was allotted 2,000 shares of £1 each in the Company. Immediately before the said allotment to the petitioner there were 6,500 issued shares of the Company. These were held as to 3,000 thereof by the respondent Simon William Mitchell, as to 3,000 thereof by the respondent Kim Richard Lane, and as to 500 thereof by the respondent Victoria Judith Dixon.
11. By a letter to the Company dated 25th of March 1988 the petitioner resigned her employment with the Company with effect from 30th of September 1988 pursuant to the terms of the employment contract.
12. At the annual general meeting of the Company held on 15th August 1988 the petitioner was removed from her directorship of the Company on a show hands by 3 votes to 1.
13. During the period 1983 to 1987 inclusive, dividends of 20p per share were declared each year at annual general meetings of the Company.
14. The profits of the Company in the year ending 31st of May 1988 available for distribution were at least £65,000, in the year ending 31st of May 1989 at least £70,000 and in the year ending 31st of May 1990 at least £25,000. Notwithstanding such profits being available for distribution, the Company has not declared any dividends after 1987.
15. The respondent Simon William Mitchell's remuneration from the Company in the year ending 31st of May 1988 was £42,000, in the year ending 31st of May 1989 it was £48,000 and in the year ending 31st of May 1990 it was £60,000. The respondent Kim Richard Lane's remuneration from the Company in the year ending 31st of May 1988 was £19,000, in the year ending 31st of May 1989 it was £24,000 and in the year ending 31st of May 1990 it was £30,000. The respondent Victoria

Judith Dixon's remuneration from the Company was £4,000 in each of the years ending 31st of May 1988 to 31st of May 1990.

16. The Company's accounts for the year ending 31st of May 1990 were made available to the petitioner on 10th of February 1992. These accounts showed that during the year ending 31st of May 1990 a further 3,000 shares had been allotted to the respondents Simon William Mitchell and Kim Richard Lane at par each, and a further 500 shares had been allotted to the respondent Victoria Judith Dixon at par. No further shares at that time were or subsequently have been offered to the petitioner.
17. In the premises the actions of the respondents Simon William Mitchell, Kim Richard Lane and Victoria Judith Dixon as directors of the Company have been deliberately designed to damage the petitioner's interest in her shares in the Company by ensuring no dividends are paid while the respondents are able to draw remuneration as directors and by diluting the petitioner's shareholding in the Company from 23.5 per cent to 13.3 per cent of the issued share capital.
18. In these circumstances the petitioner submits that the affairs of the Company are being conducted in a manner which is unfairly prejudicial to the interests of some part of the members including the petitioner.

THE PETITIONER therefore prays as follows:

(1) that the respondents and each of them may be ordered to purchased the petitioner's shares at a fair value to be determined by the court;

(2) that the Company may be ordered to pay a dividend for the year ending 31st of May 1991 if profits are available for that purpose;

(3) that there be an inquiry ordered as to what dividends ought to have been declared by the Company in the years ending 31st of May 1988 to 31st of May 1990;

(4) and that such other order may be made as the court thinks fit.

NOTE

It is intended to serve this petition on:

(1) Simon William Mitchell of 11 Prospect Road, Exeter EX4 4DD

(2) Kim Richard Lane of 22 Pennsylvania Crescent, Exeter EX3 6HJ

(3) Victoria Judith Dixon of 11 Prospect Road, Exeter EX4 4DD

ENDORSEMENT

This petition having been presented to the court on 12th of March 1993 let all parties attend before the Registrar in Chambers on:

Date:	30th April 1993
Time:	3 p.m.
Place:	Room 112, Thomas More Building, Royal Courts of Justice, Strand, London, WC2A 2LL

for directions to be given.

The solicitors for the petitioner are:

Name:	Messrs Allen and Dickson
Address:	11 Queen Street, Exeter EX4 6DR
Tel No:	0392 263377
Reference:	Alc/Smith

Index

A

Articles of Association
- alteration 6, 8, 39, 94-96
  - motive 70
  - *bona fide* 74-75
  - variation of
    - class rights by 6, 10, 12, 97
    - by court order 126
- breach of 7, 10-11, 14, 41-44, 80
- conduct in
  - accordance with 52, 54-56
- contractual effect 10, 31, 41-44
- declaration of dividends 87
- exhaustive 47-48, 140
- legitimate expectation,
  - giving rise to 34, 49
- provision for
  - share purchase 36, 61-69, 141
- purchase price fixed by 132, 134-135
- removal of directors,
  - provisions prohibiting 79
- rights under 1-2, 10-14
- Table A 18, 27, 86
- *ultra vires* 2, 27

B

Breach of Memorandum and
- Articles of Association 7, 10-11, 14, 41-44, 80

C

Cadbury Committee 8, 9, 37

Class Rights
- variation of 6, 10, 12, 97

Cohen Committee 2, 15, 16, 18, 31

Company
- separate status from
  - its members, having 10, 28

D

Derivative action 1, 3-4, 42-44, 81
- alternative to
  - unfair prejudice remedy 70
- costs of 9, 120
- *prima facie* case 7
- unfair prejudice, and 43-44, 70, 120-121
- use of
  - representative form 6, 49
- wrong done to company 3-4, 6, 7, 41-44

Directors
- duties of 40, 71,75, 80, 82-83
  - *bona fide* exercise of 75-76, 80, 96
  - breach of 11, 13, 25, 40-46, 72, 80-86, 89
  - *mala fide* exercise of 4, 13
  - owed to company 11, 120
  - owed to members 40, 71, 88, 120
  - takeover, during 44, 82, 88-90

Discovery of documents 8, 113-114

Discrimination
- against minority shareholders 4, 6, 57, 73-76, 96

Dividends 12-13, 31, 35
- inadequate 37-38, 87-88
- non-payment of 16, 57
- reduction of 75

Draft Fifth EC Directive 88, 141

F

Foss v Harbottle 1, 3, 6-7, 9-11, 15, 41, 45, 52, 72, 77, 81, 83, 121, 139-140
- exceptions to 1, 3, 52, 77, 81, 83

Fraud
- minority, on 1, 3-6
  - breach of director's
    - duty, and 40, 41, 42 81, 82, 83
  - meaning of 4
  - personal right, and 12
  - problems of 6-10
  - proof of 8
  - public company, by 45
  - wrongdoer control 5-6
- pleading of 8

G

Group
- detrimental act to 42
- majority rule and 3
- representative action 1, 10

Groups
- afloat, keeping 76
- company affairs of 25, 26

I

Injunctions 108-111

J

Jenkins Committee 2, 16, 18, 23

Jenkins Committee (cont) 31, 36, 44, 46, 51, 83, 126
Joint ventures
breakdown 79
expectation 35
no expectation 47
prejudice 54
pro rata, valuation 130
probity, lack of 99

L
Locus standi
derivative action, of 5, 10
lack of 35
s.459, under 17, 65
transferred or transmitted by law 20, 21

M
Majority rule 2-3
exceptions to 2-6
Memorandum & Articles of Association see Articles of Association
Members of company 18-20
Minority shareholders
fraud against 3-6, 41, 120
negligence, as victims of 4, 8, 15, 45-46, 83-86
rights of 1-3, 9, 11-12
costs 9, 119-122

O
Oppression 2, 15, 16, 22, 23, 25, 31, 51, 52, 57, 77, 80, 83-84, 86-87, 139

P
Practice Direction 1990 14, 118-119
Procedure 101-124
costs 119-122
indemnity 119-122
security 122
courts 101
escape clause 123-124
injunction 108-111
prima facie case 109-111
interest 123
interlocutory orders 108-113
petition
advertisement 108
alternative to winding up 116-117
parties 104
serving of 103
out of jurisdiction 106

Procedure (cont)
petition (cont)
stay of proceedings 106-107
striking out 106-107, 115-119
prescribed form 102, 143
procedural rules 101-104
return day 102-103
receiver 111
interim payment 111-113
Public company 33, 35-36, 43, 45, 48, 82, 93, 128, 141

Q
Quasi-partnership
appointment of receiver 111
breakdown, winding up 117
legitimate interests 34
alteration of Articles of Association 40
excessive remuneration 37
exclusion from management 35, 36, 79, 140
inadequate dividends 37
not transmitted by law 50
retaining shareholding 39
takeover 38
offer to buy out 61
prejudice 54
probity, lack of 98
qua member requirement 22, 33
valuation 130
pro rata 130
discount 131

S
Shareholders
agreement among/with 32, 72
proportionate shareholding 39
personal rights of 10, 11, 12, 13, 80
academic debates 31
breach of director's duty on 13, 40-44
class rights 97
legitimate interests, as 49
takeover, in 89
rights of 1
actions for breach of 6
interests, and 42, 71-72
legitimate interests, as 34, 36
restricted to legal 46-48

Shareholders (cont)
rights (cont)
unfairly prejudicial
exercise of 56
Shares
dilution of holding 39
locus standi of 21
offer to buy out 61-69
purchase order 126-128
escape clause 123
transferee 21
Valuation, see
Valuation of shares
Status quo
alteration of 55

T

Takeovers 38, 88-90
breach of city code 94-95
compulsory purchase 90-93
legitimate expectation in 35
misleading information 88-90
unfair prejudice 44, 82

U

Ultra vires decisions
and transactions
personal action for 2
unfair prejudice, and 27
Unfair prejudice remedy
act or omission of
the company 26-28
application 79-99
alteration of articles 94-96
autocratic conduct 97-98
breach of directors' duties 80-86
excessive remuneration 86-87
exclusion from management 79-80
inadequate dividends 87-88
information requested 98
negligent management 83-86
probity, lack of 98-99
takeover 88-94
variation of class rights 97
company's affairs 23
groups 25-26
concept 51-52
illegality 52
impropriety 52
legitimate interests
alteration of articles 39-40
breach of director's duties 40-46
excessive remuneration 37
exclusion from management 35-36
inadequate dividends 37

Unfair prejudice remedy (cont)
legitimate interests (cont)
non-transmissible 49-50
personal rights, and 49
proportionate holding 39
takeover 38
trading at a loss 46
locus standi 17-22
member 19-20
members erroneously
registered 22
persons transferred or
transmitted by law 20-21
prejudice 53-54
affecting all members 57
exercise of legal rights 54-56
qua member requirement 31-34
section 459 17
history 15-16
unfairness 58
alternative remedy 69-70
'clean hands' 139
delay 76
motive 70-76
offer to buy out 61-69
petitioner's conduct 59-60
pre-emption provisions 63-67
withholding money owed
to subsidiary 76

V

Valuation of shares 128-138
basis of 130-133
discount 131
pragmatic approach 132-133
pro rata 130
date of 135-138
elimination 137
order 136
petition 135
prior to petition 136
factors affecting 133-135
contractual minimum
price 134
petitioner's conduct 134
value of shares 129

W

Winding up
advertisement of, petition 108
alternative to
unfair prejudice petition 117-119
just and equitable 2, 13-15
pre-emption provisions 67
striking out 107, 115

MINORITY SHAREHOLDERS' PROTECTION

A STUDY OF [illegible] IES ACT 1985

S H Goo, LLB, LLM
Lecturer in Law
University of Exeter

First published in Great Britain 1994 by Cavendish Publishing Limited, The Glass House, Wharton Street, London WC1X 9PX
Telephone: 071-278 8000 Facsimile: 071-278 8080

British Library Cataloguing in Publication Data

Goo, S H
Minority Shareholders' Protection
A Study of Section 459 of the Companies Act 1985
I Title
344.206666

ISBN 1-874241-04-X
Printed and bound in Great Britain